AN EXTRA...
GATHERING OF ESSAYS
ABOUT LESBIAN
SEXUALITY, CULTURE,
AND POLITICS TODAY

BY TURNS FUNNY, SCATHING, ANALYTICAL, AND IMPASSIONED, this chorus of bold new voices offers powerful testimony to the vitality of lesbian culture today. Lourdes Arguelles extols the virtues of "crazy wisdom" in her memoir about growing up Cuban and queer in the late '50s. Editor Arlene Stein describes lesbian erotica that would have been unthinkable during the '70s and asks whether it heralds the next stage in an unfinished sexual revolution. In a stirring meditation, Jackie Goldsby moves from slave narratives to beauty pageants to discuss her coming of age as a black lesbian. *Sisters, Sexperts, Queers* is an eclectic, free-spirited anthology that is provocative in the best sense of the word.

EDITED BY ARLENE STEIN

SISTERS, SEXPERTS, QUEERS

BEYOND THE LESBIAN NATION

UCD WOMEN'S CENTER

A PLUME BOOK

PLUME

Published by the Penguin Group
Penguin Books USA Inc., 375 Hudson Street, New York, New York 10014, U.S.A.
Penguin Books Ltd, 27 Wrights Lane, London W8 5TZ, England
Penguin Books Australia Ltd, Ringwood, Victoria, Australia
Penguin Books Canada Ltd, 10 Alcorn Avenue, Toronto, Ontario, Canada M4V 3B2
Penguin Books (N.Z.) Ltd, 182–190 Wairau Road, Auckland 10, New Zealand

Penguin Books Ltd, Registered Offices:
Harmondsworth, Middlesex, England

First published by Plume, an imprint of New American
Library, a division of Penguin Books USA Inc.

First Printing, June, 1993
1 2 3 4 5 6 7 8 9 10

The editor gratefully acknowledges permission to reprint lyrics from "Folksinger"
by Phranc (*I Enjoy Being a Girl*, Island Records, 1989), copyright © Folkswim
Music (BMI).

"Dykotomies" by Alisa Solomon is reprinted by permission of the author and *The
Village Voice*.

 REGISTERED TRADEMARK—MARCA REGISTRADA

LIBRARY OF CONGRESS CATALOGING-IN-PUBLICATION DATA
Sisters, sexperts, queers : beyond the lesbian nation / edited by
Arlene Stein.
p. cm.
ISBN 0-452-26887-7
1. Lesbians—United States. 2. Lesbians' writings, American.
I. Stein, Arlene.
HQ75.6.U5S58   1993
305.48'9664—dc20   92-38902
                                                          CIP

Printed in the United States of America
Set in Eurostile and Garamond Light

Designed by Steven N. Stathakis

PUBLISHER'S NOTE
People mentioned in this book are gay, lesbian, bisexual, and heterosexual. In the
absence of a specific statement herein concerning the sexual orientation or personal
practices of any individual mentioned in this book, no inference with respect thereto
is intended and none should be implied.

CONTENTS

ACKNOWLEDGMENTS ix

INTRODUCTION xi

PART ONE **SEX AND OTHER GAMES** 1

SPEAKING IN TONGUES 6
CAMILLE ROY

THE YEAR OF THE LUSTFUL LESBIAN 13
ARLENE STEIN

BUTCH-FEMME AND THE POLITICS OF
IDENTITY 35
TRACY MORGAN

IDENTITY CRISES: WHO IS A LESBIAN,
ANYWAY? 47
VERA WHISMAN

PART TWO **IMAGINING OURSELVES** 61

ANYTHING BUT IDYLLIC: LESBIAN FILMMAKING
IN THE 1980S AND 1990S 67
LIZ KOTZ

A FREAK AMONG FREAKS: THE 'ZINE SCENE 81
S. BRYN AUSTIN WITH PAM GREGG

ANDROGYNY GOES POP: BUT IS IT LESBIAN
MUSIC? 96
ARLENE STEIN

QUEEN FOR 307 DAYS: LOOKING B(L)ACK AT
VANESSA WILLIAMS AND THE SEX WARS 110
JACKIE GOLDSBY

PART THREE **LOOKING FOR HOME** 129

A QUESTION OF CLASS 133
DOROTHY ALLISON

PARENTING IN THE AGE OF AIDS 156
KATH WESTON

LESBIAN MARRIAGE . . . (K)NOT! 187
CATHERINE SAALFIELD

CRAZY WISDOM: MEMORIES OF A CUBAN
QUEER 196
LOURDES ARGUELLES

PART FOUR **COMMUNITY AND ITS
DISCONTENTS** 205

DYKOTOMIES: SCENTS AND SENSIBILITY 210
ALISA SOLOMON

BITCHES IN SOLITUDE: IDENTITY POLITICS AND
LESBIAN COMMUNITY 218
LISA KAHALEOLE CHANG HALL

NEW ALLIANCES, STRANGE BEDFELLOWS:
LESBIANS, GAY MEN, AND AIDS 230
RUTH L. SCHWARTZ

WANDERING THROUGH HERLAND 245
MARIA MAGGENTI

NOTES 257
ABOUT THE CONTRIBUTORS 263
INDEX 267

ACKNOWLEDGMENTS

THIS BOOK WOULD NOT HAVE BEEN POSSIBLE WITHOUT THE resources of the Lesbian Herstory Archives in New York, the archives of the Gay and Lesbian Historical Society of Northern California, and the rich body of literature produced during the last two decades by lesbian and gay historians, theorists, and community journalists.

The San Francisco Lesbian and Gay History Project has, for the past several years, provided a valuable context for the discussions that spawned this book, as have friends and colleagues at *Out/Look* magazine, and at the University of California at Berkeley. The audience at a talk I gave at Iowa City Gay Pride Week in June 1990 provided valuable feedback on my own pieces in this book, as did an audience at the University of California at Santa Cruz. Dozens of other women, too numerous to name, gave me their time and shared ideas, contacts, and written materials.

I am also very grateful to those who read and commented on various parts of this book: Cheryl Cole, Deborah Gerson, Jackie Goldsby, Nina Hagiwara, Sabine Hark, Rachel Pfeffer, Sarah Schulman, Nancy Solomon, Shari Zeck, and my literary agent, Jeffrey Escoffier. Susan Rogers edited the entire manuscript and improved it immensely. Nancy Solomon kept me sane.

IN SAN FRANCISCO TODAY, THE HOTTEST LESBIAN CLUB HOSTS a once-a-week splash that unabashedly features go-go dancers on pedestals and patrons clad in leather miniskirts. Across town sixty or seventy women gather each week in a dusty church basement to discuss the legal ins and outs of donor insemination, foster adoption programs, power of attorney contracts, and parenting. There are many other signs of lesbian life in this great gay mecca, but few seem to capture the spirit of the moment so completely as the femmes strutting around in their lipstick and high heels and the prospective mothers worrying about the quality of the school systems.

Women are trying to carve out lesbian identities at a moment when many of the certainties of the past have eroded. As one twenty-three-year-old New Yorker told me, "What I am is in many ways contradictory. I don't belong in the straight world, though I'm a privileged white girl. But I don't really belong in the feminist world because I read lesbian porn and refuse to go by a party line. But I think of myself as a feminist. It's a set of contradictions." The simple opposition—assimilationism versus separatism—which once guided our thoughts and our political strategies no longer seems to apply.

If the goal of the lesbian feminist movement of the 1970s was to reveal the contours of oppression, to encourage coming out, and to create a common culture and identity to counteract that oppression, today the vision of a Lesbian Nation that could stand apart from the dominant culture and provide a haven in a heartless (male/heterosexual) world seems distant. The young, predominantly white and middle-class women who built the lesbian feminist movement are aging, undergoing life changes, and settling into families and careers of various stripes. A younger generation of women is coming of age that possesses few loyalties to the utopian visions of the past and fewer connections to the shadow world of the closet.

Those who once dreamed of a lesbian refuge from society's ills somewhere between metaphor and reality survey the landscape with wonder and more than a little remorse. A fortysomething mother of two boys told me that "in the old days" she could go to a particular place—a café, a women's center—to find the lesbian community in her medium-sized town. By the late 1980s, when she broke up with a longtime lover, she went out searching for that community and couldn't find it.

The month after I spoke with her, the *San Francisco Examiner* reported on the demise of the last lesbian bar in the city. How strange, the columnist noted, that "more lesbians than ever live in San Francisco but that the last lesbian bar was set to close." Bemoaning the loss of a "home base" for lesbians, the former owner of the bar said, "It's a victim of the lesbian community becoming more diverse. There is an absence of a lesbian community in the presence of a million lesbians." Others spoke with alarm about the number of friends they had lost to heterosexual conversions, convinced that more and more women were forsaking their lesbianism in exchange for the seeming security and respectability of lives with men.

They saw women intent on shedding their anger and fitting in, on flaunting their sexuality and renouncing faith in a lesbian counterculture. "We used to talk a lot about lesbianism as a political movement—back in the old days when lesbianism and feminism went together, and one heard the phrase lesbian feminism," warned philosopher Janice Raymond in the pages of a women's studies journal. "Today we hear more about lesbian sadomasochism, lesbians having babies and everything lesbians need to know about sex."

We are, in many respects, emerging from a period of retrenchment. The policies of the Reagan/Bush era took their toll on many community institutions; calls for "family values" drowned out demands for sexual freedom. But the death-of-community scenario described by Raymond and others can't explain the existence of my twenty-year-old friend Angel, who wears her lesbianism as a proud badge of difference. For me, Angel is living proof that in some pockets of this country, the feminist vision of making women the masters of their own sexuality has in fact come to pass. Nor can Raymond's scenario explain my own complicated history.

At the end of the 1970s, I was in college in western Massachusetts, a member of the first class of women at a formerly all-male bastion of WASP gentility. At the time, I was desperately trying to come out. I was convinced that the personal was indeed political, and yet I struggled to reconcile the widespread conviction that "cock rock" was a tool of the patriarchy with my undying love of the Rolling Stones. I realized that my desire for women made me in some important sense different, but I longed to see that difference as one part of the complex, contradictory reality of who I was—a lower-middle-class Ivy Leaguer, a Jewish rock and roll devotee, and a cynical idealist.

At the time, the ideal of a women's counterculture, a Lesbian Nation, provided many women with the strength and support they needed to proclaim their desires for one another. It allowed them to leave abusive situations and permitted freedoms never before possible. Lesbian communities across the country served as a refuge for those for whom assimilation into the dominant

culture was tantamount to social death, and spawned a movement and culture which irrevocably changed the national
landscape.

But at their worst, those communities hardened the boundaries between those who belonged within them and those who
did not, set up rigid standards for living one's life, and excluded
many of those who might have been able to take advantage of
their shelter. Particularly after the mid-1970s, many lesbian communities in towns and cities throughout the nation became
private enclaves, far removed from the mainstream. As a budding
baby dyke, I found myself torn between the pressures to make
my lesbianism a primary identity which would always set me
apart and the hope that at some point that difference would not
seem so great.

As it turned out, I wasn't the only one facing these dilem-
mas, a fact that became clear to me in the early 1980s, as an
explosion of discussions about sex and race echoed across the
country. These discussions were most charged when it came to
pornography and sexual imagery. Some women challenged the
assumption that lesbian life could ever stand completely outside,
or apart from, the structures of the patriarchal culture, and called
into question the once uncontested relationship between feminism and lesbianism—in which the latter was assumed to grow
naturally out of the former. They affirmed the differences of
race, ethnicity, class, and sexuality that have always existed
among us. The geography of the Lesbian Nation would never
be the same.

A year after we first met, I bumped into the fortyish mother
of two boys again. She told me that after her initial dismay, she
had come to realize that the community had not in fact disappeared. "We are everywhere," she said, echoing the words of
an early gay liberationist slogan. In cities across the country,
there are lesbian parenting groups; new, often graphic sexual
literature; organizations for "career women" and lesbians of
color; and mixed lesbian/gay organizations where women play
very visible roles.

But gone is the hope that we can somehow withdraw from

the mainstream and create ourselves anew—increasingly, we are finding out how impossible such a task is. The first phase of our struggle involved a rediscovery of roots and a preoccupation with identity and with building communities in opposition to the mainstream. Today we are discovering how much we are actually embedded in the culture from which we have tried to escape, and how important it is for us to learn to live with the contradictions—while pushing up against them. The dolled-up dykes and lesbian mothers, for better or for worse, are two of the clearest signs of these realities.

Recently, I talked to a coming-out group at a lesbian/gay community center in Berkeley, California. A woman asked me, point-blank: "How can I learn how to be a lesbian? Is there a book I can read?" She was completely in earnest. While I had to chuckle at the thought that one book could ever encapsulate the complexity of the lesbian experience, her question reminded me of how invisible we remain, how difficult it is to obtain information about our lives, and how important is the task of building and sharing the information we have, both inside and outside our communities.

When I began thinking about putting this collection together, I perused the few existing anthologies of nonfiction lesbian writing, published in the early 1970s, during the heyday of the lesbian and gay liberation movements. I was struck by the optimism that pervades much of that writing, by the virtual absence of contributions from women of color, and by the paucity of any explicit discussion of sexuality—the products of a very different historical moment.

Certainly many of the questions posed by those early books still are worth asking: How can we live as lesbians in a society that tries to marginalize us? What sorts of communities do we wish to create to provide support for our difference? But many of the earlier assumptions about the ease of answering those questions, it seems to me, have become much more complicated. Young women (and men) coming out today, in a period of relative conservatism, do not have the expectation that they are going to remake the world in a matter of weeks, or even years. The structures of the dominant culture have proved more intractable than we once thought, the difficulties of unifying lesbians much more relentless.

As I was gathering material for this book, I was faced with a nagging question: to what extent can we even talk about a lesbian *community?* Often I found myself speaking of "lesbian culture" or "lesbian politics," knowing full well that the vast diversity of class, race, ethnicity, geography, and even sexuality among us makes describing such coherent entities difficult, if not impossible. To paraphrase Gertrude Stein, I found myself reflecting on whether there is really a "we" there.

Many write about the "lesbian community" as if it were a monolithic whole. This leads them, I believe, to focus on the most out, most articulate, most politically conscious members (typically white and well educated, and living on the East or West Coast) and assume that they represent all lesbians. It also leads them to exaggerate the impact of the most visible ideologies or trends on all people who call themselves lesbians. I knew how dangerous this was, having taught an undergraduate class at Berkeley, where the differences among women who identified themselves as lesbians were often as great, or greater, than those between lesbians and women who called themselves straight. Several women in the class called themselves lesbians on the basis of very little sexual and even less political experience; others lived gay lives and yet refused the label altogether.

It is true, however, that as lesbians we all live under the yoke of the dominant heterosexual culture. Because of this, and thanks to the historical development of our communities and our movement, in the United States in the early 1990s being a lesbian is much more than simply a matter of sexual preference. Often it has to do with subtle, shared codes of understandings, such as an exchange of glances as we pass one another on the street, or local traditions, such as an annual softball game or women's music festival. These codes and traditions vary with region, race, ethnicity, class, and other factors, but they share in common the sense of being "other."

This book, like all works on the subject, is primarily the story of the most self-conscious and politicized sectors of the lesbian world, with fewer contributions from the less conspicuous, less noisy parts. I've tried my best to compensate for this by seeking out a diversity of voices. For example, many of the contributors to *Sisters, Sexperts, Queers* belong to the younger generation; approximately half came of age in the 1980s.

This book examines the current state of lesbian cultures and politics by focusing on four overlapping themes: sexuality and its relationship to lesbian identity; the representation of lesbianism in art and popular culture; the meaning of family in our lives; and the legacy of identity politics and community. It includes original material from well-known and little-known writers, theorists, and activists, along with some previously published pieces from the lesbian/gay and alternative press. It is an eclectic mix. Many of these essays were inspired by the recent burgeoning of lesbian and "queer" studies on college campuses, but they are written in a style accessible to those who may not be familiar with the theoretical debates. There is much in the way of creative, critical thought in these pages, but little in the way of ideological unity or a party line—reflecting the fact that at this moment lesbian culture is itself decentered, and up for grabs.

PART ONE

SEX AND OTHER GAMES

THE PARADOX IS THAT IF WE DON'T NAME OUR DIFFERENCE IN explicit, sexual terms, we remain invisible as lesbians—but if we do name it, we're typecast as little more than sexual beings, and the vast complexity of our lives disappears. So, as we have proclaimed our desires, we have often downplayed their sexual nature—at least publicly. In the 1980s, that seemed to change. A tidal wave of writing, thinking, and arguing about sex swept over many lesbian communities.

This first section assesses the impact of these discussions. According to Camille Roy, what is being constructed is a new "sexual dialect." Lesbian porn and sexual self-help books, and urban sexual subcultures such as s/m have opened up new space for discussion and experimentation. In a sense, this emergent sexual dialect challenges the notion of lesbianism as either a politically pure identity or simply a private sexual choice.

Two of the best known lesbian "sexperts," women who are

helping to disseminate this new sexual dialect, are Susie Bright and JoAnn Loulan. Through their writings, speeches, and videos, they are telling lesbians to reject deeply rooted patterns of female socialization and take up their unfinished sexual revolution. In "The Year of the Lustful Lesbian," I discuss the sexperts' origins in the "sex debates" on pornography and s/m, which shattered the feminist consensus that male and female sexualities are diametrically opposed, and I compare the in-your-face sexual libertarianism of Bright to Loulan's self-help sex therapy. Their efforts to foment a lesbian "sexual revolution" still encounter resistance. However, Bright, Loulan, and others are helping to fundamentally reshape how we see ourselves.

While pronouncements on a lesbian "sexual revolution" may be premature, in the end the most lasting change wrought by this new sexual discussion may be its impact on lesbian identity—how we see ourselves. Lesbians, by our very existence apart from men, challenge accepted notions of gender and conventions of femininity. But recently, many women are also recognizing and playing with gender in a very self-conscious fashion. The butch-femme tradition has long been alive and well, particularly in working-class lesbian subcultures. As Tracy Morgan tells us, roles are an indigenous lesbian institution—a reflection of the dominant heterosexual culture and *also* an attempt to subvert it. Still, there's little consensus as to what they really mean. Are they just a matter of personal style—what clothes we wear, what we like to do beneath the sheets—or are roles more deeply rooted than that?

It is ironic that while our sexuality has been the basis of our commonality, it is also one of the primary sources of our differences. As political restrictions on butch-femme roles, bisexuality, s/m, and other previously marginalized sexual practices loosen somewhat, thorny questions spring up for all of us. Who is a lesbian? What is a lesbian? Today, Vera Whisman writes, it is becoming harder and harder to answer many of those questions.

Viewing feminism as the repressive mother, many younger lesbians have come to frame their identities on the basis of a shared "queerness" with gay men. The new queer culture appears to offer younger women new freedoms, writes Whisman, but she cautions that it may also trade purity for kinkiness. Rather than exchange one set of standards for an equally exclusionary set, we should reject membership requirements altogether and acknowledge that there is no essential, timeless lesbian but that "we place ourselves within that category, drawing and redrawing the boundaries in ever-shifting ways."

SPEAKING
IN
TONGUES

WHEN I CAME OUT IN 1975, A FRESH-FACED NINETEEN-YEAR-old dyke, "lesbian sex" was so foreign a term it was practically phallic. Drop the "lesbian" and it wasn't much better. In those early days, after make-out sessions on the couch in my communal household, if my girlfriend said the S(ex) word, I'd place my index finger over her lips, gently commanding silence. She'd sputter protests at my ridiculousness but it did no good: silence was my law. I was much more comfortable between the sheets of our bed than trying to grope my way into a dyke form of sexual speech.

And so my first lesbian experiences were an inwardly shocking form of body talk: *So I can feel this? And that?* The urge to compare notes is strong, and soon the self-imposed and culturally imposed silence became a strain. Eventually, the body and language intersect.

Actually, you might say they breed, producing stories, rumors, gossip, and, among lesbians, a sexual dialect, or dialects, at once playful and sharp, contradictory and passionate. Among lesbians the story is a form of sex talk—whereby the community and the couple become part of the same body. This conversation has shaped me even as I have tried to influence it.

I remember Kay, a roommate, curling up on a big chair in the living room and inventing names for her butch girlfriend. "*It* is taking me out tonight," she'd tell me. Over time *It* evolved into *The Creature*, which became *Helen*, and finally, most gloriously, *Wanda*. For me the memory of *Wanda* has almost erased the woman's real name. Now Kay has a new lover, also named Kay, so my friend refers to their combination as *Mr. and Mrs. Kay*. Mrs. Kay (my friend) is the sharpest player I've known in what I'm calling a lesbian sexual dialect, so when I began preparing my thoughts for this essay I immediately arranged a get-together over coffee. What, I asked Mrs. Kay, should I say about lesbian sex? "Just don't make it jiggle jiggle jiggle and lick lick lick," she replied. Then she went on to describe the dildo she and Mr. Kay had just bought, and its nickname—*The Family Jewels*.

My conversations with Mrs. Kay—some silly, others profound —work the territory of taboo, and isn't that what comedians do? Finally, the audience is hysterical, laughing at its own stupidity. This reminds me of my sexual history—played out by word of mouth, something tasty to give and receive. Over time, conversations, rumors, and jokes among lesbians revised practically everything I had thought possible about sex.

Mari, for example, taught me "how insatiable a woman could be," at a party which I spent mostly on her lap. She had her hand on my hip; occasionally it would slyly drift under my sweater. That night Mari was wacky and radiated heat, her eyes shining, as she entertained us with tales of her sexual exploits. Once, she related, she had sex in a phone booth on the corner of 18th and Mission, opposite the Doggy Diner, where the whores used to stroll. It was early on a summer evening. When we acted incredulous she gave us the details: the phone booth painted up to the waist, the other woman on her knees, etc.

Perhaps I think of what has emerged among lesbians as a sexual dialect because my only parallel is the Black English I heard growing up on the South Side of Chicago. It was a mark of dispossession yet also a creative stream of speech, and far livelier than what anyone else could talk. Irony, play, antagonism stretched the sound and meaning of "Standard English," and there was something in its style that made even my grim neighborhood yield.

What has happened may be the opening up of an erotic conversation whose roots go back to the 1950s, the era of butch-femme. "I did not learn a part," Joan Nestle writes of coming out at that time, "I perfected a way of loving." The mix of play and display she describes (in *Heresies,* "Sex Issue," 1981) reminds me of my friends today. But her stories also remind us how the butch-femme couples in the Village during the fifties were far more vulnerable to assault. She explains, "My understanding of why we angered straight spectators so is not that they saw us modeling ourselves after them, but just the opposite—we were a symbol of women's erotic autonomy, a sexual accomplishment that did not include them." Nestle further describes the "code language" that developed for their erotic world:

> *I loved my lover for how she stood as well as for what she did. Dress was a part of it—the erotic signal of her hair at the nape of the neck, touching the shirt collar; how she held a cigarette; waved her hand . . . all these gestures were a style of self-presentation that made erotic competence a political statement in the 1950s. . . . Butches were known by their appearances, fems by their choices.*

I think of this quote as I step out into the street in heels, fishnets, reddened lips; my lover in black or gray, a glossy dark shirt with a narrow collar, a leather jacket. Her hair is graying, her eyes are dark blue. She hops on her motorcycle, I settle behind, my hands around her hips or secretly exploring her pockets. It is not the elements of display but their combination that gives me a sly pleasure. Like I've stolen something.

During the 1970s, the women's movement completely absorbed this sexual underground. Lesbianism became commonly understood as a "political statement." Because we were part of the women's movement's struggle for legitimacy, lesbian sex had to be reconstructed in politically "pure" terms. In an ironic twist, lesbianism had to appear untainted by power plays in order to be incorporated into a feminist agenda for power.

The key issue for me is one of language. The lesbian dialect of the fifties was underground, and had a quality of expressive freedom in pursuing erotic pleasure as the focus of community life. With the surge of feminism in the seventies, as women adopted the language of social and political power, this was suppressed. The women's movement, wrote Amber Hollibaugh in the same *Heresies* issue, "became this really repressive movement, where you didn't talk dirty and you didn't want dirty. It really became a bore. So after meetings, we *ran* to the bars. You couldn't talk about wanting a woman, except very loftily."

The problem was rooted in the language of power. It has rules, among them that evidence of pleasure undermines authority. An executive must keep "a grip on himself" to control others; dominance starts under the skin. Power is always imitating itself, is really individuals "acting like" a sequence of images. Their self-control is a social agreement and a means of entitlement. In public the powerful can be counted on to act like "figures of authority," and they maintain their position in part by reproducing that image. But under an economy of control, pleasure in community life drifts to the margins.

And here, at the margins, is where lesbians are, among

others. Yet there's an imaginary quality to this lesbian location, perhaps because we are invisible perverts—society isn't looking at us, so our game of "acting like" is about experiment and arousal, not social power. New configurations become possible.

I'm reminded of Lee, a woman who fascinated me for a period because, though butch, she's a masochist. Never having run into that combination, I wanted to know more. We got together for coffee before a party. From the café I watched her walk up the pavement, with a curious stiff-legged stroll. She was wearing a man's suit from the forties, with baggy pants; blue smoke curled from the tip of a thin cigarette. Her round cheek was so soft it reminded me of one of those pictures of Colette in drag. I felt mildly giddy. At the party we drifted from corner to corner, passing sly flirtatious comments back and forth. After an insult I slapped her face, lightly, as a joke. She tilted her head, rubbing her chin thoughtfully as her eyes closed, and a smile came onto her lips. "That was interesting," she said, "but you only slapped one side." So I slapped the other, with my fingers instead of my whole hand. "You did it differently that time," she observed, and I watched her soft cheeks flush. "I want to keep you off balance," I said.

I want to draw attention to something that is not there. A peculiar feature of the lesbian community is our invisibility; thus I've heard butch women described as "the image that can't stand the light of day." This is a mark of oppression but it also gives us a kind of buffer zone, or breathing space, outside the demographic. No advertisements aim to sell lesbians feminine hygiene spray. The smiling faces of ads are a form of control through resemblance; but a community of female sexual perverts resembles nobody, and nobody desires to resemble us. We possess a quality of ironic freedom, simply because we're not a target of that scrutiny.

The *Oxford English Dictionary* defines "marginal" as "close to the limit . . . beyond which something ceases to be possible." An accurate description of our location, I think, where we are not "real" women and certainly not "real" men. The powers of definition are exhausted at this boundary. They cannot cross, except through parody. So, for example, there is the view of a butch lesbian as an inadequate man. It reminds me of a butch-femme meeting I once attended with my beloved. One woman—a femme, with kinky blond hair that she pushed out of her face with a defiant thrust of her wrist and chin—described how thrilled she was by her girlfriend's "mascoolinity." Over and over, she pronounced "mascoolinity," until I was giddy.

Whether butch or sadomasochism or extremes of gender —what can't be represented is the locale for invention and exchange. Probably, it is the most taboo and "disgusting" elements that give the lesbian dialect its expressive power.

Lesbian sex doesn't produce "real women." The surplus meaning generated by violated taboos is itself a kind of pleasure, bringing forth tattoos, piercings, rumors, more jokes.

Bette and Ruth are sitting on the stairs, telling me a funny story—something they're not supposed to be talking about, the "French maid" they were with at a sex party. "Her French accent," Bette begins, and Ruth finishes, "was so bad!" They lean forward, laughing so hard they can hardly breathe. It's not ridicule moving them, more the presence of the ridiculous. So we're all part of it.

This sexual dialect has a quality of improvisation. It is urban. Unsettling. Un-doing. An expressive explosive moment—understanding words of sex in relation to my body. So how about some dirt on me?

"Get dressed," she says (today it'll be black lace and some big fake pearls) "and then come here and do just what I say." Which is exactly what I want. "Spread your legs, honey." There's a kind of happiness in this today for me, I don't feel it's unendurable at all. It's weird, though, to be known so well, like she's got my story in her hands. "Give it up," she says, and off I go, melting into a blue sky that throbs with the chords of hard-rock guitar. The boy next door plays heavy metal, and today it's a redone classic: "Somewhere over the rainbow," trills a thrilled

Dorothy, through our walls—and that somewhere is suddenly exactly here, where I can be thoughtless and noisy. How did I get here?

A misgiving draws my thoughts to a close. As I translate this material into an essay, an intimacy is lost and recollecting it becomes only nostalgia.

I want to insist on this: the principle of "You had to be there." Then I can recall Tattoo Blue on stage at the Baybrick, doing a strip to "Why don't you come with me little girl, on a Magic Carpet Ride." The roll of her hips is so generous I'm undone, and I settle back, encircled by my beloved's arms. I like it as it is, a place invested with desire, undoing what we usually know as fact. My feeling is: *What is happening here is happening all over the world*. This contentment has an ornamental quality, its arrangement shifting according to multiplicative desires. A minute and energetic democracy, all style.

ARLENE STEIN

THE YEAR
OF THE
LUSTFUL
LESBIAN

In living amorously together, two women may eventually discover that their mutual attraction is not basically sensual. What woman would not blush to seek out her amie *only for sensual pleasures?*

—COLETTE,
The Pure and the Impure

Woman has sex organs just about everywhere. The geography of her pleasure is much more diversified, more multiple in its differences, more subtle, more complex than is imagined.

—LUCE IRIGARAY

WOMEN DON'T TEND TO ATTRACT ALL THAT MUCH ATTENTION IN the gay male ghetto. But when six-foot Susie Bright, in high heels and a slinky cocktail dress, turns the corner and saunters toward the Castro Theatre, the dozen or so men perched in a café sipping after-work cocktails let out a flurry of catcalls. "Susie, Susie!" they call, as she adjusts her schoolmarm glasses, smiles politely, and marches up the street.

It is the 1989 San Francisco Lesbian and Gay Film Festival, the gay community's answer to Cannes. Dozens of women, most of them in their twenties and early thirties, are milling around outside the theater, frantically trying to scare up tickets, while hundreds scurry inside, packing the cavernous hall. It has all the trappings of an event writ large, right down to the theater marquee, which reads, in giant bold letters: SUSIE BRIGHT! ALL GIRL ACTION!

Thirty-year-old Susie "Sexpert," a sort of lesbian cross between Dr. Ruth and Al Goldstein (of *Screw* magazine fame), has become a familiar face in this neighborhood, hawking vibrators and other sex toys, reviewing videos for *Penthouse Forum*, and for five years editing *On Our Backs*, the first and largest national lesbian sex magazine. She has emerged, through no small effort of her own, as perhaps the most visible leader of a movement to create a public erotic culture for lesbians.

Inside the red velvet deco-kitsch auditorium the fifteen-hundred-strong audience is guided through a ninety-minute cinematic tour of sleazy straight porn, big-budget Hollywood productions, and homegrown lesbian-made videos, in search of images of lesbian sex. The audience watches with rapt attention. There are few men in attendance—a fact underscored by the high-pitched titters emanating from the crowd at various points during the evening, proof that the voyeur role is one to which women are not yet accustomed.

It is an evening of strange juxtapositions. A bored housewife is pinned to the bathroom floor by a female maintenance worker who ends up servicing more than the kitchen sink. Two French schoolgirls fondle each other in the bushes. The lovers of *Desert Hearts* learn their way around each other's bodies. Bright punctuates the movie clips with a narrative mix of feminist theory and porn-film history. Midway through the evening, she calls on the audience to acknowledge the work of all "the wonderful porn actresses," who, she says, are "part of our lesbian erotic heritage."

Several years earlier, those would have been fighting words. Feminists tarred pornography as evidence of the degradation of women. Women Against Pornography and its national affiliates organized slide shows of violent antifemale images and widely publicized junkets through urban porn districts. The equation of pornography and violence, resting on the belief that women's complicity in that world was the result of coercion, or of false consciousness at the very least, was simple yet powerful. For many women porn seemed to symbolize the fear that stalked them through the routines of daily life, from their interactions with strangers on dimly lit streets to their relationships with men at work and, all too often, at home.

That Susie Sexpert found receptive ears in this crowd is a signal of political shifts in feminist and lesbian culture. There is an increasing reassessment of an earlier feminist orthodoxy that held all sexual representations of women to be degrading. At the same time, there is a burgeoning lesbian conversation that sets itself apart from earlier feminist critiques, brandishing sexual representation to make its point. In the aftermath of the "porn wars," and in an age of AIDS and sexual limits, censorship battles, and injunctions to "just say no," a growing chorus is arguing that women should seek sexual freedoms rather than reject them. Through their writings and speeches, films and videos, self-proclaimed "sexperts" such as Susie Bright and JoAnn Loulan are telling lesbians to reject deeply rooted patterns of female socialization and begin the next phase of their unfinished sexual revolution.

In the final part of the program at the Castro Theatre, Bright shows a series of clips from recent lesbian-made porn, seeming to offer them up as the crowning achievements of the last twenty-five years of film erotica—arty pastiches and campy romps which recall the humor (and limited production values) of early straight porn. "You're the frenzied generation," she teases the audience, mocking 1970s lesbian-made "erotica" for substituting images of flowers, seashells, and gentle female embraces for rough-and-ready sex. "Tenderness, gentleness, and reciprocity are really nice qualities in and of themselves," says Bright. "People would give their eyeteeth to have those qualities in their sex life, just to have someone be sweet to them. It's just that they don't have much fire because there's no passion, or conflict."

In *Clips*, a classic porn narrative is given a lesbian twist as the femme, a leggy blond (who also happens to be the publisher of *On Our Backs*) dressed in a pale pink negligee and stockings, is sprawled out on a mauve La-Z-Boy armchair trying to tempt her partner away from the television set by masturbating. The butch, reading the business news, suitably attired in striped shirt, suspenders, and pants, remains uninterested. Microphones veer off course, and the acting is self-conscious. But as the femme fingers a large clear dildo the audience remains engaged.

By the time the butch disrobes, the femme has come single-handedly, in an acrobatic feat which may go down in cinematic history as the definitive "G-spot ejaculation." It is an obvious play on the male cum-shot, the hallmark of straight porn films, and a parody of the convention that says that the cum shot reveals real arousal in men. It is also an attempt to signify lesbian sexual prowess. See, the video says, we can wield our sexuality as source of power rather than victimization.

If the scene tonight is any indication, it appears that Bright has gained a host of new converts to the cause. Some stalwart feminist bookstores still refuse to carry lesbian porn, and the appearance of leather-clad lesbian sadomasochists at women's music festivals can cause a stir. But the fiery battles have flickered out, the antiporn organizations have—for the most part—closed shop, and Susie Sexpert, in her slinky black dress, has emerged as a viable, even respectable, lesbian spokesperson. On this sultry summer night, the once inevitable feminist pickets are noticeable only by their absence; the ideological debates and emotional clashes of the past have faded to a distant memory.

If a lesbian sexual revolution is in the making, its most recent phase began in the early 1980s, when some women, primarily in New York and San Francisco, began to question the literal fashion in which many pornographic images were being interpreted by many feminists. Certainly, they admitted, violence against women was a pervasive fact in our society. But hadn't all the attention on sexual danger minimized the possibility of pleasure? They criticized the blanket equation of objectification with violence, and proclaimed that "feminist porn" was not a contradiction in terms.

The polarized battles raged on in the pages of feminist publications and in public clashes—sex radicals branded their antiporn, anti-s/m opponents as good girls, who in turn tarred the bad girls as antifeminist and tried unsuccessfully to codify their views into law—and came to a head in the unlikely setting of a highbrow conference at Barnard College in 1982, when anti-s/m activists picketed a forum on "politically incorrect" sex.

For lesbians, who could be found on both sides of the fray, these debates held a forceful, if ambiguous, resonance. Visual representations of lesbianism, from the early twentieth century sexologists onward, have been uniformly unidimensional, depicting lesbians as either sexless spinsters or mannish characters who stalked innocent women and seduced them into their ways. In contemporary popular culture, pornographic images were primarily responsible for linking lesbians indelibly with their sexuality.

Responding to this legacy, in the 1970s feminists tended to downplay the queerness of lesbianism. "Men who are obsessed with sex are convinced that lesbians are obsessed with sex. Actually, like other women, lesbians are obsessed with love and fidelity," declared poet Judy Grahn. Lesbians were not crazed perverts but very good friends—and the vanguard of the feminist movement to boot. The downplaying of sexuality was strategically brilliant, allowing lesbians to claim legitimacy and space in a homophobic culture, and at the same time recruit converts to the cause. If lesbianism was redefined as woman-identification, in some sense anyone could be a lesbian—you needn't even touch another woman where it counted (though it helped). What was once feminism's "lavender menace" became its vanguard.

The public desexualization of lesbianism emerged out of the realization that for lesbians, unlike gay men, sexual orientation was an insufficient basis on which to build a culture and a politic. It echoed a tendency among some feminists to see sexual liberation as the undoing of women's liberation, as a male invention, a "phallic" concept that bore little relationship to the actual experience of women, rarely as goal-directed, and orgasm-centered, as men. When lesbian feminists affirmed the erotic publicly, they did so in a holistic sense, in the words of poet Audre Lorde, as the creative energy or "life force of women."

But as Susie Bright and other heirs to the prosex legacy of the sex wars see it, somewhere in the midst of defining sexuality as male, and lesbianism as a blow against the patriarchy, desire—and all its wayward incorrigibility—seemed to drop out of the picture. Down-and-dirty public discussions of sexual practice were skirted in favor of talk of eroticism, friendship, and softer pleasantries. The specificity of lesbian existence—as a *sexual* identity—seemed to get lost.

"The traditional notion of femininity as gentle and nurturing creates the stereotype that lesbianism is just a hand-holding society," Bright says. "Lesbians don't have sex, the story goes. Or if they do, it is this really tiresome affair—five minutes of cunnilingus on each side, with a little timer nearby, and lots of talking about your feelings and your career." In *On Our Backs* and in Bright's lesbian-sex road show, *All Girl Action*, that vision of politicized sex serves as the dramatic foil.

Heralding 1984 as the "Year of the Lustful Lesbian," trumpeting "sexual freedom, respect, and empowerment for lesbians," and featuring erotic stories, graphic illustrations, and unmitigated boldness, *On Our Backs* appeared on the stands announcing itself as "Entertainment for the Adventurous Lesbian" and gleefully ruffling some prudish feminist feathers in the service of sexual libertarianism—right down to its name, a not-so-subtle play on the radical feminist publication *off our backs*. It was a family affair, of sorts. Susie Bright was working at the local women's sex-toy shop when she got to know publishers Nan Kinney and Debi Sundahl (who were girlfriends). She contributed a tongue-in-cheek column that probed the ins and outs of dildos and vibrators. Other friends took photographs, wrote erotic stories. Early reader response was effusive, if not overwhelming.

Bright, the daughter of a prominent linguistics scholar and herself a former antiporn activist, quickly became the flamboyant and eloquent mouthpiece of the magazine's philosophy. Each installment of her column, "Toys for Us," a compendium of safe-sex tips, sex-toy consumer reports, and lesbian trend-watching, featured a different photograph of her, somewhere between goofy and sexy. Susie sucking her finger. Susie raising her T-shirt over her head. Susie getting a piercing. If many lesbian feminists scorned celebrityhood, at least in theory, on the grounds that it was unsisterly and elitist, Bright courted it.

She quickly mastered the art of the media bite, with pithy quotes like "penetration is only as heterosexual as kissing," and told the press on more than one occasion that she believed that her mother had never had sex after Susie, an only child, was conceived. Bright also played bit parts in several porn films, including the Mitchell Brothers' safe-sex feature, *Behind the Green Door II*. In German director Monika Treut's 1989 film, *The Virgin Machine*, she played a caricature of herself: a fast-talking, bright-eyed sexpert expounding on the virtues of dildos and vibrators. She even got up before a packed lecture hall to ask the intellectual savant Susan Sontag what she thought of lesbian porn. "The shocked expression on her face," says Bright, "made it well worth the effort." More than anything else, it is controversy, she says, that gets her "hot."

In the fall of 1988, an article assessing the state of lesbian life in the 1980s appeared in *OOB*, along with three drawings by cartoonist Alison Bechdel. The first showed a demure woman in skirt and saddle shoes clutching a copy of *The Ladder*, the newsletter of the prefeminist lesbian organization Daughters of Bilitis; the second was of a cigarette-smoking hippie dyke circa 1973, a woman's symbol around her neck, a copy of *off our backs* stuffed in her overalls pocket. The final image was of a woman in black leather and cowboy boots, a heavy industrial chain around her miniskirt, holding a copy of *On Our Backs*, as if to say: we represent the lesbian of today—sexy, self-assured, and ready for action.

The editors of *OOB* are supremely conscious of their place in history. It is, some say, a revisionist one, which pits renegade sex "radicals" against their bad "feminist" mothers and, in the process, simplifies the complexity of lesbian history, which was never quite as sexless as they make it out to be. But complexity doesn't sell magazines; provocation does—though perhaps not quite as many as *OOB*'s editors would like. Since 1984, circulation has grown modestly but steadily, to almost ten thousand paid subscribers (and possibly as many as twenty thousand unpaid ones, the editors are quick to point out), making the magazine perhaps the most widely circulated lesbian publication in the nation. Other lesbian sex magazines, such as *Bad Attitude, Power Exchange*, and *Outrageous Women*, also cropped up, but none ever equaled *OOB*'s influence, which far exceeds the numbers.

While 1970s feminist "erotica" distanced itself from porn in both form and content, *OOB* tries to subvert the genre on its own terms. Yet the magazine has a sort of homey look, hardly the glossy stuff of big-budget commercial magazines, and pale by comparison to most gay men's porn rags. Indeed, the most noteworthy thing about it, some have remarked, may be its very existence. Lesbian-made porn makes the lesbian the subject as well as the object of desire.

Bright scoffs at the suggestion that most women prefer the sublimated masochism of romance to explicit pornographic material; the feminist view that porn embodies a male gaze to which women cannot possibly respond, she believes, is misguided. It was in commercial pornography that she herself first found images of lesbians that were exciting, realistic, and at times even funny—"wild s/m lesbians, aggressive biker-chick lesbians, nymphomaniacs who couldn't get enough"—images of sexual infantilism, wayward desire, aggressiveness, and fantasy, repressed in popular and in feminist culture. These images led her to believe that the problem is not porn per se, as her feminist predecessors had charged, but who controls it. Women objectify other women—whether they admit it or not.

Bright wants to take these feminist critiques and turn them on their heads. She'll admit that commercial porn, filled with blond WASPs with perfect figures and lesbian sex that is rigid and formulaic, doesn't do justice to women, who are rarely shown as powerful subjects of desire. Mainstream pornography never found out, she says, "that people are very subversive in their likes and dislikes." But she discards the conviction that capitalism cheapens sexuality by offering up a vision of good orgasms in exchange for the debasement of women. Porn's failings come from the fact that it is made by men, with male consumers in mind; its production, therefore, should be seized by those who have been disenfranchised from it—women. Magazines such as *On Our Backs*, Bright says, derive from the same self-help impulse as the feminist health-care movement. "What that movement tried to do for women's health," she says, *OOB* attempts to do for sex. "Everyone assumes we started the magazine because we're nymphomaniacs. They had no idea it was a big political statement."

But if it is political, it is politics of a postmodern stripe. Politics, for second-wave feminists, meant a search for authenticity and truth, the communication of the reality of women's lives, and the forging of community. Politics, *On Our Backs*-style, places fantasy above reality, artifice and style above the "truth," and individual desire above community rules. The magazine is less an attempt to convey what "lesbians really do" than to depict fantasies never fully realized. Rather than reassuring women with soft, sweet sensuality, as did 1970s lesbian erotica (and the new genre of heterosexual "feminist" porn produced by Candida Royalle and others), *On Our Backs* goes out of its way to be daring, pushing up against the parameters of politically correct fantasy, reappropriating the imagery of heterosexual, gay male, and prefeminist lesbian culture, and transposing them into the lesbian context.

And while the magazine has not radically redefined the boundaries of conventional beauty—young, femme, white, typically svelte models predominate—it has sometimes made gallant efforts to do so. *OOB* ran a "Bulldagger of the Month" photograph in its first issue, an image that was a far cry from the *Penthouse* ideal. In June 1990, the magazine featured a layout of three voluptuous women over sixty. "We don't show nontraditional images because we're trying to be politically correct," says Bright. "We do it because they're hot."

In fact, whether or not something is hot—at least in the

eyes of its editors—is pretty much the sole criterion for what gets published. Since one woman's nightmare may be the next woman's fantasy, anything, or just about anything, goes. If feminists held up lesbian sex as the favorable alternative to an oppressive heterosexuality, in Bright's book all orgasms are created equal and all are good. This conviction, perhaps more than any other, lies at the base of Bright's view of lesbian sex. The extreme pluralism it implies often raises the hackles of even those who are mostly sympathetic to the project of creating a lesbian sexual culture, and feminist critics have accused her and others of failing to question the relationship of porn to sexual violence, and to sexism in general. Black women, in particular, have said that she and other "sexperts" fail to acknowledge the historical associations of sexualized images of black women.

But then subtle distinctions, as one critic put it, are not Bright's forte. Anything less than total freedom, says Bright, tarring feminist censors with the same brush as official thought policeman Jesse Helms, is "totalitarian piggery." After all, what counts in the end is pleasure, isn't it?

If Bright represents an in-your-face sexual libertarianism, JoAnn Loulan may be greatly responsible for its widespread dissemination to the more faint of heart. Bright relies on shock value, championing the most outrageous images just to push buttons and stretch the boundaries of acceptable sexuality; Loulan, in her early forties, is the more respectable go-between, melding lesbian feminist sensibilities and 1980s therapy-speak onto the brave new world of lesbian sexual abandon.

While the pages of *On Our Backs* depict a fragmented world, filled with anonymous sexual encounters and forbidden fantasies, the archetypal reader lurking behind JoAnn Loulan's sexual primers is a Midwestern dyke, possibly coupled, whose sex life is on the rocks. She is someone probably not unlike Loulan herself, whose small frame, shoulder-length permed hair, and impish face present a package as different from Bright as one can imagine. "Compared to Susie Bright, I'm your grandma," says Loulan, whose folksy persona and comfortable suburban existence (she lives outside San Francisco with her young son) once prompted Susie Bright to call her the "Eisenhower of Lesbian Sex." Loulan's books *Lesbian Sex, Lesbian Passion*, and *The Lesbian Erotic Dance* are consistent best-sellers at women's bookstores throughout the country.

When cartoonist Kris Kovick illustrated an article Loulan wrote for *Out/Look* magazine, she pictured her in a short skirt, wielding two giant pom-poms and yelling, "Give me a *c*, give me a *u*, give me an *n*, give me a *t*," a reference to the last section of Loulan's book *Lesbian Sex* (Spinsters, 1984), titled "Be Your Own Camp Director," which features a variety of "homework exercises" ("imagine yourself very small, and crawl up inside your own vagina"). Loulan would gladly assume the role of lesbian sex cheerleader. This folksiness has allowed her to get away with all manner of statements which might otherwise be considered blasphemous.

It's no coincidence that Susie Bright and JoAnn Loulan have both emerged in the San Francisco Bay Area, known for its tolerance of sexual nonconformity, home of a graduate program in sexology, clearinghouse for sexual information, and institutional mooring for the profession of sexology on the West Coast. Humanistic sexology melds Masters and Johnson–style therapy with an eclectic mix of human potential and Reichian philosophy. According to Janice Irvine, author of a recent study of sexology, one of the cornerstones of the profession is a belief in the essential similarity of male and female sexuality. When some feminists argued in the early 1970s that orgasm was a male invention, sexologists dedicated themselves to the goal of teaching women to have more and better orgasms.[1]

JoAnn Loulan, who emerged out of this sexual model, first seized upon the idea of bringing lesbian sex to the masses while she was teaching health-care professionals at the University of California Medical School in the mid-1970s, an experience she calls "sex boot camp." She says, "I was appalled at the way medical professionals talked about sex, in such dry, clinical terms," and she was troubled by the lack of knowledge about lesbians. "All the models we had were heterosexual." In 1975 she took a six-month course taught by a variety of liberal sex therapists and educators, some of whom were gay. Tee Corinne and Pat Califia, two veteran lesbian sex experts, were her teachers. It sparked her crusade for lesbian sexual literacy. She began working as a private sex therapist, mainly counseling lesbians, giving occasional talks in the community. At first, she got lots of flak for talking about sex out loud; the ones who weren't angry were usually embarrassed. But her blend of stand-up comedy and sex therapy eventually caught on.

Today she delivers about twenty talks a year and is a veritable star on the lesbian lecture circuit, having sold over a hundred thousand books to lesbians who find their sex lives lacking. On her 1988 tour, which featured a talk titled "An Evening of Provocative Comedy and Lesbian Sex Education," Loulan wore a long, flowing gown, matching pantyhose, big hair, and dangly earrings, and proceeded to outline the archetypal lesbian relationship. First comes the LIP (Lesbian Insanity Phase), in which you don't get out of bed for months on end; which often leads to MIP (Moving In Phase), in which you begin to merge but end up arguing about whose pictures to hang on the wall; which frequently declines to LBD (Lesbian Bed Death), in which a yeast infection is an excuse not to have sex for six months, which can end up turning into six years.

Onstage, this was all presented with the help of mime. There was the "going down on your lover" routine, the "coming out to the neighbors at the bus stop" mime, and the "stimulating the clitoris" scene, among others. In the final part of the evening, Loulan coaxed a volunteer onstage for a twenty-minute demonstration of "safer sex," which involved the placement of a dental dam on a fully clothed woman as Loulan pointed and announced, "That's your pussy, this is your clitoris, and here is your asshole."

Some criticize her folksy manner, contending that she talks down to her audience. Loulan admits that she is not a particularly profound thinker. "Being esoteric is all well and good and interesting, but when do you plant the corn and when do you pick it? I want to know a little bit of the background and information of how I got here, but I really want to know what I can do with the pain that I'm in." This matter-of-factness, coupled with her concessions to feminist ideology, allows her to make anonymous sex, role-playing, and s/m fantasy palatable to even the most dyed-in-the-wool sexual ideologue.

Lesbian Sex, published the year *On Our Backs* first appeared on the stands, mixes Masters and Johnson behavioral sex therapy, liberal ego psychology, California feel-good expressive individualism, and feminist theory, and is emblematic of Loulan's approach. "There is magic in this process of becoming fully identified with our lesbian selves," she writes. "For so long we have given our sex lives away to the closest person, family member or government. We don't have to do that anymore. . . . You can have what you want out of sex." The basic premise of the book, and of much of Loulan's work, is not particularly original: Lesbians are caught in a double bind. They are raised in a culture that teaches women that they cannot be sexual. At the same time, they learn that their identity is determined by their sexual partner. This creates a great deal of anxiety and ambivalence, particularly in a homophobic society, as they are torn between being "good girls" and claiming a lesbian (read: sexual) identity. Following the behavioral model in which she was trained, Loulan believes that "if you change one part of the whole, the rest will change." It is an optimistic vision. Far from waiting until after the revolution, you can fight homophobia now—by having a good fuck.

About lesbian self-esteem Loulan has written: "I do not understand not wanting to have labels—the truth is, if you eat pussy, you eat pussy." On difficulty with dating: "Don't say 'would you like to go on a date?' if you mean 'would you like to fuck.' " And on sexual reticence: "We trap ourselves with shoulds. Sex should be sacred. Sex should be a spiritual union between two people. I don't know about you, but I have done some things during sex that are not all that sacred, and I wouldn't particularly say my spirit was unified with the other woman. I got off."

Lesbian Passion: Loving Ourselves and Loving Each Other
(Spinsters, 1987), was culled from a series of Loulan's talks and
includes fifty pages of sex homework. "I like to make real practical applications," writes Loulan. The book continues many of
the earlier themes of *Lesbian Sex* in a somewhat talkier style,
punctuated with the ever-present language of the "recovery"
movement. In a chapter titled "Healing the Child Within," Loulan
insists that many of us have "an inner child with a broken heart,"
afraid to show her vulnerability, and she even admits that "many
of us feel we have a little boy inside." There is a continuum
between active physical child abuse and "inner child abuse,"
she reminds her readers; "your heart wasn't necessarily broken
from incidents of incest or the death of a parent . . . it might
have been something as normal as leaving home for kinder-
garten." We are all, in a sense, abused.

Unlike many feminists, however, she draws a distinction
between consensual and nonconsensual abuse. Referring to the
often vitriolic lesbian debates about s/m, she writes: "We have
a history of going after each other like crabs in a bucket. The
sex wars, particularly around s/m, are just another way to divide
us. I'd like the wars to be dialogues." She believes that the
feminist position (which saw s/m as an example of violence
against women) was overstated; the women who are against
s/m are "torturing" the women who are into s/m. Still, Loulan
wonders whether s/m isn't just another form of "getting stoned"
and laments the fact that "a lot of younger women are becoming
indoctrinated into it."

If many prosex activists of the early 1980s had a vision of
sexuality that acknowledged danger along with pleasure, in the
"sex wars" which ensued, the sides were often loudly polarized,
pitting "good girls" against "bad girls," libertarian sex radicals
against prudes. If there was any middle ground, any acknowledgment of the emotional pain which many women associate
with sex, even as they desire it, it was hardly spoken. JoAnn
Loulan, one might say, recognized that market and cornered it.
By equating lesbian sexual prudishness with sexism and homophobia, placing a value on individual sexual expression, and

acknowledging the pain that many women associate with sex, Loulan is able to mediate between feminist "prosex" and "antisex" positions, carving out some comfortable, if at times shaky, middle ground.

"Some women enjoy giving up control to someone they know and love," she writes, singing the praises of dildos and harnesses. "Some people say, now that's really male-identified. I say why not? Why should men be the only ones who get to put something into a woman's vagina and still keep two hands free?" She is a good girl who occasionally harbors bad thoughts, a prudish Ohioan with libertarian impulses. While she finds a kindred spirit in Susie Bright's work, Loulan believes that "sex radicals" often wrongly frame sex in terms of a political battle pitting the whores against the prudes. Loulan isn't looking for any battles; she believes that sex should be roundly depoliticized. She offers good old-fashioned American individualism, in new therapeutic clothing.

Her latest book, *The Lesbian Erotic Dance* (Spinsters, 1990), is a rethinking of butch-femme roles, an aspect of sexual orientation unique to lesbians which, she believes, has been trampled underfoot by homophobia. The feminist insistence that roles were male-identified and retrograde, Loulan writes, was a product of lesbians' shame about being visible. The problem is, she writes, "in the lesbian community you can walk into any group and say something about butch-femme and everyone knows what you're talking about. It's a lesbian cultural phenomenon, but when you sit down and ask what those words mean, no one knows. We all know what it means on an emotional level, but we don't have language to explain it to one another."

For a woman who has made her career as a sex therapist, it is perhaps ironic that Loulan has railed on more than one occasion against the "tyranny of orgasm," admitted that "most people in the world are sexual a small percentage of their lives," and suggested that lesbians' sexual identity "overemphasizes sex." If pushed, she might even say that lesbians' problems don't really center on sex at all; sexual problems are simply symptomatic of other difficulties. But in the end the liberal therapist in Loulan wins out. "There's a new paradigm being talked about, a new language being created," she writes. "It's all part of a process which is revolutionizing lesbian sexual practice. We're more willing to talk about sex, more willing to express it, and that's important."

While Loulan dedicates *Lesbian Passion* "to lesbians everywhere" who must "band together in our clan," Bright walks a fine line between celebrating the lesbian community and mocking it. For Bright, the discussion began early in 1975, when she was in college and lesbian separatism was at a fever pitch. She never identified with separatism, in large part because of her bisexuality, which many women around her assumed to be simply a phase in her coming-out process, and a political affront. "I had been wearing dyke buttons since I was fifteen, but slept with men and women the whole time," she recalls. "I used to get into terrible sobbing fights with women over bisexuality. I knew that the way those women characterized sex with men was stupid—the qualities people were talking about could apply to men or women."

Though she never stopped calling herself bisexual, she started calling herself lesbian because she wasn't having sex with men, not because she wasn't attracted to them. "They were just kind of out of the picture. I had a very busy little lesbian life," she recalls. But the controversy reared its head again a few years ago, when, in an interview with a San Francisco gay paper, she was quoted as saying that it was all right for lesbians to sleep with men. The response this time, she says, was much more favorable than ten years earlier. "A lot of lesbians called me up and confided in me that they were having a secret affair with some guy, or that they had had a one-night stand two years ago, or a secret marriage." Still, many women remain leery.

In 1990, when writer Jan Clausen published an article in *Out/Look* that attested to her newfound relationship with a man and defended her right to retain her lesbian citizenship, a flood of letters to the lesbian/gay quarterly called her a traitor to the cause. Even as there is increasing acknowledgment of sexual difference among lesbians, bisexuality is still taboo in many quarters. Lesbians who sleep with men (termed "hasbians" by the feminist publication *off our backs*) are often seen as turn-coats, betraying their lesbian sisters and unable to deal with their "true" desires. Some have even been accused of import-ing AIDS into lesbian communities. For ideological as well as personal reasons, the desire for sexual consistency remains strong.

Because bisexuality may call into question the notion of sexual identity as necessarily being fixed, consistent, and either homosexual or heterosexual, it makes some lesbians uneasy. In a society where heterosexuality is the norm and lesbianism is still stigmatized, bisexual boundary crossings often lead to hurt feelings, as when a woman is left by her female lover for a man. Particularly suspect, and confusing, are women like Bright who sleep with men but maintain a lesbian identity, navigating the turbulent waters of two often contending worlds.

In this debate, as in others, JoAnn Loulan assumes the me-diator's role. "Lesbian identity goes much deeper than our gen-itals," she admits. "For some lesbians, sex with men is a wonderful adjunct to their ongoing sexual relating to women." She recognizes that discussions about lesbians sleeping with men may be coded debates about the loss of community and meaning of lesbian identity, the generational lament of baby boomers who are now finding their once supportive commu-nities gone, transformed into fragmented couples and isolated individuals without firm mooring. "It's harder to be a lesbian these days," writes Loulan. "We're not hanging out together, supporting each other as much. As you get older, it's harder and harder to date."

Bright, however, will hear no such thing. She likens these fears to a "horrible *Titanic* paranoia" in which "there are only six lesbians left on the life raft, and if we lose one more person, we're all going to sink." She adds, "It's only threatening to those who are insecure, who feel as though we're losing our community." This she finds curious, as she's convinced that there are more lesbians, of all ages, coming out now than ever before. "It makes the period I came out in seem like small potatoes."

For her own part, in June 1990, after admitting to her readers that she had gotten pregnant "the old-fashioned way," she gave birth to a baby girl, silencing her critics' contention that "real" lesbians do it through insemination. "I lay on a waterbed with a real live man, someone whose genes and fatherly temperament I've been admiring for some time," she wrote in *On Our Backs*. "It was the first day of my ovulation and I remember visualizing the sperm being sucked into my cervix like a honey vacuum. It was thrilling. So many women are having babies on their own," she wrote, "with women spouses, men friends, and every other newfangled family support. It's rewarding to talk about when you dispense with the old stereotypes."

These old stereotypes have a lot to do with sexual boundaries. While some would like to narrow the definition of "lesbian" to those who limit their sexual practice to women, Bright would like nothing more than to erase the boundaries, admit anyone into the club who wishes to be a member, even those who occasionally embrace phalluses—of either the rubber or the human variety.

She is one of a growing number of intellectuals and activists who have begun to call on gay people to subvert the medical categories, to deconstruct the notion of homosexuality, to begin to speak of "practices" rather than identities. In the pages of *On Our Backs*, Bright exhorted her readers to "start talking about what we do instead of who we supposedly are. Don't say 'I'm an s/m lesbian,' when you could be saying, 'I fantasize about eating out my manicurist on the bathroom floor with her mouth gagged by a rubber ball,' or, 'I pinch my nipples when I masturbate until they're hard as points,' or, 'Fist me until the sweat drips off my lip.' Isn't that much more enlightening?"

Calling herself a lesbian while living a bisexual life, championing the rights of sexual minorities of all sorts while writing columns for a heterosexual porn magazine—and viewing it all as perfectly consistent—Bright herself is perhaps the best exemplar of a post-Stonewall, post-identity lesbian politics that has little respect for sexual borders or good behavior.

As JoAnn Loulan, Susie Bright, and others announced the onset of a lesbian "sexual revolution," some observers wondered whether lesbians were picking up where gay men had left off. Relatively unscathed by the AIDS crisis—if reports were accurate that woman-to-woman AIDS transmission was rare—lesbians seemed uniquely poised to reclaim female pleasure. And many did. Lesbians, critic Cindy Patton wrote, "have adapted the hanky code of sexual options, and the randy attitudes that go with them, from gay male culture," and may represent the reinforcements for a sexual liberation movement badly damaged by the right wing and AIDS. "We got off on fighting back, while gay men got off on putting out," she wrote. "But sex is political, and sex lib theory rings false without some good, sweaty praxis."[2]

Some activists tried to build a renewed interest in prefeminist lesbian culture and reverse the feminist insistence that butch-femme roles were simply reflections of patriarchal values. Butch-femme relationships—"strong, fierce lovemaking: deep, strong givings and takings, erotic play challenges, calculated teasings," wrote Joan Nestle, "were complex erotic statements, not phony heterosexual replicas."[3] Like butch-femme roles, s/m embodied sex as performance, a far cry from the sundappled, hand-holding images of the past, providing an endless supply of fantasy images, and a gendered archetype for the sort of erotic tension required by the emerging model of lesbian sex.

Lesbian sadomasochists took their cause to numerous conferences, forums, music festivals, consolidating themselves as beleaguered minorities within a minority, and mobilizing new recruits, leading s/m advocate Gayle Rubin to report that in 1982 there were about as many sadomasochists in most lesbian communities as there were radical feminists in 1970.[4] By 1990 there were organizations for s/m lesbians in at least fourteen cities across the nation, with names like "Bound and Determined"

(Hadley, Massachusetts), "Power and Trust" (Portland, Oregon), "Southern Kink" (Decatur, Georgia), and "Urania" (Somerville, Massachusetts). San Francisco's "Outcasts" vowed, in the words of Pat Califia, to be "male-identified, objectifying, pornographic, noisy and undignified," and claimed as many as a hundred members.

In a striking historical irony, sadomasochists made dykes with dildos, once pathologized as man-hating perverts, hip. They represented a sort of class revolt—the rising up of a less "civ-ilized" working-class sexuality against middle-class, "ladylike" feminist norms. Drawing on the iconography of prefeminist lesbianism, gay male culture, and heterosexual porn, this lesbian sexual fringe introduced a new vocabulary of lesbian desire, a world of dildos and harnesses, butch and femme, tops and bottoms, lust and intrigue—symbols of a queer female culture and reminders of a lesbian past that, for all intents and purposes, had disappeared from public view by the 1970s.

By the end of the decade, sadomasochism had crept into the vocabulary of "vanilla" culture, as some lesbian therapists began to prescribe a diet of sexual dominance and submission to guard against the stultifying effects of the much-touted "Les-bian Bed Death"; more and more women experimented with butch-femme and other forms of sexual role-playing, or at least talked and wrote about it. Mail orders for harnesses and dildos skyrocketed, propelled by a new lesbian market; and a new playfulness about sexuality came into view in urban areas with large gay populations, especially among younger lesbians, who embraced dolled-up dyke fashion and new dance clubs which featured miniskirted go-go dancers. If their older sisters claimed power by renouncing lipstick, coquettishness, and even por-nography, by 1990 many lesbians asserted their sexual power by reclaiming them, and by withholding access from the con-ventional male beholder.

But some cautioned against overstating the extent of the revolution. Throughout the nation, women wrote outraged let-ters to lesbian and gay newspapers, scoffing at the suggestion that lesbians had any intention of mimicking the sexual excesses of their gay brothers. And as many lesbian therapists could tell you, for all but a feisty sexual fringe, the sexual revolution was probably more about changes in representations of sexuality than about changes in behavior.

"If you read *On Our Backs*, you think that things are changing rapidly," cautions Seattle therapist Elizabeth Rae Larson, "but it's important to recognize that few people actually do what appears in its pages." Most of her clients, she says, "are overwhelmed when handed stuff like that. It bears no resemblance at all to what they are doing." Like the pronouncements of a society-wide sexual revolution in the 1960s and 1970s, the notion that a lesbian sexual revolution is occurring today, she and others contend, may be exaggerated. Old patterns die hard. The combined effect of a still conservative dominant culture and the deep roots of individual sexual patterns make behavioral change slow.

On Our Backs and other sexual materials may "provide comfort," but all the dildos, harnesses, and new sexual techniques in the world, says therapist Larson, probably won't alter patterns that are "deeply rooted in the fact of being a woman, and being gay in this society." Because sex is so private in our culture, particularly lesbian sex, the few public representations which do exist tend to dominate the scene, distorting our perception of actual change. The growing visibility of lesbian-made representations of lesbian sexuality, and the rise of a sexual fringe, may be more indicative of the fact that a sexually active vanguard is becoming more visible than that such attitudes and practices are trickling down to the grass roots.

This realization has led some to ask whether the new model of the "lustful lesbian" may be leading to a "pleasure imperative" which is insidious in its own right. "It's great and it's playful, but it's not the only way," says therapist Marny Hall, warning of the arrival of a new set of standards. Writing in 1988 in the radical feminist journal *Sinister Wisdom*, Marilyn Frye chided lesbians for answering questionnaires that ask us "how frequently we 'have sex,'" contending that "they are leading women to become dissatisfied with ourselves and with our re-

lationships because we don't 'have sex' enough." In a dig against
Loulan and other sexperts, she proclaimed: "We are so dissatisfied that we keep a small army of therapists in business trying
to help us 'have sex' more."

Hall agrees: "There's a fundamental problem with hooking
our identity onto genital sex. What I would like our identity to
be hooked to is our incredible ability to reinvent ourselves. That
is our great strength." She is not alone in her ambivalence.
Today, most lesbians will admit that while porn may have made
a big splash within the lesbian community, if the truth be known,
it has never really taken off. In San Francisco, the lesbian strip
shows, so popular for a year or two, have exhausted their audience and closed. Even Susie Bright has left *On Our Backs* to
devote herself to writing and mothering.

The sexperts have revealed a partial truth: that women are
not as different from men as many feminists had asserted the
decade before—though neither are they identical, as current
resistance to the "lesbian sexual revolution" attests. While many
women welcome the advent of a new prosex lesbian culture
and applaud the license it affords, others hold out for a "kinder,
gentler" alternative free of domination, subordination, and pleasure imperatives.

TRACY MORGAN

BUTCH-FEMME AND THE POLITICS OF IDENTITY

THE TOPIC OF BUTCH AND FEMME HAS BECOME A KIND OF CON-versational refrain among certain sectors of the lesbian community. Walk into any lesbian bar in New York City on a Friday night, and you're pretty much guaranteed to overhear one dyke say about another: "She's such a femme," or "Look at that butch girl coming out of the ladies' room." But check out the "femme" or "butch" in question, and you'll see (in either case) a lesbian in a leather jacket, work boots, and a muscle T-shirt. At such moments, it's hard not to wonder what is being referred to: whenever I hear the words being applied to women who aren't especially—dare I say it—masculine or feminine, I get suspicious of this butch-femme refrain and how women are using it to identify each other. And I wonder at whose expense the nouns "butch" and "femme" have been turned into adjectives to describe not beliefs or behaviors but certain styles of lesbian dress and demeanor.

To hear it from the women who comprise the Butch-Femme Society, butch and femme are not identities you get up and decide to put on in the morning: butch or femme is who you are, not roles you play. As I listen to the story of the cross-dressing butch who was "found out"—by the lack of hair on her face, a softness about her hands—by a group of men at a gas station and threatened with rape, or the femme who had to prove she was a lesbian before being allowed to use the bathroom in the Community Center—she ended up pushing aside the dyke who'd denied her entrance, saying, "Get the hell out of my way"—I wonder what they would make of the women I run into on my Friday nights out.

Stereotypes and misconceptions about butch-femme abound. Nonetheless, a lot of dykes who don't necessarily belong to organizations are speaking with a great deal of authority on butch-femme. And as women who adhere to the traditional identities of butch-femme are organizing, becoming visible, and learning to take care of their own, it's only a matter of time before these two worlds collide. Like the lesbian sex wars of the eighties, which shattered illusions and ultimately forced discussion of lesbian sex out into the open, the debate over butch-femme promises to provoke similarly strong feelings and ignite equally strong reactions. The issues at stake—sex, power, class, race, parody, drag, and a new kind of identity politics—are ones most dykes seem ready and willing to jump right in the middle of and take to town.

Ever since I first came out, and before I knew all that the word could mean, I have been a femme. It's a part of my identity I've been hated and loved for—have loved and hated—but cannot deny. Even in my toughest boy-outfit, butch and androgynous dykes always nail me for what I am. Especially the butches.

I was born ten years before abortion was made legal in this country; I came out fourteen years after Stonewall. Both facts are significant; the change in the political climate, combined with the growth of lesbian-feminism and women's studies programs, made me the dyke I am today. I did not come out as femme. I did, however, come out with a butch.

The first twenty years of my life (a time I've now come to recognize as two decades of deprivation), I never came across anyone my own age anything like the woman who brought me out. Cris had a quietness and deft grace that made me feel my idiosyncrasies and excesses would be understood and respected. To me, my first butch lover was a source of tremendous desire and pride. To others, we were freaks.

The way my lover dressed was constantly used to discount her feminism, which was radical and incisive—born of rage. My women's studies cohort used to put her down by asking, "If she's such a feminist, why does she dress like a man?" Yet I never thought of my lover's pressed white shirts and wing-tips as objects for discussion: they were just *her*. She was a dyke who saw herself very much connected to the lesbians of the past, and she was not about to turn her back on her history.

When I came out, I was told that I was not a "real" lesbian. It was a constant refrain, sung by queer friends who offered me but conditional acceptance, by non-queer parents who threatened to disown me. And when the flannel-shirted dykes at the bar made it clear (verbally and otherwise) that I did not look like a real dyke, I began to feel very unentitled to the lesbian identity I so desperately needed. My lesbianism, I was told, was just a phase I was going through. When I walked my Mobil-uniformed lover to her job at the gas station, we always held hands.

I took my first few political arrests, with WHAM! and ACT UP, wearing a skirt. (This not only gave me the rare opportunity to fuck with cops' heads, it also gave me a certain degree of security, since the police obviously had no idea what to do with a woman in a dress sitting in the street, screaming her head off.) Almost everyone else dressed the same—in leather jackets, jeans, and big boots, with lots of political buttons and short haircuts for all. Since my attire provoked derogatory comments from the other activists (from a sneering "Why are you wearing a skirt?" to a chilling "You look straight"), I often ended up feeling like an outcast among people I was supposed to be fighting the same battles with. Once more, I quickly learned that being femme was hardly an identity I should want to claim.

In my work with ACT UP, I felt that somehow to appear femme, and to work exclusively on women's issues as I did, would put me at a great disadvantage. The all-too-popular confusion of femininity with hysteria did little to ease my fears about being taken seriously as an activist working on issues I cared deeply about. The price of admission? A look of greater authority: boots, jeans, and leather. My safety as an activist depended upon my being easily recognizable to other comrades. This recognition, this authority, has done wonders for lesbian visibility, but the look has been decidedly more butch than femme—and more like gay men than anything.

The place of butch-femme as central to lesbian history is only now beginning to be explored. Its Western origins are often traced back to the advent of sexology, the late-nineteenth- and early-twentieth-century study of human sexual behavior. Sexologists labeled those with queer tendencies "inverts" (among other names); from them we get our concepts of mannish women (the butch) and womanly women (the femme). The most common criticism of sexology is leveled against its initial homophobic purposes: to categorize and contain the proliferation of homosexuality. If, for example, "mannish" girls could be identified and "cured" at a young age, the problem of the mannish woman would be no more. The womanly woman, like a good infiltrator, remained perpetually elusive and uncategorizable.

The beginnings of butch identity can be traced to the history of women who cross-dressed for survival. Dressing as men has always been a strategy for female survival, especially for women who have no interest in marrying or who seek to make a living for themselves the best (or only) way possible.

For women who wanted more than the nineteenth-century ideal of romantic friendship—indeed, for women who wanted lesbian sex—wearing masculine attire was a way to signal desire for other women. Amid the poverty of early lesbian identity, cross-dressing was an act of daring and self-assertion.

By the forties and fifties, butch-femme had shaped itself into a lesbian institution, in which specific sexual codes, styles of dress, distinct mannerisms, bravado, bar culture (as well as the routine realities of police harassment, Mafia involvement, and fear of disclosure) constituted an entire world, one for which women were willing to risk their jobs, homes, and families in order to follow sexual desire. As Joan Nestle writes in her 1981 article "Butch-Femme Relationships and Sexual Courage in the 1950s" (in *Heresies*), women labeled ourselves as part of our cultural ritual, but "the words which seem so one-dimensional now stood for complex emotional exchanges" at the time. Butch-femme gave order to a group of people who had limited visibility. It indicated sexual preference and sexual desire and provided continuity in a world that regularly sought to uproot and disband a nascent lesbian community. Butch-femme poured the concrete for the identity upon which many of us now stand.

By the seventies, feminism had sanitized lesbianism. Lesbophobia forced lesbians to cling to feminism in an attempt to retain respectability. However, in the eighties, discussions of sadomasochism permanently altered the relationship of many lesbians to feminism. When lesbians started to explore bondage, wear harnessed dildos, and investigate issues of power and dominance in sex, the gloves came off, and an often difficult, often thought-provoking communitywide debate was begun.

The new debate in the lesbian community, currently eclipsing sadomasochism, is about butch and femme. Every dyke I interviewed for this article had more than a little to say about the topic. Two dykes, Milyoung Cho and Nancy Brooks-Brody, are presently making videos about butch-femme. Joan Nestle edited a mammoth butch-femme reader; Madeleine Davis and Liz Kennedy's long-researched book on butch-femme bar life in Buffalo in the forties is eagerly anticipated. NY Femmes and the Butch-Femme Society, providing support and social activities for women who identify as butch and femme, are both less than five years old and have several hundred members. Donahue has had shows about female cross-dressers, further testimony to the rebirth of interest in butch-femme, even among in-the-dark heterosexuals.

At the last few Lesbian and Gay Studies Conferences, a barometer of what the middle-class lesbian is thinking about, several panels gave butch-femme serious attention. Throughout a recent conference, butch-femme was used as a reference point for identity. Many dykes began their statements with disclaimers of "I'm not a femme but . . ." or "I'm not a butch, although . . ." At a lesbian-sex symposium, on a racially diverse panel of eight women, there was only one self-identified butch and no self-identified femmes. When some panelists trivialized butch-femme, calling it an identity that could be taken off before entering the bedroom, an uproar ensued. One butch got up and left the room. Immediately thereafter, Joan Parkin, a smartly put-together self-identified femme, threw down the gauntlet with this succinct manifesto: "People are speaking about butch-femme as identities you put on and take off. There is no such thing as butch on the streets, femme in the sheets. It's butch on the streets, butch in the sheets. And I am afraid of all the femme-bashing that takes place. No one wants to identify as a femme on the panel, but I think that femme identity has the power to redefine femininity."

Most dykes see the renewed discussions of butch and femme to be primarily about sexuality and lesbian identity and an outgrowth of our newfound power as a part of a queer community. Risa Denenberg, a self-identified femme, thinks that "identity politics are making a comeback, only this time they are emerging for us as individuals and not as political groups. The past decade has been a really repressive one, so if you are going to be out at all, you have to know who you are." Butch-Femme Society founder Yvette Schneider has a different but complementary understanding: "Everyone is talking about this because we are coming out of the woodwork. Word is out. Butch-femme is back."

But for many dykes, butch-femme has never gone away. Josephine Rosa, who came out as a butch in a Puerto Rican community in Brooklyn, spoke of having a butch role model when growing up who "adopted" her, teaching her how to act, dress, and survive. And today, in her community in Bushwick, where she lives with her femme lover, Alida Gonzalez, she is a role model for baby butches. When asked if any of the lesbian feminist debates on the political correctness of butch-femme had had an impact on their community or identities over the decades, they said no. "It took a normal role in my household," Alida laughed. But Josephine, who does AIDS education in homeless shelters where the numbers of gay homeless people are enormous, sees things a little differently: "It's like a trend. Some people are curious. They try it and stay in the life."

For those who just "try it," the butch-femme refrain marks a part of a larger exploration of lesbian sexuality. Lisa Winters, founder of NY Femmes, a support group for femmes who are primarily attracted to butches, says that lesbians are "thinking more about the locus of their desire in general—and so we are talking about butch and femme." Nancy Brooks-Brody adds, "Lesbians are coming out like never before. We are proud of our sexuality and butch-femme is a part of it."

For women outside of butch-femme, the use of the term to discuss sexuality is shorthand for talking about what goes on inside, rather than outside, the bedroom: active/passive, top/bottom, s/m. For these women, clearly the terms' value lies in their metaphoric power. But the sexuality of many butch and femme women is not so rigid; often it bears little resemblance to the words "butch" and "femme" when used to describe sex. As Polly Thistlewaite, a self-identified butch, put it, "I like to roll over too, you know." Further untying this knot, Ara Wilson, an androgynous lesbian, adds, "This confusion arises because butch-femme has been conflated with sexuality but, as I understand it, it's about personality, looks, *and* how you fuck." Are we using the butch-femme refrain to avoid talking explicitly about the sex we want to be having? Does our yanking the term out of history also damage our ability to see clearly the lives of those who came before us?

The lack of tolerance displayed toward butches and femmes is disturbing, considering the increasing communitywide use of the terms. Just as many gay men use the term "queen" endearingly for friends, while remaining dismissive of drag queens themselves, women who talk about butch and femme all the time frequently perceive women who identify as butch or femme as dinosaurs.

Many dykes claim that these social and sexual roles are, in Cathy Chang's words, "obsolete and unnecessary." But the discrediting of butch-femme may come less from a position of power than from a place of fear. As Desi Del Valle says, "I think being androgynous can sometimes be a copout, for people like myself, who don't want to identify one way or the other because of the stigma involved." Other lesbians fear the constraints imposed by butch-femme identity. "What happens when your behavior no longer fits your identity?" wonders Monica Pearl.

Nevertheless, Valerie Walker, a black lesbian who does not identify as butch or femme, thinks that part of this renewed discussion has to do with "lesbians needing some guidance— you know, how to walk, talk, and act." Indeed, for many college-educated dykes, schooled in postmodern theory, the notion of identity has been completely confused. Roni, a black femme, has noticed that "there seems to be a real return to butch-femme, and you have to identify as one or the other. There's a kind of panic about who people are." Jill Harris, a self-identified butch, thinks that "butch-femme is a pretty solid identity for dykes who feel that identities are so mushy now," but adds, referring to her butch identity, "To me, it's not something that changes."

Indeed, for many of us who identify as butch or femme, it's not about role-playing or a conscious choice. According to Josephine Rosa, her male peers accused her, at age fourteen, of wanting to be a man. "I would try to explain to them—I'm not trying to be a man. This is just me." Many of the dykes I interviewed spoke about being able to tell if a woman was butch, even when she was in a cocktail dress and heels. Nancy Brooks-Brody says, "It's almost a scent—like something you can smell," making butch or femme seem almost inherent.

But there is also a great reluctance on the part of many butches and femmes to see our identities as completely immutable, fixed, or innate. Our destinies, as women and as lesbians, have been tied for too long to biology. Even so, some of us feel so pushed against the wall by those who question our right to butch and femme identities that the temptation to raise the flag of biology is not easily resisted.

Many of the dykes I interviewed felt that butches and femmes in the fifties and sixties made it possible for them to learn how to survive. But many also stressed differences between the meanings of butch and femme intergenerationally. Mostly, it was the butch women I spoke with who were eager to address this issue. According to Nancy Brooks-Brody, it is a lot easier for women to be visible as butches now than in the fifties simply because clothing has become more unisex. "Even wearing a skirt suit in the forties made a woman kind of butch," she says. But beyond the realm of clothing, where discussions of butch-femme often get stuck, the difference lies also in the arena of flexibility. "In the fifties, the older butch style was more regimented. It was about survival, and we benefited greatly from their trials," says Yvette Schneider. "But now I can say that I'm a butch and I like to cook."

To some degree, the femmes I spoke with had less to say about the changes in the meaning of femme identity over time. Speaking for myself, there is no way I can avoid hearing a feminist critique of the cosmetics industry each time I put on some lipstick. In many ways, feminism has unalterably transformed all women's relationships to femininity. Nonetheless, femmes, probably more than butches, take the heat for not being feminists, because we may wear "dressed to be killed" heels or "just got punched in the mouth" red lipstick. We are also accused of passing as straight. But as Ara Wilson insightfully joked: "Drop a bunch of femmes in a bridal shower and you'll see the difference between femmes and the straight women. Probably most of the femmes would end up feeling pretty butch in that environment."

Race and class profoundly affect the way butch-femme identities are constructed. For many women, variances in class background altered the ways in which they initially claimed their identities. Joan Parkin, a white middle-class femme, came out as "a radical dyke," but, she adds, "When I went to the bars, in working-class, suburban Massachusetts, they were real butch-femme and everybody pegged me for a femme, so it was an identity that attached itself to me, that I took up as mine." But working-class black and Puerto Rican women spoke of coming out first as butch or femme and then as lesbian. In fact, many reject the term "lesbian," according to Marie Declet, because "it's so white." Contrarily, Valerie Walker thinks that, due to multiple oppressions, working-class black women "have not had as much time" as middle-class women of color like herself to develop sexuality for themselves and so end up relying on a lot of stereotypes.

Janet Gino and Ronda Cohen, two butch women, agreed that it is more common to find butches in working-class jobs. As Gino asked: "Where can a butch work? I mean, how can you become a part of a corporate world if you don't wear a skirt suit?" Of the femmes I spoke with, there were, among others, academics, secretaries, a psychiatric nurse, and a teacher. These jobs do indeed fall within the realm of traditional female employment. On the other hand, butches, working frequently in male-oriented working-class jobs, often have access to unions and higher pay than their femme counterparts. Cohen spoke also of having little trouble being accepted in her job as a butch: "I've had a lot of positive experiences being butch. I'm managing a warehouse now and I like it."

In my experience, it's a rare man, gay or straight, who is not, at some level, extremely threatened by butch usurpation of male posturing. Amanda Prosser, a butch, described what is for many butches a typical incident: Leaving a meeting one night, she watched a gay man kiss goodbye all the straight men and women and all the gay men and androgynous lesbians—and skip over her.

Certainly, as a femme, I can pass if I need to. The same is not true for a butch. Yvette Schneider spoke of butches being fired or harassed on the job, and of men threatening to rape her, "to turn me into a real woman." Such stories of harassment and brutalization have rarely come to the attention of a queer community that, as a matter of course, marginalizes butch and femme. Despite this inattention, activism has taken root: to take one example, the Butch-Femme Society has organized to confront the management in workplaces where members have experienced discrimination.

Far too many butches told me of their being threatened at gunpoint, drugged, abducted, and raped for refusing to compromise their sexual identities to adhere to their culture's standards of femininity. My first lover was physically threatened on a continual basis by her stepfather for being a baby butch. A year ago, my short-haired lover was beaten by a gang of teenagers on the street, with a girlfriend who wore her hair long. Butch-femme couples are not mistaken for anything but the dykes we are. We don't pass as androgynous, crunchy-granola, or countercultural.

Femmes spoke of feeling protected by their butch lovers; butch women spoke of feeling protected by femmes. But the protection comes at a very specific price: femmes are often invisible as lesbians, and butches carry all the weight of being visible.

When I asked Alida Gonzalez whether she had concerns about being out in her Bushwick Brooklyn neighborhood, she said no. She described her relationship with her lover, Josephine, as one of great visibility, saying, "Everyone in the neighborhood knows that we are lovers." When asked if she has any fear of violence, she let me know, in no uncertain terms, that she did not, saying, "I will lose my temper. I've always controlled the streets. I've always fought my own battles. Anyone that hassles us, deep down inside, I know that they feel intimidated by our relationship."

For all of Alida Gonzalez's strength and power, for all of the strength and power of so many femmes I know, I am plagued by our lack of visibility—especially when we are butchless femmes. Roni, a black femme, married two men before knowing she could be a femme. "It's hard to tell who is a femme, and I wish it weren't so difficult," she laments. "If only I had known I could be femme, I would've been gay a long time ago." Our queer community has at long last committed itself to visibility as one path to confronting our annihilation: where, in this landscape and enterprise, does the femme fit? Lisa Winters takes this question quite seriously, saying, "I love coming out to people —and I do it all the time." As a femme, coming out to people means opening your mouth and telling them you are a lesbian. Butches, often through dress and demeanor, announce themselves without speaking.

In the past five years, lesbian visibility has been connected to our activism in the streets, primarily about AIDS, primarily with ACT UP. This visibility has come through our attachment to gay men and our melding into a group, forming a queer, rather than a lesbian or gay, identity. I believe that by reexamining and reclaiming butch and femme, we can reclaim an identity that offers dyke visibility, historical connection with older lesbians, and an overt form of lesbian sexuality.

VERA WHISMAN

IDENTITY CRISES: WHO IS A LESBIAN, ANYWAY?

Stillwater, Oklahoma, 1977. I am at my first women's music festival. Twenty-one and freshly out, I am amazed by the sight of hundreds of women baring their breasts in the sun. There's not a man in sight. The crowd is young (though mostly older than I) and nearly entirely white. A woman onstage in a crew cut and no shirt sings, "If the package ain't too pretty, it's because I'm not for sale," and the crowd cheers loudly. The air is charged with erotic and political passion, and with promise.

New York City, 1991. I am watching slides of homemade lesbian porn flash over the dance floor at the Clit Club. Downstairs, slick sex videos compete with the pool table for my attention. The crowd is young (at thirty-five, I'm at the high end) and ethnically diverse. Many are wearing makeup and black leather; the woman who checks my coat sports a revealing sheer black blouse. She smiles sweetly at me, belying her "bad girl" appearance. The air is charged with sexual desire, and with possibility.

These two scenes are separated by more than time and space; the players in them enact two conflicting visions of what (and who) is a lesbian. The women at the music festival in 1977 saw themselves as a vanguard living out a new and radical conception of lesbianism, much like the women at the Clit Club today. Where they differ is that today's "bad girls" rebel as much against their feminist predecessors as against male power.

Lesbian feminists of the 1970s emphasized their solidarity with straight feminists, taking on the name "woman-identified-women" to signify that bond and their common stand against the patriarchy. Today's younger lesbians, in contrast, often make their alliances with gay men, and are as likely to call themselves "gay girls" or "queers" as "lesbians." Stylish, sexy, and impatient with the politics of their forebears, they tend to write about sex more than political theory and often define themselves as "not-lesbian feminists," as the following letter in *Out/Look*, the national lesbian/gay quarterly, revealed:

> *Lesbians are doing and talking about things we have never done or talked about before. We are moving beyond the realm of Sisterhood into the world of the nasty, the tasty, and the sexy. We are pushing the boundaries of what is acceptable lesbianism. We use the word "fuck" like the boys used to, we wear lipstick, and we lust openly and pridefully. . . . It is not simply that we are finally able to voice certain questions about desires that the self-righteous atmosphere of political correctitude and erotophobia we called lesbian-feminism kept us from uttering; our new culture is actually producing new desires.*[1]

This clash between lesbian feminist and lesbian queer styles and ideologies is only the latest in a long string of efforts to articulate the meaning of lesbianism, to draw boundaries around our communities. We can't be evenly divided into sheep and goats; relatively few lesbians are a part of either of these middle-class and largely white "in crowds." Nonetheless, as we make culture—art and institutions, style and theory—we articulate the tensions and contradictions that are felt far beyond these enclaves.

This process of defining who is a lesbian is much more than a word game. It is a collective attempt to make sense of our history, figure out our present, and strategize for our future. It lurks beneath contemporary debates about bisexuality, butch-femme roles, and s/m sexuality. It haunts our discussions of political strategies, such as separatism and assimilation. And lately, this process of definition is posing vexing questions which seem ever more difficult to answer.

The theory of lesbian feminism once promised an alternative to patriarchal culture, where differences of race and class would disappear under the force of sisterhood, and where differences in sexual tastes would disappear under the force of consciousness-raising. But many women not only refused to ignore difference, they actually began to embrace it, and to rub up against the boundaries. We haven't all rallied around a shared identity as lesbians; today we don't even agree on what the word means. Does that mean our movement is losing its base—or that the base is becoming broader and more diverse?

Is the lesbian world really so polarized? Few of the women I know fit neatly into one category or another. Some of them attend both the music festivals and the Clit Club; many have little interest in either world. I find that both scenes simultaneously attract me and offend me. Over the years, my lesbian identity has felt empowering, exhilarating, consuming, joyful, angry, and occasionally even irrelevant. But lately it feels like a tug-of-war.

DRAWING THE BOUNDARIES

In 1969, when psychologist Dr. David Reuben wrote, "One vagina plus another vagina equals zero," he was echoing the time-worn belief that female sexuality is passive and receptive, and virtually nonexistent without a man. Before the nineteenth century, the lesbian was often characterized as a woman with a huge clitoris who penetrated another woman with it. In this male-centered view, a woman's lust for another woman was practically inconceivable; no penis equaled no sex.

In the late nineteenth century, medical men conducted "scientific" studies of sex, dropping the notion of the clitoris-as-penis literally, but keeping it in spirit. They defined the lesbian as a man trapped in a female body, an "invert" or member of a "third sex." It's hard to say how popular these ideas were among the women they described. At the time, a number of working-class women "passed," dressing, working, and marrying as men. But how they (or their "wives") thought about themselves is lost to history, as are the recollections of nearly all women of color. It is the work of white, upper-class, literary women that survives, much of which used the sexologists' theories to define a shared identity and subculture.

The best known of these efforts is Radclyffe Hall's 1928 novel *The Well of Loneliness*, whose protagonist, Stephen Gordon, is a "true invert," masculine in thought, feeling, and desire. Her body—broad shoulders, narrow hips, flat chest—is only rudimentarily female. By the end of the novel, her typically feminine lover, Mary, marries a man (after Stephen tricks her into it, nobly sacrificing their relationship so that Mary can have a "normal" life). Lesbians, Hall implies, are trapped in the lonely, no-woman's-land of gender gone awry. They have less in common with "normal," feminine women than with heterosexual men. And, according to this definition, it's unclear whether women like Mary count as lesbians at all.

By midcentury, both "experts" and lesbians themselves had switched from the lesbian-as-invert model to lesbian-as-female-homosexual and to lesbianism as a sexual preference. If the notion that lesbians had much in common with straight men lived on, the belief that they were men trapped in women's bodies became less and less convincing. A neatly symmetrical set of categories described the sexual possibilities: female or male, homosexual or heterosexual. But the symmetry did not imply equality; the homosexual remained the "deviant" or "variant."

Variant was the label of choice of the Daughters of Bilitis, the first lesbian organization in the United States, which was founded in 1955. The DOB saw its mission as educating the public, participating in research, and assisting "the adjustment of the variant to society." That program of adjustment discouraged the embrace of butch-femme styles, seeking to teach butches, in particular, "a mode of behavior and dress acceptable to society." DOB founders Del Martin and Phyllis Lyon recall that they knew "too many lesbians whose activities were restricted because they wouldn't wear skirts."[2] Seeking to gain legitimacy by defining lesbianism as a sexual preference rather than a gender inversion, they wanted their members to look the part.

In the 1960s, many "sex experts" abandoned the concept of inversion, adopting the idea of the "female homosexual" and popularizing the view that lesbians are attracted to women in much the same way that gay men are attracted to men. Lesbianism became firmly established as a sexual orientation, the female version of homosexuality. If that definition seems straightforward and painfully obvious it's because it has permeated our thinking.

But by the early 1970s lesbian feminists conspired to challenge such definitions, proclaiming that lesbianism was no "mere sexual preference." "What is a lesbian? a lesbian is the rage of all women condensed to the point of explosion," wrote the Radicalesbians in 1970.[3] In a strategically clever reformulation, they responded to straight feminists' homophobia by defining lesbianism as a form of female revolt and woman-bonding, dissociating it from male homosexuality. In the idea of the "lesbian continuum," Adrienne Rich included "a range . . . of woman-identified experience; not simply the fact that a woman had or consciously desired genital sexual experience with another woman."[4] Cheryl Clarke wrote that such passion would "ultimately reverse the heterosexual imperialism of male culture."[5] If feminism was the theory, lesbianism was the practice.

The women's music industry, women's centers, rape crisis hotlines, battered women's shelters, and the lesbian feminist press were all more or less explicitly part of the project of constructing lesbianism as the quintessential feminism. In the 1970s, as more and more feminist activists came out, at times it appeared that Jill Johnston's proclamation that "all women are lesbians" would prove literally to be true. But as this women's culture became more clearly articulated, its borders became less and less permeable. For if the personal was political, then no part of one's life—including preferences for clothes, food, or even sex—was off-limits to scrutiny by the movement. No longer was it sufficient to simply be a lesbian; some ways of being were clearly better than others. And so commenced the Lesbian Olympics, wrote Jacquelyn Zita, where competing lesbians are ranked, categorized, accepted and rejected:

> *The criteria for ranking vary with the community— downward mobility, chemical purity, non-monogamy, proximity to men, number of cats, runs-batted-in, ritualistic obscurity, quality of exotic sexual forays and others. . . . Winners of the Olympics are named the real lesbians; runners-up lesser lesbians; and losers remain losers—immoral, inauthentic, and politically corrupt.[6]*

East Coast Lesbian Festival, 1991. I overhear a woman in her early forties say, "There were lots of excesses in the way we did things. We came down too hard on each other. It's no wonder there's this young generation of lesbians who seem so angry with us. We need the balance."

SIGNIFICANCE AND SIGNIFICATION

Every definition has placed some lesbians in the blessed inner circle and some outside it. Is a woman who identifies herself as a dyke but who's never slept with a woman a lesbian? Is a lesbian who sleeps with men really a lesbian? What about a woman who sleeps with women, but has had a primarily heterosexual past? If she becomes involved with a man next year, was she ever a true lesbian?

Lesbian theory has often worked its way through this minefield by making a distinction between "real" and "false" lesbians, explaining away those women whose experiences don't fit our definitions. When the real lesbian was the invert, her partner was not quite the authentic article. Typically she was portrayed in feminine dress and manner, signifying that she could pass as straight and often did, whether she wanted to or not. She was more likely than her partner to have been involved with men (she was possibly even married) and was widely believed to be able to go back to men at any time. Since her gendered appearance obscured the stigma of her sexuality, could she really be counted on? Mary, the femme to Stephen's butch character in *The Well of Loneliness*, seems loyal enough, but in the end her lesbian allegiance proves to be too weak.

Given lesbian feminism's penchant for downgrading and dismissing certain varieties of lesbian experience (notably butch-femme relationships), it may be difficult to remember that lesbian feminists, too, have been relegated to the "false lesbian" category by those who see themselves as "born lesbians." Sex therapist JoAnn Loulan explains:

What I have heard, from "old-time" lesbians, if you will—seventies and sixties lesbians who came out in the sixties and fifties, is that . . . they've felt the community has been overwhelmed and inundated with women who weren't really lesbians but who felt it was the cool thing to do. They've been expecting a shake-

down, for the trendiness to lose its appeal, and for the
real lesbians to emerge again.[7]

The most recent version of the "false lesbian" label adheres to
dykes who sleep with men. In 1990, a widely discussed article
by longtime lesbian feminist activist Jan Clausen declared her
involvement with a man and argued for her right to maintain a
lesbian identity nonetheless. A series of angry letters followed.
One woman wrote: "The bottom line is: I don't consider any
woman a dyke who sleeps with a man. Period." Another declared: "These women refuse or are afraid to own their own
bisexual identity. They dilute and pollute the very definition and
essence of lesbianism."[8] Using the real/false lesbian distinction
to patrol the borders of lesbianism raises the question, "What's
a false lesbian to do?" The implied answer is clear: be straight.

Confessions of a false lesbian: I was married to a man when I
first came out, and when I fell in love with a woman I searched
my past hard and long for evidence that I had "really" "always"
been a lesbian. Much more eager to prove to myself that I was
a lesbian than to find evidence that I wasn't, I just couldn't say
to myself, "I choose to be a lesbian." I was afraid I'd have to be
straight unless I could prove I wasn't.

The popular distinction between "real lesbians" and those who
appear to be lesbians but actually aren't is rooted in essentialism.
The notion that lesbianism is the expression of an inherent
(maybe even biological) essence underscores much thinking
about sexual identity. Lesbianism, we say, is an orientation—a
"true self"—which, in every time and place, clearly distinguishes us from them.

But the lesbian feminists of the early seventies tossed out
the notion of the "true lesbian self." They hacked away at the
conceptual boundary between lesbians and straight women,
promising, in Alix Dobkin's words, that "any woman can be a
lesbian." In the process, they welcomed into the fold many
women whom more essentialist definitions had portrayed as

"false" lesbians. An extensive heterosexual history did not preclude you from claiming dykedom.

But even as they created new, more fluid conceptions, lesbian feminists invested in rigid understandings of the "true essence" of women. They believed that they were constructing a movement that expressed that essence—and the real interests of women. Women, they said, weren't *really* interested in casual sex, or body adornment, or men. Of course, some women didn't see it that way. But they were covered by lesbian feminism's own category of the false: male-identification.

Since they collaborated with the enemy, heterosexual women were male-identified. But lesbians could also be male-identified—if they identified too closely with the cultures and practices of gay men, or if they "emulated heterosexuality" by relating as butches and femmes. The strongest denouncement was reserved for s/m lesbians, who were accused of replicating the dominant culture's linkage of sex and violence.

Such charges of male-identification were rooted not only in antisex attitudes (which seem to have since softened), but also in essentialist understandings of womanhood. For lesbian feminists it was an article of faith: women's authentic sexuality is process-oriented and egalitarian rather than genitally focused.

So much has changed, and so fast, that it's difficult to remember what I felt in the early 1980s, when I was trashing lesbian feminism and brandishing "incorrect" politics at every turn. My criticisms are more tempered now, and my enthusiasms less blind. For one thing, lesbian feminism has become an easy target, and easy targets are no fun. But more to the point, those things that are real dangers—random, vicious violence against women and gay men and people of color, the decimation of a generation from AIDS and complacency, the slow, sure destruction of the air and water and land, the misery of urban poverty, and the latest wars—weren't created by lesbian feminists. Increasingly, I wonder whether we take each other on because we've lost faith in our ability to fight the big fights.

NEW LESBIANISM, OLD QUESTIONS

If lesbian feminists bought into essentialist beliefs about gender difference, today's lesbian queers have not. They see gender as a game, played with signs and symbols, whose meanings are constantly shifting and negotiable. Their wardrobes read like a list of lesbian feminist horrors: leather and chains, high heels and stockings (worn over shaved legs!) and lacy push-up bras. Appropriating the symbols of gender, they announce: I can wear a dress and lipstick or have a pierced nipple. It has nothing to do with helplessness, the cult of beauty, or mutilation. As an *On Our Backs* model put it: "I don't wear 'fuck me' pumps. I wear 'fuck you' pumps."[9]

The new lesbian's understanding of what it means to be a woman may emphasize choice and change, but, in many respects, her understanding of sexual identity is actually quite traditional. Lesbianism, she believes, is about sexual preference. That is what distinguishes lesbians—and gay men—from the rest of the world, as one member of the direct-action group Queer Nation put it: "I just want to say, 'I'm queer.' That's the only term that matters—I'm a sexual minority, I'm not straight, and my relationships are not legitimized by the straight world. I'm an outsider; I'm queer; I'm different."[10]

In many ways, the 1990s word "queer" looks like a more defiant and prouder version of the 1950s word "variant," signifying sexual deviance. But there are signs that these new lesbians are willing to define lesbianism in more slippery terms than their older sisters. The acceptance, in some circles, of lesbians who engage in sex with men is a case in point. But that acceptance seems to come more from a conviction that "anything goes" sexually than from any questioning of the *idea* of sexual preference. Some may play around with men, but lesbian queers see themselves as more like gay men than straight women.

New lesbians make their chief political and cultural alliances with gay men, arguing that lesbians and gay men are two sides of the same coin. If we're all queer, it means that we locate ourselves, according to activist Charles Fernandez, "exclusively in opposition to the category of heterosexual."[11] Gender opposition disappears. But when lesbianism is defined as a sexual preference—the female version of homosexuality—women get the short end of the stick. Being a lesbian does not immunize us from things like rape, harassment, or poverty. Moreover, the tendency in homo-land, as elsewhere, is to take male behavior as the yardstick, the norm, the lens through which all other behavior is viewed. By these standards, lesbian queerness is not "true" queerness.

Lesbian queers sometimes buy into this, enacting their own nineties version of the Lesbian Olympics, taking other lesbians to task for being less hip, less sexual, in other words—not like gay men. Susie Bright, writing in *On Our Backs*, asks:

> *Are lesbian audiences ready for their own drag shows? Are lesbians afraid to show and admire their masculine selves? I'm afraid I'm going to have to sissy-bait all you pussies out there until I see some results. When are we going to learn to enjoy the sexuality of gender instead of being terrorized by it?*[12]

In this version, lesbian sexual culture is not like gay men's because lesbians, as women, are sexually repressed. By extension, male sexuality is unrepressed, authentic, the norm. Obviously, women are encouraged to control their sexuality, to use it as a means to some other end, such as love or money. But men's sexual ways are also shaped by their situation. It's simplistic to think that some "authentic," "unrepressed" lesbian sexuality would look like male sexuality—even of the gay male variety. The females of the emergent Queer Nation seem to have forgotten that we're not just fighting for access to what the boys have.

Certainly new lesbians, on the streets and in the sex magazines, have expanded the pleasures and possibilities of lesbian sexuality as never before. Ten years ago, it was tough to find lesbians talking about sex toys, s/m, role-playing, and fist-fucking, to say nothing of engaging in them. That's the good news.

The bad news is that for all its embrace of the kinky, the new lesbian definition of sex is pretty narrow. In Susie Bright's words, the only sex worth having is the "sweat-pouring-off-you, the *She's Gotta Have It* variety." Lesbian feminists were rigid and dead wrong in claiming that lesbians wanted only a diffuse, process-oriented sexuality. But when lesbian queers try to liberate sexuality without recognizing that some women *do* want that sort of sexuality, they just erect a new barrier, and a new category of the false: false lesbian sex. (You may think that what you're doing is having sex, but it's too tame to be the real thing.)

Lesbian feminists opened the door to letting women be lesbian in ways that were specifically female, but over time, the realm of the "woman-identified" became more and more restrictive. Today, by allying with gay men, lesbians end up as the lesser queers, as the deviant deviants. Neither alternative will do. Lesbians are not the female version of (male) homosexuality. On the other hand, the boundary between lesbians and straight women may be permeable, but we usually know when we've crossed it. The truth is, most of us sometimes feel incredibly queer, at other times indelibly female. Some of us identify more centrally with racial or ethnic identities. What neither lesbian feminists nor lesbian queers seem to understand fully is that sexual identities, and the political affiliations that arise from them, are always shifting and contingent.

The foundation of identity politics—the belief that, as lesbians, we share an identity and therefore a politics—is crumbling. The post-Stonewall mainstream gay and lesbian rights movement was founded on an essentialist gay identity, which claimed that gay people are the equivalent of an ethnic minority. The feminist movement, too, was grounded in the shared identity of all women as "women." This conception of identity politics has been challenged by women of color, and by others for whom community allegiances and identities originate from more than one source—by those for whom, as Jackie Goldsby wrote, "splitting our affiliations just won't do."[13]

Identities are often difficult to pin down. They are diverse and multiple. It's impossible to identify with a single conception of a "woman" or a "lesbian." For we can only believe in "the lesbian" by downplaying differences, by obscuring parts of our lives. In the 1970s, lesbians who would not ignore gender chose lesbian feminism over the gay rights movement. Today, a generation of younger lesbians, refusing to ignore differences of sexuality, are helping to construct the new queer culture. Women from both age cohorts are claiming the importance of their ethnic, racial, and class identities. And, increasingly, we are all realizing that identities are multiple and complex.

As Shane Phelan, a philosopher, puts it, "The struggles of lesbians over the past thirty years should tell us that people are not 'actually like' anything."[14] But if there is no timeless and essential lesbianism, what is the proper hook on which we can hang our political actions? What, in other words, are our common interests? What do lesbians *really* want? If "the lesbian" is nothing more than a shifting definition, is there any way to answer these questions?

If we can answer them at all, we may have to do so in a tentative fashion, specific to our time and place. That means dealing with contradictions. It means abandoning the search for consistency. To use critic Ann Snitow's term, sometimes we need to "minimize" lesbian identity by constantly pushing against the borders; at other times we need to "maximize" it.[15] We minimize identity when we refuse to be controlled by it, when we expand the ways to be a lesbian. There are ways in which both lesbian feminists and lesbian queers dream of a world without sexual identity, a world where homosexuality doesn't exist because heterosexuality doesn't exist either.

But even dreamers have to deal with the world, a world where it is at times necessary to maximize our shared lesbian identity, to proclaim our common needs and demand that they be met. Our politics must negotiate this duality; neither maximizing nor minimizing lesbian identities is sufficient in itself.

We have seen the problems of the maximizing approach —the construction of rigid, suffocating, and at least implicitly racist understandings of "the lesbian" and her culture, ethics, and politics. But wholesale minimizing runs the risk of making us disappear before we've changed the world. If *we* deconstruct before *they* deconstruct, we end up in a situation where "the rich as well as the poor are forbidden to sleep under bridges," where equality is defined as blindness to real difference. We have to minimize *and* maximize, create unities and simultaneously see them as false, build boundaries around ourselves, and, at the same time, smash them.

Years ago, I pried myself loose from a white, middle-class, vacuous culture and ran into the protective arms of the "lesbian community." Now, as the basis of that community is revealed to be a fiction, I feel cut adrift. I ask my lover, "Where does all of this leave us? Out there?" But she cannot talk. She's out on strike and is on her way to walk the picket line. In her union, she has pushed for domestic partner benefits, for a sexual harassment policy, and for the biggest raises for the lowest-paid. Through her efforts, I'm beginning to acknowledge that it is not uniformly ugly "out there." But the path that once seemed clear to me has more twists and turns now, and I can only see what's just ahead.

What is a lesbian? Who is a lesbian? One woman says it's her lust that makes her a lesbian, even if she admits that she likes men, too. Another says that it's her choice to surround herself with a community of women. A third talks in terms of her deeply felt sense that she is different, queer. In the end, a lesbian must simply be any woman who calls herself one, understanding that we place ourselves within that category, drawing and redrawing the boundaries in ever-shifting ways. For there is no essential and timeless lesbian, but instead lesbians who, by creating our lives day by day, widen the range of possibilities.

PART TWO

IMAGINING OURSELVES

LESBIAN LIFE IS INDISTINGUISHABLE FROM OUR IMAGES OF IT. Not only do the mass media shape how we see ourselves, but they also determine in large part how others see (or don't see) us. This second section focuses on the shifting relationship between lesbian culture and popular culture, and on the ways in which lesbians working in film, producing their own magazines, and making music are constructing new images of lesbian life.

While gay and bisexual men have long made their mark in popular music, in literature, and in many other areas, lesbians continue to stand on the sidelines. In many respects, quoting writer Joan Nestle, we remain citizens of "a restricted country." At the same time, as a community, we have little consensus as to how we should represent ourselves. Some believe we should create only "positive images," which are most palatable to the mainstream. Some think we should represent the full spectrum of our lives—warts and all. Others contend that we should create an alternative lesbian culture that can stand completely outside the mainstream, while still others assert that we should struggle to make inroads into mainstream film, music, and the like. This section looks at historical shifts in the ways in which we represent lesbianism—to ourselves, and to those outside our communities.

It is perhaps fitting that videos and homemade photocopied magazines called " 'zines" emerged as the two most potent lesbian-made media in the 1980s. Both are relatively cheap and easy to produce—necessary criteria in a community that tends to lack the resources for more costly endeavors. Both lend themselves to mixing and matching a variety of cultural influences, which may help explain why they are embraced by younger women who are fashioning lesbian representations that draw on elements of, among other things, 1970s lesbian feminism, 1950s butch-femme, and punk.

Looking at the evolution of lesbian filmmaking, Liz Kotz focuses on the films of four women—one from the 1970s and three from the 1980s and 1990s—to show how lesbian filmmakers, once concerned almost entirely with creating art that would be free of the language and imagery of the dominant culture, are now increasingly making links between lesbian culture and the "mainstream." In contrast to an earlier period, today's filmmakers are less likely to make "lesbian films" and more likely to produce works that explore lesbian themes in relation to popular culture.

Similarly, in the new genre of 'zines, younger women are expressing themselves by embracing and at times also mocking dominant cultural images of the "lesbian." In "A Freak Among Freaks," S. Bryn Austin and Pam Gregg provide a survey of lesbian 'zines, from their beginnings in punk culture to their more recent proliferation in lesbian and gay communities. 'Zines may exemplify the predicament lesbians find themselves in in popular culture today: children of television, they have grown up surrounded by mass culture, and yet find themselves curiously alienated by its content.

Twenty years ago, the founders of women's culture tried

to create new forms that would stand outside, and in opposition to, the dominant culture. Many young lesbians today situate themselves, ironically, inside *and* outside it. They "use guerrilla strategies to fashion their own icons and histories from scavenged pop cultural information," write Austin and Gregg. And they wholeheartedly embrace sexual imagery.

In "Androgyny Goes Pop," I explore what appear to be new openings for "unconventional" women performers and audiences in the commercial music industry. In contrast to those who were part of the women's music network of the 1970s, few of these women see themselves as self-consciously making "lesbian culture." Rather, many see themselves as lesbians making culture, and they don't believe they owe any particular allegiance to a lesbian "community." k.d. lang plays "for the girls as well as the boys." Michelle Shocked sings a love song to a woman —and to a man.

Who would have thought that a woman swaggering in a man's Western suit and singing torch songs would achieve mainstream success in an industry that likes to keep its women glossy and available? As feminist styles are incorporated into pop culture and the boundaries between "mainstream" and "women's" culture blur, some lesbian performers find an unprecedented degree of freedom to construct their images as they please. Perhaps it is a testimony to the maturity of lesbian culture that filmmakers and musicians no longer believe they have to make their lesbianism the central overriding feature of their work. But barriers imposed by the film and recording industries— and the artists' own ambitions—still prevent many from "speaking" lesbianism.

On the one hand, a young lesbian today can see images in the mainstream that closely resemble her. On the other hand, since lesbianism is still rarely spoken and the vast majority of the population can't "read" the codes, the heterosexual norm remains, for the most part, unchallenged. Often it seems as though the only performers who are "allowed" to speak lesbianism are those, such as Madonna, whose heterosexuality is seen as unwavering.

The problems go deeper when we add questions of race. It's no coincidence, Jackie Goldsby writes, that a white performer like Madonna can embrace lesbian imagery and transgress gender and sexual boundaries, while Vanessa Williams, a black woman, was castigated for it. In "Queen for 307 Days," Goldsby analyzes the fall from grace of the first black Miss America, dethroned for her associations with sexually explicit lesbian photos. That incident, Goldsby argues, is far more consequential than one might think. For women of color, particularly lesbians of color, every representation of sexuality is also a representation of race. That lesbian feminists were curiously silent on Williams's fall from the throne exemplifies a larger problem in feminism, and in lesbian discussions of sex, says Goldsby: we tend to ignore the historical connections of race and sexuality. For black women, as for lesbians, sex in public is taboo. Black lesbian sexuality may be doubly taboo.

LIZ KOTZ

ANYTHING BUT IDYLLIC: LESBIAN FILMMAKING IN THE 1980s AND 1990s

Someone must always be more powerful, someone is always more or less powerful. It can be me or you, one woman or another, but power is always there, it is never, ever, absent. Right now, I have it, you're listening to my words and you recognize my strength. . . . It's because we've lost power that we need each other like this.

THESE WORDS ARE UTTERED TOWARD THE END OF *LET'S PLAY Prisoners* (1988), Julie Zando's provocative and haunting video about love, control, and submission between women—as lovers and friends, as mother and child, or even as artist and viewer. In this video made fifteen years after the beginning of independently produced lesbian media in this country, Zando starts from an assumption of the complete interrelation of power and sexuality—an assumption that couldn't be further from the representations of utopian lesbian worlds found in many of the films, novels, and narratives of the mid-1970s.

Despite fears of censorship, and antifeminist and antigay backlashes during the past decade, more lesbian artists are "out" in public, and more and more often they are taking on controversial issues and experiences. At the same time that the idea of a unified, distinct "lesbian community" has been thrown into question, lesbian filmmakers and videomakers are exploring worlds that are complex, conflicted, and anything but idyllic. An idealized and often painfully sentimentalized "up with lesbians" film aesthetic has, in the past few years, given way to a number of works that probe darker and, at times, distinctly dystopic aspects of women's relationships and communities.

Lesbian film and video provide a corrective to the attitudes, stereotypes, and models of Hollywood films, television, and the popular press, but they also respond to the representations which have been produced within the lesbian community. Films, videos, and art about aspects of lesbian identity are more numerous now than ever, yet the nature of these media—the kinds of audiences they were made for, and the kinds of roles they play—has clearly changed.

Once strongly based in, and accountable to, self-defined "women's communities," lesbian film today is often made by individuals who may feel deeply ambivalent about their relation to these communities—particularly younger women, women of color, or others whose lives are distant from the lesbian feminist utopias envisioned and made visible during the mid-1970s. Often, these filmmakers seek out mixed or lesbian/gay audiences in the context of gay film festivals, the independent film community, or the art world. In the fields of independent and experimental film and video especially, many of the most visible and most successful artists are gay women who create work that sometimes does, and sometimes doesn't, explicitly address lesbian subjects or issues.

Early lesbian experimental cinema of the 1970s sprang up at the intersection of several historical forces: a tradition of American experimental cinema committed, against the narrative conventions of the larger culture, to self-made "personal" filmmaking; an emerging feminist documentary practice, made possible by the development of lightweight, portable equipment that allowed "direct" recordings of events and personal testimonies; and an increasingly separatist lesbian feminist community which, although predominately white and middle class, tried to distance itself not only from the dominant culture, but also from other "deviant" communities, such as gay men and prostitutes.

If any shared trait marked lesbian culture and experimental film culture of the 1970s, it was something like a "tyranny of the radical," in which anything believed to be inherited from the dominant culture was energetically purged. Reacting to the depiction of women in heterosexual pornography, mainstream movies, and advertising, feminists criticized or even proscribed erotic or objectified images of women. These restrictions on content and form made it difficult, for instance, to explore lesbian subjectivity in relation to popular culture, to the cultural and political contradictions of present-day American society, or to diverse ethnic and racial histories. Emerging in response to the modern feminist movement, lesbian experimental film tried to free itself from the repressive, "patriarchal" culture and create a "new language" of lesbian desire and identity. Yet, in its own way, it was unavoidably situated within and shaped by this culture.

The most visible and most prolific producer of early lesbian cinema was Barbara Hammer. Starting in the San Francisco Bay Area in the early 1970s, she has produced almost fifty short experimental films, many of which have been screened internationally. Like that of many feminist artists of the period, Hammer's work initially revolved around the development of a specifically female aesthetic focused on questions of gender and female community. Formally her films are lyrical and imagistic, working with metaphor and superimposition. Thematically, they investigate autobiography, the body, and sexuality, and are often situated in a mythic, pastoral landscape.

Hammer's *Dyketactics* (1974) presents a group of women in nature enacting a communal ritual that celebrates sensuality and lesbian collectivity. By representing the sexual completely divorced from any of the genre conventions of pornography, the film elaborates a tactile, sensual aesthetic. It juxtaposes shots of hands and bodies, water, grass, and women having sex, all situated in an almost mythically pure rural setting, compressing many of the elements that are now seen as stereotypical of this period. In *Double Strength* (1978), Hammer adopts a more explicitly autobiographical form to represent her relationship and breakup with trapeze artist Terry Sendgraft. The camera records an interplay between the two women that is lyrical, harmonious, and egalitarian. The "breakup" occurs offscreen, evoked through metaphor but not recorded directly.

Hammer's 1978 film *Women I Love* is a classic compendium of 1970s-style cunt imagery, represented directly and through various floral and natural symbols. While the intent may be to glorify women's sexuality, the cumulative effect of the images, at least at this historical distance, is deeply romanticizing—a strategy perhaps necessitated by the politicized suspicion of sexual imagery among many feminists. Ironically, much like porn, this idealized iconography of women's bodies and sexuality has the effect of isolating sex from everyday life, from relationships and all their inevitable emotional and political complications. The tendency to locate sexual expression within this pastoral, mythical realm may say a lot about how distant any public expression of sexuality has been from most women's lives, particularly within the kinds of urban spaces that gay men have long had access to. Other films by Hammer, *Menses* (1974), *Superdyke* (1974), and *The Great Goddess* (1977), documented and celebrated various elements of this mythically oriented 1970s lesbian culture.

While many of these once-exploratory tropes became quite conventionalized in 1970s lesbian feminist culture, Hammer helped originate this aesthetic, and her works often have a lyrical power and rhythmic intensity. *Dyketactics*, in particular, was a groundbreaking film, one which helped set the agendas, for better or worse, to which much later lesbian cinema would respond. Energetically embracing sexual expression at a time when many feminists, including lesbians, were unwilling to accept lesbian visual imagery, Hammer's films of the 1970s responded to a complex historical moment full of contradictory possibilities and restrictions. The films are unabashedly gay liberationist, exhibiting all the separatist, experimental, utopian tendencies of the movement in Northern California in the 1970s. These tendencies were rooted in, and contributed to, a model of women's culture which strove to be almost completely outside the structures of "patriarchal," capitalist American society —distinct from the consumerist, urban-based gay male culture of the late 1970s.[1]

Clearly, imagining another world served a purpose. But this retreat from history and from cultural specificity became increasingly problematic. The narrative of "coming out," which dominated much lesbian and gay filmmaking of the 1970s and 1980s, reflected this belief in sexuality as the basis for personal identity, prior to any other cultural or social affiliation. Such a focus on the personal and autobiographical often fit neatly with American individualism and voluntarist strategies of political change. As gay historian and theorist John D'Emilio argues, there has often been "an overreliance on a strategy of coming out" in gay culture, one which has "allowed us to ignore the institutionalized ways in which homophobia and heterosexism are reproduced."[2]

By the 1980s, lesbian artists in many disciplines came to question the predominance of autobiographical genres and the reliance on the coming-out story as the defining narrative of lesbian work. It is easy to see how such devices had become deeply clichéd, with all the romanticized tales of women breaking with repressive families and the falseness of straight society to find harmony, happiness, and their "real selves" within the lesbian community. Feminist documentaries, in particular, had tended to rely on "talking heads"–style presentations of women telling the "truth" of their own experiences. These strategies, which were believed to create a truer, more immediate, and more self-defined representation of women, tended to deny the mediation and manipulation inherent in any filmed and edited representation.

Yet such naive assumptions, however common, are not inherent in autobiographical work or coming-out stories. A good case in point is *Susana* (1980), by the Argentinian-born San Francisco filmmaker Susana Blaustein Munoz, who went on to make the highly acclaimed documentaries *Las Madres: The Mothers of the Plaza De Mayo* (1986) and *La Ofrenda: The Days of the Dead* (1989) with Lourdes Portillo. A self-reflexive and probing look at family and coming out, *Susana* shows how issues of sexual identity and self-determination can be situated within larger cultural and social histories. Even viewed more than ten years after its making, little except the clothing and hairstyles seems dated. A bittersweet work about Munoz's tentative reconciliation with her family, the short film implicitly questions the documentary techniques it uses. As Munoz records the reminiscences of her family and close friends, the process of filmmaking produces a tense encounter between the subjects and the filmmaker, one which often verges on emotional violence.

The film works through disjuncture, probing conflicting points of view rather than creating a seamless narrative flow. Susana's mother recounts her combined love for and rejection of her daughter. She recalls Susana's upbringing in Mendoza, a small town in Argentina, and tries to figure out what went wrong with her smart, headstrong daughter: "Her only problem was to be stubborn. . . . I'm trying to be honest and just, but when I look back on my child's life, I can't find any problem with her." Confronted with her daughter's lesbianism and her departure from the strictures of small-town life, Susana's mother puts it into terms she can understand: "Mendoza was too small for her."

What is at stake, from the outset, is who gets to represent Susana, and how: what genres, narratives, and histories her life will be shaped and understood by. Visually, the film combines Munoz's photographs of herself with home movies and baby pictures, presumably taken by her parents. Even though this is her film, it is clearly not her story only. The film counterposes the perspective of the filmmaker, who sees her parents as having rejected her, with that of her parents, who see their daughter as having rejected them and their way of life. Switching back and forth between speakers, *Susana* probes not only these conflicting opinions but also their irreconcilable ways of making sense of the world. "Yes, Mother," Susana responds with some irony, "I guess Mendoza was too small for me."

The film's most poignant moments focus on Susana's younger sister Graciela, to whom the film is dedicated. Sequences of Graciela reading her written statements are intercut with scenes of two of Susana's lovers. As Graciela describes her fear of Susana, who, her parents have told her, is a "sexual deprivate" and dangerous, Susana's ex-girlfriend recalls how Graciela's visits, as an emissary of her parents and their expectations, would set back Susana's growing self-acceptance. Yet Susana's emerging lesbian identity is not romanticized or idealized. Karen, Susana's first lover, recounts that Susana gave photographs of Karen as presents when they first got involved; one day, after a fight, Karen came home to find her face had been "torn into pieces." Though the violent emotional conflicts between the two lovers are not downplayed, they are shown to be very different from Susana's ruptures with her sister and mother. Munoz, as she presents herself within the film, is tough and angry, but also resilient.

At the end of the film, Susana enters the frame and the two sisters confront each other onscreen. Graciela asks Susana what she thinks, whether they can be friends. "Well, you know, 'friends' is a funny word," Susana replies. "If I do this it's because I think people can communicate. But do you think I really have to change?" When Graciela answers yes, she still thinks Susana must change, that there is no future for her without a man, it is clear that the conflict is as much Graciela's as Susana's. Although she knows she is bolstered by social convention, Graciela paradoxically still looks for her older sister's approval. The relation of power between the two remains ambiguous, and in the end Susana appears to triumph.

Juxtaposing stories and perspectives, the film represents different parts of Susana—her cultural identity as an Argentinian and as a Jew, her family's heritage, her sexual identity, her life as an artist—as conflicting and yet completely interrelated. With its model of personal identity as a composite of disparate, intersecting social forces and narratives, *Susana* foreshadowed much of the lesbian filmmaking that followed in the 1980s.

Like Munoz's *Susana*, the work of New York experimental filmmaker Su Friedrich offers a set of subjective reflections on family and cultural history. Friedrich's works have ranged from the silent, nonnarrative *Cool Hearts, Warm Heart* (1979) and *Gently Down the Stream* (1981) to later works incorporating dramatization, narrative, and documentary techniques, such as *The Ties That Bind* (1984), *Damned If You Don't* (1987), and *Sink or Swim* (1990). Often loosely autobiographical, her films locate the individual in a web of intersecting histories and narratives, chance events, and fantasies, in which forces of empowerment and entrapment cannot fully be separated.

Gently Down the Stream uses text and rephotographed imagery to interweave themes of sexual conflicts, troubled relationships, and Catholic guilt. Based on dreams Friedrich recorded in her journal over a number of years, the film meditates on moments of anxiety, doubt, and everyday trauma. The text is scratched word by word into the emulsion, leaving the spectator in a state of waiting and uncertainty: "I / wake / her / She / is/angry/Smears/spermicidal/jelly/on/my/lips/NO!" "I/draw/a/ man/Take/his/skin/Get/excited/Mount/it/IT'S/LIKE/BEING/IN/ LOVE / WITH / A / STRAIGHT / WOMAN." As the film progresses, the anxieties take shape, offering different glimpses of Friedrich's psyche and probing these traumas and tensions. The lesbian experiences evoked by the film are anything but idyllic.

The film's form is itself fractured and disturbed; bits of white leader and punched-out holes insist on the vulnerability and incompleteness of the medium. Series of images—feet walking, water viewed from a boat, a woman rowing, religious artifacts—shift from full-frame to reframed presentations in irregular patterns and rhythms. Their relation to the text is not illustrative but suggestive and oblique, intersecting erratically to create new sets of associations and subjective impressions. The structure of *Gently Down the Stream* is highly permeable, conveying a sense of random and unpredictable encounters that approximate dream logic, as the film proceeds in a stream-of-consciousness flow with constant interruptions and eruptions of unprocessed, sometimes obscure material.

In one of Friedrich's more recent films, *Damned If You Don't* (1987), she returns to the subject of Catholicism, telling a story of a nun's seduction by another woman. Somewhat more conventionally narrative in structure, the film incorporates historical materials into its story: footage from *Black Narcissus*, a 1946 film about nuns; a friend's taped reminiscences of a Catholic-school girlhood; and testimonials from Judith Brown's book, *Immodest Acts: The Life of a Lesbian Nun in Renaissance Italy* (Oxford, 1986). Yet this time, the relationship of lesbian desire to the traditions of Catholicism is more ambiguous. Rather than simply condemning the repressive nature of such religious traditions, the film performs a loosely historical investigation of nuns as embodiments of suppressed and displaced female desires.

Turning the tables on the symbols and structures of institutionalized repression, in its final seduction scene the film gently eroticizes the religious vestments, portraying them as covers hiding potential pleasure and abandon. Sensuality and physical pleasure appear at every turn, as the nun is unable to escape her desires. She flees her pursuer to visit an aquarium, only to be confronted by a pair of beautiful white whales twisting through the water. Throughout the film, the implicit sensuality and perversity of the baroque Catholic iconography is used to create an erotic fascination with concealment and repression. The other woman finally accomplishes her seduction through a gift, a small needlepoint image of Christ with only the mouth embroidered, which she leaves in the nun's room, an eroticized *détournement* of the religious icon.

The underlying strategy of the film revolves around recovering—for pleasure, for suspense, and for fantasy—the mechanisms, anxieties, and twisted representations of the oppressive culture. Rather than questioning the "truth" of its assembled documents, Friedrich probes their pathologized narratives as sources of both history and fascination, documents whose aesthetic excesses and ambiguous powers can be undermined and resituated in a modern tale of "girl gets girl." The structure of the film works to appropriate filmic clichés of voyeuristic pleasure, female sexuality, and happy endings into its highly personal and even humorous meditation on lesbian erotic pursuit and guilt-drenched lust. Rather than using its fragments to create a new fiction of lesbian identity free from repression, the film plays itself out on the level of suggestion and allegory. Perhaps more than anything, it is about fantasy and the processes by which repressive experiences and traumas, when reworked, become turn-ons. Like *Gently Down the Stream*, *Damned If You Don't* explores the subjective processes of memory, anxiety, and fantasy.

In this alternation between critical and almost nostalgic stances, Friedrich's film explores how a modern lesbian subject is positioned in relation to these representations. *Damned If You Don't* seems to revolve around the possibilities for creating pleasure in the discards of a repressive and constrained past, and of moving beyond feminist critique to selectively reinvest these images and memories with private and erotic meanings. With its sensual and suggestive intercutting, the film probes the complex interplays of voyeurism and identification, guilt, pleasure, and shame, at work in their cautious reappropriation. As Scott MacDonald notes in his discussion of Friedrich's films:

> Damned If You Don't . . . *energizes feminist deconstruction by locating it within a context of at least two forms of (redirected) film pleasure: the excitement of the melodramatic narrative and the sensuous enjoyment of cinematic texture, rhythm and structure. Friedrich's decision not only to include a representation of female sexuality but to use it as the triumphant conclusion of the film is central to her new direction. Friedrich has cinematically appropriated the pleasure* of *women* for *women*.[3]

Another artist who in recent years has probed the dense interplay of repression and desire in female relationships is videomaker Julie Zando. Zando's videos raise interesting questions about what constitutes a lesbian work, especially since they don't explicitly focus on sexual relationships between women. Yet the questions she addresses, about female masochism, erotic obsession, and victimization, are clearly located in contemporary lesbian discussions of sexuality and power. Artful and complex, her videos probe the shifting relations of dominance and submission, which are not reducible to the dualistic male-female axis of power on which most earlier feminist analyses were based. Definitely not feminist fairy tales, Zando's works look frankly at desire, submission, and cruelty between women.

Conceptually blurring some of the boundaries between lesbian and straight subjectivity, Zando's films explore how lesbian identity itself is constructed in relation to larger sets of family and social relationships, but without retreating into the closet in the process. *Let's Play Prisoners* (1988) explores power between women through a story about two girls whose childhood rituals and dares take on a distinctly sadomasochistic tone. The story, read by an adult woman (the story's author, Jo Anstey) sitting on a couch, tells of childhood games of imprisonment, physical restraint, humiliation, and pain from the victim's point of view, probing how the girl's masochism and desire for approval compel her to comply with her friend's increasingly cruel requests.

The play of control in the story is echoed in the control exercised by the director in relation to the woman reading the story. Rereadings of lines, interruptions, and instructions from the director are exaggerated, and Zando's hand frequently enters the frame to prompt or adjust Anstey. Combined with the aggressively intrusive and manipulated camera work, this interplay forces the viewer to witness the tension between the two women and to comprehend the making of the video as itself an act of power and seduction. The story is repeated in fragments by a young girl, who is prompted, more gently, by her mother.

As the girls' games become increasingly sadistic, the tension between the storytellers and director also intensifies. At first, the two girls play a simple game of prisoner and guard; then they make an excursion into the forbidden territory of the boys' playground, where they must pull up their skirts so that the boys can see their underpants. Eventually, the friend tells the narrator that they must refrain from going to the bathroom all day and then both wet their pants. Torn between humiliation and an intense fear of rejection, the girl becomes distressed, refuses to comply, and provokes her friend's anger and abandonment.

Exploring this dense relationship between power and love, the video probes the edges of acceptable or comfortable experiences of submission, approval-seeking, and control. It sets up a series of reverberations between the need of the girl reading the story for approval from her mother, the need of the girl in the story for approval from her friend, and the author's need for approval from the director. The video's visually poetic and emotionally gripping play on the inescapably complex and contradictory relations of power forces the viewer to confront her own involvement and complicity in the games of voyeurism and control enacted in the tape.

While many earlier experimental works made by women, such as Hammer's, portray an unproblematic trust and intimacy between filmmaker and subject, and a faith in a direct, unmediated form of representation, Zando's video probes the highly charged undersides of such relations between women, insisting that *all* representations involve some level of control and manipulation. Zando's work implies that this space between women is seductive, but it is not "safe."

Unlike Zando's more psychoanalytically-oriented explorations of power, Indian-British film- and videomaker Pratibha Parmar has investigated levels of racist and colonialist violence in many of her works. Parmar's early video art tape *Sari Red* (1988) poetically examines how the ever-present threat of violence intrudes on the lives of Asian women. Interweaving the account of a racist-motivated murder of a young Indian woman with sensuous images of Asian women in private rituals, *Sari Red* probes the interrelation of public and private spheres and

the inseparability of private lives from global forces of colonialism and racist violence.

The tape develops an experimental language, based on
South Asian iconography, to explore the intimate spaces between women. Parmar reframes the image of the sari, an icon
of Asian female submissiveness in white racist discourse, in
order to reclaim it as a symbol of Asian female power, visual
pleasure, and cultural identity. While never explicitly sexual or
lesbian, the video implicitly politicizes the fragility of this space
between women, this possibility for intimacy and subjectivity.
The sensuality and lyricism of the images, which suggest an
almost erotic embrace of beauty, make the horror of the murder
all the more violent and disturbing.

Parmar's more recent work, *Khush* (1991), is an experimental documentary about the lives of South Asian lesbians and
gay men. Shifting from Britain to North America, to India and
back, the film explores the interplay of cultural identity, racist
repression, and sexual desire, and relates the difficulty and danger of coming out for many Asian gays, for whom the family
and community are a vital protection from racist societies. The
men and women in the film describe the tension of feeling torn
between white-dominated gay communities and ethnic communities which, because of racism, are often conservative and
inward-looking.

Revolving around the appropriation of the term *khush* (an
Urdu word meaning ecstatic pleasure) by the emerging international community of gay South Asians, the film documents
their political and cultural self-articulation in the face of legacies
of colonialism and diaspora. The film incorporates archival footage of traditional dances, contemporary performance sequences, and images from sculptures and religious icons, to
visually evoke culturally specific experiences of sexual pleasure
and identity. Like a growing number of other films and videos
by women of color, *Khush* affirms a multiplicity of gay identities
rooted in diverse historical and cultural traditions, and probes
the contradictory intersections of ethnicity, sexual identity, and
community.

   As different as they are from one another, these works nonetheless reflect some of the shifting agendas of lesbian media. Departing from a conception of lesbian identity and community as unitary, defined by opposition to or exclusion from the larger culture, lesbian artists have over the past fifteen years established a position from which to investigate and redefine elements of both gay and straight cultures. No longer bound to the production of so-called "positive images" or idealized representations, these filmmakers and videomakers are challenging and extending contemporary awareness of the relations between power and sexuality, cultural identity and community.

S. BRYN AUSTIN
WITH PAM GREGG

A FREAK AMONG FREAKS:
THE 'ZINE SCENE

i'm a big fan of the word freak. the dictionary says something about abnormality and deviation. yeah, that's it, but as opposed to what? what is this normalcy all about? straight white middle-class america, I guess. but take that a step further—what if you're a freak within a subculture—like a queer in a predominantly straight punk scene or a queer girl in a predominantly straight male punk scene. a freak among freaks.

—*Sister Nobody (Spring 1991)*

THIS TESTIMONIAL BY A LESBIAN PUNK SPEAKS TO THE DESperation and alienation of the "freak" searching for validation but finding only disapproval or, more likely, a complete absence of images in her own likeness. In the 1980s and 1990s, this alienation spawned a grass-roots publishing form called "'zines," cheap homemade magazines rooted in the lesbian/gay and feminist communities but also defined in opposition to them.

Since the first handful of publications were established in the wake of the 1969 Stonewall rebellion, lesbian/gay and feminist newspapers and magazines have grown to number in the hundreds. As lesbian/gay and feminist publishing has flourished, small alternative publications have also proliferated, filling a need for journals that speak more accurately to the experiences of different subcultures within the lesbian/gay community—such as the African-American magazines *Blk, Black Lace*, and *Aché* and the Asian-American publications *Phoenix Rising* and *Shamakami*.

What distinguishes the 'zine genre from other small, alternative publications is its location in youth culture, its punk roots, its exaltation of unpolished, raw presentations of ideas and images—and its taste for the outrageous. 'Zines tend to have a format antithetical to the design and editorial style of conventional publications. They also reject political and aesthetic orthodoxies of all sorts, and have created a new forum for exploring perspectives not represented in straight, gay, or feminist presses, or in the dominant culture at large.

Crucial to the growth of 'zines was the photocopier-and-personal-computer revolution of the 1980s, which gave renegade publishers a quick, easy, and accessible medium to work with. (The majority of 'zines are photocopied with smatterings of computer text mixed in with handwriting and graphics.) A number of lesbian and gay and alternative bookstores also began to carry the homemade publications, thereby greatly increasing the visibility of the publications and planting the 'zine seed in the minds of other potential editors.

The history of 'zines begins in the early 1980s, when punks generated publications such as *Maximum Rock N Roll* and *Flipside*, tailored to their own music, heroes, and culture. These were called "fanzines"—a fusion of the words "fan" and "magazine." In the mid-1980s, lesbian and gay male punks used the fanzine model to begin to identify their own community, one step removed from both the straight punk scene and the mainstream lesbian and gay community. *J.D.s*, (short for juvenile delinquents), a punk 'zine founded in 1986 in Toronto by G. B. Jones and Bruce La Bruce, a lesbian and a gay man, was the first of its kind and is now considered an institution in queer 'zine publishing.

Today there are dozens of queer 'zines in the United States and Canada, and new ones continue to appear in bookstores. About ten currently being published are exclusively lesbian, and

twice that number are cogender, ranging from mostly-male publications with an occasional lesbian contributor to those with a
strong feminist bent and an earnest commitment to lesbian/gay
collaboration.

Most 'zines are created in major urban areas—Los Angeles,
Chicago, Toronto, Montreal, New York. Close to twenty come
out in San Francisco alone. But a few other cities, namely Eu-
gene, Oregon, Ann Arbor, Michigan, and Minneapolis, have been
leaders in 'zine production since the early years. The cities that
generate the most 'zines tend to have an active lesbian/gay youth
culture, centered particularly in such direct-action groups as
Queer Nation.

As much as queer 'zines are rooted in punk fanzines that
are not explicitly gay, they are also rooted in (and against) the
gay/lesbian and the feminist presses, of which the largest and
best-known publications—*The Advocate*, a national gay and lesbian news magazine founded in 1967, and *off our backs*, a
national feminist news journal founded in 1970—have been in
existence for over twenty years. 'Zines such as the cosexual
Bimbox, from Toronto, deliberately situate themselves against
this legacy:

> *Lesbian and Gay publications which are available only
> by purchase lose vision. . . . Magazines like* The Ad-
> vocate *and* Out/Look *have but one mandate: to sys-
> tematically render the entire international Lesbian
> and Gay population brain-dead. Only a handful of
> small "alternative" publications stand in the way of
> the complete labotomization [sic] of our culture. BIM-
> BOX is one of those publications. (Summer 1990)*

For many lesbians, magazines such as *The Advocate* are read as
a two-decade legacy of male content, perspective, and aesthetics.
Because of this, some 'zines, such as Chicago's *Madwoman*, take
a somewhat separatist line, resisting interaction with the gay
male press, which has long been controlled by male editors,
dominated by articles on male issues, and packaged in beefcake

covers. But for many lesbian 'zine makers, established feminist/ lesbian publications are not much better, as *Sister Nobody*, a dyke punk 'zine from San Francisco, reveals:

> *Standing in A DIFFERENT LIGHT bookstore, looking through the magazine racks for something— ANYTHING—with cool, funny, homo, intelligent, punk content by and for girls. i don't find it in ON OUR BACKS, OFF OUR BACKS, UP OUR BUTTS, or in any number of feminist-journal-poetry-mags. all i find is SISTER! and minimal girl input/content in HOMO-CORE. the inspiration comes from the gaping void that needs to be filled—as in the utter lack of cool girl stuff—but the apathy kicks in when i wonder if anyone, male or female, even notices that void or gives a shit if its filled. (Spring 1990)*

Lesbian 'zine creators seek to fill that "gaping void." In the process, they are helping to extend the parameters of what is considered "lesbian." Situating themselves within (and against) popular culture, and deghettoizing marginalized sexualities within lesbian communities, they are reshaping lesbian publishing and, along with it, notions of lesbian identity and culture.

LESBIAN FEMINISM MEETS THE ABSURD

In the 1970s and 1980s, a movement to render lesbians visible, and to create a lesbian "home," led to the emergence of a public lesbian community and culture. Now young 'zine makers respond to what they perceive as the exclusion by the lesbian community of identities deemed problematic or undesirable. Dyke 'zines such as *Hysteria*, published by lesbian punks in San Francisco, seek to disrupt the regimentation of political thought and behavior that their writers see in the larger lesbian community.

*Am I the last punk in this city? What's the matter isn't
it fashionable to have colored hair and to be broke?
And how come almost all the dykes in this city all
follow each other in trends (music, clothing, jewelry,
hair, etc, etc, etc)? Hardly anyone is an individual. Are
we scared to be ourselves? Oh no maybe someone wont
like us anymore if they find out how we really feel.
Please. Why are we so uptight and boring? . . . Sorry
I'd rather not partake in the dyke drama thank you.
Anyways I hope this 'zine will get some of you thinking.
Try to take a joke and stop being so uptight. (Spring
1990)*

Minneapolis artist Karen Platt created a poignant satire on the
political rigidity of the lesbian community in her 1989 *Dolo
Romy*, a cross between a 'zine and a graphic novella. It tells the
story of a "21-year-old educated, vagrant" lesbian who chances
on an underground lesbian city/police state. In her description
of the origin of the city, Platt draws obvious parallels with lesbian
separatism: "A group of ladies in 1973 got an idea that they
needed a special place to nurture women, like Lesbos. Except,
instead of an island, they went underground."

On first seeing the city from a secret passageway perched
high above the main floor, our heroine comments, "If I didn't
think those were all women down there I'd swear Bush was
involved." The women she sees are all dressed in military-style
uniforms. By the end of the tale, disgruntled citizens rebel
against the military rule, staging an insurrection to overthrow
the ruling queen, and our heroine leaves, disillusioned with the
underground lesbian society.

'Zine makers also respond to what they see as a feminist
reticence about "speaking" lesbianism. For example, when lesbian feminists adopted the terms "womyn" and "wimmin" to
emphasize women's independence from men, these terms often
appeared in the feminist press in instances where the term
"lesbian" would have been more accurate. *off our backs* is
known officially as a women's publication, although it has been

dominated by lesbian volunteers, contributors, and readers. Arguably, terms specifying gender but not sexual orientation have been used as euphemisms for the more sexually loaded "lesbian."

By making sexuality a *cause célèbre* and aiming to be as crass and "obscene" as possible, 'zine makers attempt to counter the perceived ambivalence of the feminist press toward explicit sexuality. The lesbian porn magazine *On Our Backs*, founded in 1984, censured *off our backs* for what its editors perceived as its singular support of antiporn feminist politics. Several years later, a San Francisco lesbian 'zine, full of material about menstruation, took the spoof of somber feminist publishing one step closer to the ridiculous with the choice of its title—*On Our Rag*.

In the past, many lesbians and gay men wasted no affection for each other's perceived sexual norms and practices. Now, as a celebratory and inquisitive sexual climate is becoming pervasive in many lesbian communities, particularly among young, urban women, some lesbians are finding a renewed basis on which to connect with gay men.

The first decade of the AIDS epidemic, from the closing of bathhouses to the sanitizing of sexual exchanges with latex barriers, dealt a harsh blow to gay male sexual institutions. Sexual content in gay male 'zines reflects a trend in the larger gay male community toward more explicit sexual representations. Particularly in the culture around the direct-action groups AIDS Coalition to Unleash Power (ACT UP) and Queer Nation, there has been a deliberate attempt to resurrect and reaffirm the homoerotic spirit, and to retaliate against the sexophobic and virulently homophobic climate of censorship spearheaded by North Carolina senator Jesse Helms and the right wing.

Lesbian 'zine makers are as earnest in their resistance to the current right-wing purges of the arts as their gay male counterparts. But possibly even more integral to the lesbian 'zine focus on sexuality is the specific history of the antiporn feminist movement, and the more recent lesbian foray into unabashed sexual representation. For example, the introductory editors' statement in *P.C. Casualties*, an Ann Arbor cogender queer 'zine, criticized "puritanical, anti-sex crusaders," making a well-worn (though problematic) segue from the far right to antiporn feminism, effectively conflating the two movements in order to invalidate that brand of feminism.

> *As if bullying prank phone calls from those young Republican shitheads weren't enough now we have half-assed, pseudo-radical academics playing the same old power games as well. Hey, you and your "analysis" can fuck off. On second thought, I suppose they can't. Can't FUCK that is. After all sex is great fun, but like right-wing, Puritanical, anti-sex crusaders, these boring people think sex, like everything else good in this world, should be a guilt-ridden affair. Yeah, you've got all the "correct" answers, and even a little power in your corner of this political ghetto. But you're all fake. The right-wing press gives you way too much credit. All you've managed to do is torture and maim those you really ought to be caring for—your own brothers and sisters. The bodies of P.C. Casualties lay strewn all over, ghosts of dreams too afraid to materialize, and whispers too fearful to make a sound. They're women banned from the Michigan Womyn's music festival for practicing sm. They're bisexuals whose voices have been silenced because "bisexuals aren't oppressed enough." (Spring 1991)*

In the format of a conventional call for submissions by a feminist press, *Scream Box*, a Los Angeles lesbian 'zine, served up a tongue-in-cheek jab at the handling of sexuality in antiporn feminist writings:

CALL FOR SUBMISSIONS
Announcing new anthology
Pathology, Morbidity, and Decay:
Lesbian Feminists Write About Sex.

Edited by Elektra Assassin.
Send submissions to *Scream Box*. *(November 1990)*

Cunt, from San Francisco, turned antiporn rhetoric on its head, glorifying language that historically has been classified by antiporn feminists as blatantly objectifying women.

> *Let's face it. There's no better way to smash the patriarchy than by engaging in lots of radical, raunchy lesbian sex. . . . Fuck, suck, clit, cunt. These are the words of our sex, and these are the words of our empowerment. (Spring 1991)*

The preponderance of sexual material in 'zines of all types is also a testament to the relatively new connection that some lesbians are making with groups of sexual minorities, such as sadomasochists. Collections of lesbian s/m writings such as the 1982 Samois anthology *Coming to Power*, Pat Califia's *Macho Sluts*, and porn magazines *On Our Backs, Bad Attitude, Outrageous Women*, and *The Power Exchange* laid a foundation for lesbian sexual dialogue in the 1980s, but very little seeped past the s/m publishing world.

The attention 'zine makers pay to subjects such as the erotic potential of power and violence marks one of the first times in recent decades that such discussions have been explored by lesbians in a positive vein, outside of a venue explicitly defined as s/m. *Taste of Latex*, a San Francisco "polysexual" 'zine, and *Slut Mag*, a similar publication from New York, are singularly devoted to sexual content, offering stories, poetry, and graphics covering a wide range of erotic possibilities. The Los Angeles 'zine *G.B.F.* (Gay Black Female), which released its first issue in the fall of 1990, offered readers a weekly love advice column and lesbian personals. Within a few months, the 'zine had become almost exclusively concerned with the legendary De Jur, who was alleged to be the most beautiful woman in the city. Week after week, *G.B.F.* served up the latest word on De Jur, whom readers either despised or madly craved—though it was never certain that she existed.

Other 'zines explore similar topics, framed in bizarre and unorthodox writings and images, stretching the sexual discussion to the point of being outrageous, comical, and absurd. *Negativa*, self-described as "Chicago's astute lezbo fantasy mag," featured a personal essay titled "The Challenge of a Highly Formalized Martial Art," by a woman who fantasizes about having sex with her female karate instructor. Scrambled line drawings—chaotic and eerie—of two women in karate uniforms, one overpowering the other, accompanied the essay.

I wanna fuck Senpai Dana! I submit with evidence some reasons why. First of all, in a classroom situation, Senpai Dana will get right in your face when she wants to use you in a demonstration. . . . Senpai Dana may be trying to "psych" you out, suggesting by her position that she could suddenly grab your crotch, leaving you no time to react and forcing you to become engaged in an unequal "face-off." Personally, I would be able to keep my composure, being balanced in the "leaning rosewater" position and breathing rhythmically. "Smartass!" she would growl, testing my drum-tight stomach. "Now, what if your opponent . . ." she would begin, then feinting to the left, thrust her tongue between my lips, but, true to form, I inhale deeply, sucking her "knife-tongue" into my throat, and, her mouth now locked to mine, I begin to meditate. The flush rises to her chest as she realizes the strength of my will. In a brilliant redoubled attack, her knee shoots into my groin. As I topple, she pins my arm behind me and follows me to the mat. In "cow-milking" stance she smacks my backside and presses my right breast. Wouldn't you wanna fuck Senpai Dana? (Spring 1991)

More recently, a few 'zines, such as *Up Our Butts* (which boasts the motto "If the buttplug fits, wear it") and *Brat Attack*, both from San Francisco, have become devoted to s/m content, abandoning any pretense of sanitizing sadomasochism to make it more palatable to the uninitiated. An issue of *Brat Attack* featured an article titled "We're Not Knitting Doilies: Safe, Sane, Consensual and Beyond." An editor's note in *Up Our Butts* declared:

> *Up Our Butts!! supports all gay sexual styles and scenes, but we are not above making fun of them (including our own). If you choose to write us because you think this is wrong . . . make your letters as abusive as possible, we are all bottoms . . . Thanks, Editors. (Summer 1991)*

This attention to sexuality is broadening the parameters of what lesbians consider to be their issues, to include such issues as AIDS and safer sex. 'Zines have also become a sanctioned forum in which to broach taboo topics such as incest and childhood sexuality, leading to unconventional and sometimes unsettling presentations. While feminist work around the issue of child sexual abuse has been immensely important, it has often effectively precluded a complex discussion of childhood sexuality. A dialogue about childhood sexual abuse is evolving in the lesbian community, and there is now more space for women to discuss the complicated intersection of abuse and pleasure in some childhood sexual experiences. Notably, 'zines mark the shift of lesbian dialogue on child sexuality beyond an arena that is "safely" segregated by the non-s/m community into the category of s/m literature.

In an issue of *Scream Box*, a piece titled "The Incest Spread" brought together a serious poem about a woman traumatized by incest with an erotic photo (by a lesbian photographer) of an adult woman dressed as a little girl posing provocatively, alongside a nineteenth-century rhyme about an old man who

makes sexual advances on a young girl. The series concluded
with the following text:

> WHAT IF
> ... *your fantasies disturb you?*
> ... *"abuse" doesn't describe what you felt?*
> ... *it wasn't entirely bad?*
> ... *daddies, uncles, and older brothers come to mind*
> *when you masturbate?*
> WHAT THEN? *(May 1991)*

LESBIANIZING THE DOMINANT CULTURE

Lesbian artists in the 1970s, by and large, imagined a lesbian
experience outside the dominant culture, and created representations and language, such as women's music, specific to that
experience. 'Zine makers reject the conception of lesbian culture as isolated and estranged from the dominant culture. At
the same time, much like their relationship to lesbian feminism,
they have an ambivalent attitude toward popular culture—at
once rooted in it, and defined against it. 'Zine makers use guerrilla strategies to fashion their own icons and histories from
scavenged pop cultural information. They validate and exaggerate rumors about public figures until they become a type of
lesbian "truth." They make up stories and lie outright about
people. They force exclusionary texts to accommodate lesbian
subtexts and narratives.

J.D.s featured an ad for a film called *Four Girls*, supposedly
directed by *J.D.s* coeditor G. B. Jones and starring girl-girl sen-
sations Jodie Foster, Nastassia Kinski, Ina Liberace, and Kristy
McNichol. *Sister Nobody*, in an issue titled "Frida likes girls,"
turned artist Frida Kahlo into a lesbian heartthrob, showing her
leaning suggestively on the shoulder of another woman. Issue
#3 obsessed about another cult hero, Patti Smith.

As much as some are loath to admit it, the mass media
wield a powerful influence over young 'zine makers, who have

grown up with TV sitcoms and comic books. *Girlie Mag* and *Negativa*, for example, mocked the conventions of advertising by subverting Camel cigarette ads. *Girlie Mag* put a condom over the head of the camel/phallus and titled it "Safe Smoking!" *Negativa* created a female version of the camel—part ox, part vagina, and part leather dyke—and called it the "Wooly Musk Ox." Others made cultural icons from childhood, like Judy Jetson of *The Jetsons*, into objects of desire.

That television is a pervasive element in 'zine imagery is apparent in this excerpt from *Girlie Mag*:

> *After brainstorming for #2, coming up with ideas for articles, etc, we began to look for a theme to sort of tie it all together. One suggestion was a look at the 90s woman—the "Post-Mod-Broads"—which led to a heated discussion of what Post-Modernism means that left us all rolling our eyes and wishing we'd never been to college. Luckily, however, one of our staffers from Michigan thought one of our staffers from New York was saying "Maude" every time she said "Mod," and launched into an enamored recollection of beads and long vests. The confusion was eventually straightened out, and the debate over Post-Modernism abandoned, to everyone's relief. (Spring 1990)*

Few feminist scholars would consider a TV show an integral part of women's history; *Girlie Mag* goes so far as to name the contemporary era after *Maude*, the 1970s sitcom which grappled with feminist issues such as contraception and abortion rights, sexism and misogyny, and all-around bigotry. And in a blend of outrageous wit and complete seriousness, *P.C. Casualties*, in a collage of images and text, rethinks childhood pop star Barbie, asking its audience:

> *What the hell did Malibu Barbie, Barbie Dream House, Barbie Dream Boat ever have to do with anyone's reality? . . . This was a chick with a waist smaller than*

the circumference of her head. A woman who didn't need high heel shoes—she had high heeled feet. Her arms, in the permanently servile position of an A&W waitress, popped off for christ's sake. And some of us actually wanted to grow up to resemble her. (Spring 1991)

After this introduction, in a biting feminist commentary on the position of the female in society, Barbie is assigned a host of identities never considered by Mattel.

SM BARBIE—Comes with leather restraints, paddles, and three different tribal tattoos. All models complete with genitals.
LESBIAN BARBIE—Invisible.
MENTALLY RETARDED BARBIE—Will be mocked by your other Barbies.
NATIVE AMERICAN BARBIE—No longer available, since white Barbies have pushed her on the floor, stolen her belongings and killed her. Offensive white Barbie celebrated holiday in honor of this.
BATTERED BARBIE—Burdened with small children. No marketable skills and no assets. Self-esteem sold separately.
CHILDHOOD SEXUAL ABUSE SURVIVOR BARBIE—Requires assembly. Sold complete with Sensitive Therapist Barbie and her very own tattered copy of The Courage to Heal. *Does not like to be touched. (Spring 1991)*

Barbie dolls are alleged to represent a girl's fantasies and her projections of identity, and are used as a measure of what is socially acceptable; *P.C. Casualties'* "Real Life Barbie" becomes a fierce critique of the culture that reinforces the invisibility of women's painful (and painfully common) experiences.

What began as a strictly punk and most visibly white male movement has come to involve lesbians, people of color, and various subcultural segments of the larger lesbian/gay community. Chicago's *Thing* is aimed primarily at a black gay male audience. San Francisco's *Whorezine* is for sex workers of any and all sexual persuasions. And *Girljock*, from Berkeley, professes to be "the magazine for the athletic lesbian with a political consciousness."

By reviewing each other's work, 'zine makers have created their own networking infrastructure. The self-referential practice of 'zine reviews is the most culturally informed and reliable means by which 'zine editors and readers keep track of their own ilk. For years, many people outside the major cities got the word on new 'zines through the indispensable *Fact Sheet Five*, a regularly published resource guide to fanzines of all types which included a lesbian and gay section. Unfortunately, the guide folded in 1992.

Several factors, particularly national conferences and technological innovations, worked to transport 'zine making into the wider lesbian and gay community. In March 1990, the San Francisco–based *Out/Look* magazine hosted Out/Write, the first national lesbian and gay writers' conference, introducing 'zines to a cross section of lesbians and gay men. Ignoring the staid panel format of the conference, 'zine publishers, largely from San Francisco, spoke informally about their publishing activities. Empowerment was the message of the panel: *Homocore*'s Tom Jennings encouraged anyone with something to say to put out a 'zine, however unpolished and ungrammatical; new lesbian 'zines were launched, and others, like Lily Braindrop's *Taste of Latex*, were propelled into 'zine-world stardom.

In the year after the 1990 Out/Write conference, 'zines garnered national attention in mainstream gay and lesbian publications such as *Outweek* (now defunct) and *The Advocate*. At this time, there was an explosion of a wide variety of 'zines, particularly those created by lesbians, and a move away from the punk influence so prominent the year before. The 'zine panel discussion at the 1991 Out/Write conference, at which speakers focused on the trials and tribulations of such conventional concerns as distribution and personal computers, exemplified this transformation. In May 1991, Chicago's alternative arts space, the Randolf Street Gallery, sponsored "Spew: The Homographic Convergence," the first-ever convention of lesbian and gay 'zine junkies from the United States and Canada.

'Zines mark a radical shift in lesbian/gay publishing. By moving the erotic beyond the confines of lesbian s/m literature and demarcating a lesbian sensibility that mocks and subverts the dominant culture, they call out for a recognition of the complexity and centrality of lesbian experience.

ANDROGYNY GOES POP: BUT IS IT LESBIAN MUSIC?

TWENTY-TWO-YEAR-OLD NATALIE BRUGMANN OF ROCHESTER Hills, Michigan, has never heard of women's music, *On Our Backs* magazine, or even *off our backs*. She attends a monthly gay coffeehouse in Detroit, twenty miles away, when she can get to it, though she much prefers riding her motorcycle or going hunting. But Natalie remembers as if it were yesterday the day six years ago when she spotted k.d. lang on a late-night TV talk show, with a butch haircut, a man's Western suit, and no makeup. "I took one look at k.d.," she says, "and I said to myself: is that a guy or a girl? There was something about her attitude that I liked."

Natalie's room is filled with k.d. videotapes, promotional CDs, posters, autographed photos, T-shirts, and ticket stubs—paraphernalia she has collected through ads placed in magazines and bookstores. She finally got a chance to see her star in the flesh last year in Detroit, an experience she exclaims was "amazing."

"Lang thangs" like Natalie, primarily young women, mob k.d. wherever she plays. When a fan club sponsored a video night at one of the oldest women's bars in San Francisco last year, the place was packed tighter than anyone could remember seeing it before. k.d. lang lookalikes wearing bolo ties and cowgirl skirts danced the two-step. Others sat on the floor, transfixed by the large video screen, watching the collage of promotional videos and homemade footage assembled for the occasion. The glee in their faces, the longing for identification, were proof of how starved they were for celebrities to call their own.

Lang, a cross-dressing crossover artist, is not the only performer to capture the attention and imagination of lesbians throughout the nation. In 1988, Michelle Shocked, Tracy Chapman, the Indigo Girls, and Melissa Etheridge also burst on the music scene, and journalists announced the arrival of a "new breed of women" in popular music. "Neither their songs," one critic wrote, "nor the images they project, cater to stereotypical male fantasies of female pop singers."

Many of these artists initially received exposure through the nationwide network of coffeehouses, bars, and music festivals that primarily cater to lesbians. Tracy Chapman made the rounds in women's music festivals in 1986 and 1987, while the others knocked around lesbian and "alternative" clubs in Austin, Atlanta, San Francisco, and New York City. Yet once they achieved commercial success, sexuality wasn't something they were quick to mention. They studiously avoided male pronouns in romantic ballads, and carefully constructed their personas to assert a strong, sexually ambiguous female presence.

Through the subtleties of self-presentation, often indecipherable to those who weren't cued into the codes, these performers made themselves objects of female as well as male desire. Swaggering in that Western suit, k.d. lang proclaimed: "Yeah, sure, the boys can be attracted to me, the girls can be attracted to me, your mother . . . your uncle, sure. It doesn't really matter to me."

This displeased some women who had earlier made an explicit politics of their lesbianism. "Almost twenty years after Stonewall and fifteen years after Alix Dobkin and Kay Gardner issued 'Lavender Jane Loves Women,' there are still no out lesbians in the national 'mainstream' music scene," said Ginny Berson, a founder of Olivia, the pioneering women's music label. "There are plenty of out lesbians in the alternative music scene—and plenty who are not out—and plenty of closeted lesbians in the mainstream, but it seems that never the twain shall meet."

Nonetheless, a younger generation of women eagerly snapped up records by the new "androgynous" pop artists, crowded their concerts, and spread the word to friends. As a Chicago woman named Mary proclaimed in a letter in *Outweek*, "Ladies, let's be Phranc. We all love k.d., Tracy, Melissa and the Indigo Girls. Many of us knew and loved them long before they achieved their current mainstream popularity. I went to see Melissa in Chicago last week. I didn't go with my girlfriend or any girlfriends. I went with one of my little brothers. And you should have seen him dancing in the aisle!

"All this bickering," she continued, "about whether these women should come out is like asking a bewildered junior varsity basketball star to come out at a pep rally. Let's just chill and enjoy the music, shall we?"

The arrival of the new breed of androgynous pop women, propelled, in large part, by an increasingly self-conscious lesbian audience, signals the fact that some women can now defy conventions of femininity in popular music and still achieve mainstream success. But at what cost? Are "androgynous" women performers cowering before a homophobic industry, enacting a musical form of passing? Or are they pushing the limits of what is possible and, along with it, lesbian visibility?

A growing debate pits those who would stand outside the dominant culture and openly name their lesbianism (even if that naming restricts their audience) against those who, in search of broader appeal, represent their sexuality more covertly. Frequently, the sides are drawn along generational lines, with older women arguing for a more separatist strategy and younger women championing an assimilationist stance. Today's younger artists, who are attempting to carve out a space for themselves between the constraints of the industry and the imperatives of lesbian identity politics, may be somewhere in the middle.

FROM WOMEN'S MUSIC TO ANDROGYNOUS POP

In popular culture, lesbians have long had to contend with a scarcity of images. When lesbian characters appear on television or in the movies, they tend to be either unflattering (as in the typical Hollywood film) or unidimensional (as in most pornography). Writing several years ago, British pop critic Jon Savage noted that while "popular music acknowledges the sign of 'gayness,' there is not yet a whisper of female sexual autonomy, of lesbianism."[1]

As lesbians we have always found ways to "read" popular culture against the grain—changing the pronouns of songs in our heads and projecting our fantasies onto female icons. But such individual strategies do little to aid the cause of group visibility. In the 1970s, the founders of the women's music industry recognized this fact. They tried to create new cultural forms that would reflect the hopes and dreams of the communities they saw themselves building. Derived from folk, women's music was rooted in the populist tradition of social protest and in the belief that small and simple was best. It was based on the feminist rejection of the commercial music industry, and the belief that only through alternative cultural networks could affirmative images of women be produced and distributed.

Less lesbian-identified than "woman-identified," women's music was imbued with a belief in a universal female sensibility which, much as lesbian feminist fiction did, embodied an expressive realism that refused to play to the desires and expectations of men. It created images of strong, "woman-identified" women that were intended to reflect the common texture of lesbian lives—girls' crushes on their gym teachers, their feelings of love and loss.

Lesbian feminists who came of age in the 1960s and 1970s wanted to distance themselves from the image of the mannish woman, long synonymous with lesbianism in popular culture. They also wanted to distance themselves from rock and roll, which they dubbed "cock rock." In 1974, *Ms.* magazine asked, "Can a Feminist Love the World's Greatest Rock and Roll Band?" and writer Robin Morgan replied with a resolute "No!" She warned that lesbian feminists who listened to the Rolling Stones were no better than those who advocated nonmonogamy and accepted transsexuals as allies: they had all adopted a "male style" that would destroy the movement.

Even in the early days there was always controversy in the ranks. Was women's music for *all* women, or just lesbians? Was it foremost an expression of art or of politics? By the late 1970s, these questions, coupled with the waning of the movement, and financial problems, conspired to throw women's music into an identity crisis, revealing that the cohesive lesbian community was the product of a particular historical moment and that women's music rested on a precarious unity. For one thing, women's music had become firmly entrenched in what was, for the most part, a European tradition—"sucky sister" music to many women of color, who resisted the claim that it represented the authentic voice of women's, and lesbians', culture. Confirming their suspicions was the fact that albums and tours by black artists (such as Mary Watkins and Linda Tillery) failed to attract much-needed audiences.

Criticism also came from women in the punk movement. Although punk embraced a politics of anti-identity, refusing to position itself as the affirmative expression of either feminism or gay liberation, from its early days it made a politics of disrupting gender and sexual codes. Critic Simon Frith has written that punk "debunked 'male' technique and expertise" and posed a critique of glamour.[2] But, at the same time, punk's appeal to androgyny and its embrace of brash, rhythmic music were at odds with the notion of woman-identification at the base of women's music. In Boston, Rock Against Sexism announced itself as a cultural activist group comprised of "closet rock and roll fans" in the women's community. One of its founders explained: "Women's music is really peaceful, not raunchy or angry; it doesn't really excite me or turn me on or get me energized."

If an earlier belief that women's music could reflect an "essential" femaleness was becoming suspect, by the mid-1980s its undercapitalization forced it to remain rather conservative. As sales flagged, many women's music producers responded by moving away from their lesbian-feminist roots. Olivia formed a subsidiary, Second Wave, which released less feminist-identified music and broke with its commitment to use only female musicians. The dream of forming alternative lesbian cultural networks that would stand completely outside the mainstream had failed to materialize.

"I thought they were playing a funeral dirge during the intermission at the album release concert of Cris Williamson and Teresa Trull in Berkeley last month," Ginny Berson wrote in 1989.[3] "For the first time in its history at an Olivia Records concert, there were more men than women on stage. . . . I thought I knew that 'Olivia Records Presents' meant something—music about women's lives, music written by women, music performed by women. But what we had here were a few songs about women and a lot about horses; lots of songs written by men; and mostly men playing the music. Is this women's music?"

If the viability of women's music was thrown into question by a crisis of identity and by the competitive pressures of the capitalist market, its problems were exacerbated by the fact that the feminist movement had helped to create an audience that was beginning to outgrow the counterculture. Lesbian musicians of the 1970s had been forced out of the mainstream in order to achieve some artistic autonomy; fifteen years later there were signs of greater openings. In 1988, as Olivia Records celebrated its fifteenth anniversary with a series of concerts across the country, larger-than-life posters of Michelle Shocked and Tracy Chapman were plastered on every record-store wall, while Olivia Records languished in the "women's music" section in the rear, if they were there at all.

GAL PALS AND REAL WOMEN

As women's music, in an effort to reach a broader audience, looked less and less lesbian, mainstream music looked more and more lesbian, or, as the industry liked to refer to it, *real*. Tracy Chapman became a household name in 1988, selling more than 10 million albums, signed by Elektra because she was "just so real," according to a company executive. Chapman's huge success sent other record companies scrambling to find real women artists of their own. Michelle Shocked was picked up by Polygram, and Phranc was signed to Island.

If an earlier move toward androgyny among male pop stars like David Bowie was influenced by gay drag's tradition of artifice and costume, the new wave of women's androgyny was typically described, by participants as well as critics, as a move "back to the basics," a retreat from artifice and role-playing into authenticity.

Women performers, long forced into the boy-toy role, can now "be more than just prepackaged gals," says Phranc, whose 1989 album, "I Enjoy Being a Girl," showed her in a flat-top haircut (alongside a blurb that sang her praises as a "little daughter of bilitis"). It was a movement that confounded the critics. "The most astounding thing of all is that Tracy Chapman et al. even happened," mused Susan Wilson in *The Boston Globe*. "Since when did the industry that insisted its strongest women play cartoon characters . . . allow a serious, powerful, flesh and blood female to stand firm on a concert stage?"

The answer, as any informed observer could say, was simple. The "new breed" of pop women emerged once the industry was convinced that it would sell. Historically, record companies spot a trend and quickly jump on the bandwagon to claim it as their own. Subcultures have long fueled musical innovation; hugely successful commercial disco and house music has its origins in the black gay dance floors of Chicago and New York. Likewise, on the heels of the feminist movement, female performers and fans became commercially important "properties" and "markets," giving both musicians and fans a new position of power to define what they did and demand what they wanted.

The trail was blazed by such performers as Cyndi Lauper and Madonna, whose messages, though at times contradictory, affirmed an empowered female sexuality practically unseen in commercial pop. In 1984, Lauper released the single "Girls Just Want to Have Fun," a "powerful cry for access to the privileged realm of male adolescent leisure and fun," in the words of critic Lisa Lewis. Madonna exuded sexual power and invincibility, at times making allusions to lesbianism, as in her "Justify My Love" video, which was banned by MTV at the end of 1990. "Clothed in the language of heterosexuality" but "soliciting a lesbian gaze," Sydney Pokorny proclaimed in the pages of *Gay Community News*, she had transformed herself "from boy toy to gal pal."

The new androgynous pop stars took advantage of these openings in the music mainstream, and saw mainstreaming as an act no less subversive than the feminist disaffection from the industry a decade earlier. Phranc toured as the opening act for The Smiths and other popular post-punk acts, playing for mixed audiences because, she said, "It's important to reach out to the kids." Two Nice Girls, an Austin group, made lesbianism an integral part of their act, but consciously chose to record on Rough Trade, a large independent label, because, bandleader Gretchen Phillips said, "We don't want to be found only in the specialty bin at the record store. We want to be in your face." Younger than their women's music predecessors, they had been shaped by punk as much as women's music, and by a different political mood.

But there were limits to their newfound power. While women performers today may enjoy an unprecedented degree of freedom to present themselves as they please, lesbian performers are still "safe" (read: marketable) only when their sexuality is muted—a woman singing a love song to another woman is still taboo, as Phranc sang on her 1989 album, "I Enjoy Being a Girl":

> *Everybody wants to be a folk singer. They want to be hip and trendy. They want to make sensitive videos and sing about politics. Androgyny is the ticket or at least it seems to be. Just don't wear a flat-top and mention sexuality, and girl you'll go far, you'll get a record contract and be a star.*

In a homophobic culture, out gays and lesbians are not generally thought to be "crossover" material. Large record companies, organized to minimize risk, attempt to hold back discreditable information about a performer from the public. "This is a very conservative country and record companies like to steer away from potential controversy," says Howie Klein, vice-president at Sire Records, k.d. lang's label. Driven by big hits, companies often sink enormous sums of money into developing and promoting an individual artist, and are loath to take chances. Instead, they tend to seek out the lowest common denominator, hoping to turn out stars who can appeal to a broad audience rather than targeting specific markets defined geographically, ethnically, or sexually.

While a large commercial record company has yet to specifically target a lesbian audience, a few smaller companies at least recognize the existence of such an audience. In marketing Phranc, Island Records' Rick Bleiweiss acknowledges that since her "core" (read: lesbian) audience already knows about her, the company's role is to seek out the potential crossover consumers—primarily the college and "independent" music audience, and to expand her reach into a larger, more mainstream audience. But Bleiweiss acknowledges that performers like Phranc, who make their lesbianism a central part of their act (that is, they actually mention it), may have a "limited consumer base."

In a rare acknowledgment of the lesbian roots of the late 1980s folk boom, Michelle Shocked, on accepting the award for Folk Album of the Year at the 1989 New Music Awards in New York (she was nominated along with Phranc, Tracy Chapman, and the Indigo Girls), said, "This category should have been called 'Best Lesbian Vocalist.' " She told *Outlines*, a Chicago gay paper, "I resent like hell that I was maybe eighteen years old before I even heard the l-word." Yet Shocked herself later complained to an interviewer about being lumped with all the other emerging women performers. Others avoided the subject entirely, refusing to be interviewed by lesbian/gay or feminist publications.

Even as they were being applauded by the critics for their fresh, unencumbered simplicity and their return to "honesty" and "naturalness," when it came down to it, many of the new androgynous women constructed their songs and their images with a sexual ambiguity that at times verged on camp. A video of Michelle Shocked's single "When I Grow Up" features a posse of her feminist friends. Shocked sings, "When I grow up I want to be an old woman," and all the friends say, "Yeeeaah!" Then she sings, "Then I think I'm gonna marry myself an old man," and they respond, disappointedly, "Ohhhhhh." Then she sings, "We're gonna have a hundred and twenty babies," and they cheer.

On her 1989 album, *Captain Swing*, one had to listen closely to "Sleep Keeps Me Awake" to make out the fact that it is a love song to a woman.

SHIFTING LOYALTIES, MIXING IDENTITIES

"We have gone through some magnificently bizarre changes," Judy Dlugacz told representatives of the two-thousand-member Association of Women's Music and Culture, the women's music industry organization, when they met in San Francisco in 1990, "but the news is not altogether good."

As she tells the story, independent record labels close daily and women's music is being squeezed out of existence. The most loyal sectors of their audience—lesbian baby boomers—have aged, shedding some of their political commitments to alternative women's culture, while others have left the fold altogether. The number of women in powerful positions at the major labels, and in the music industry as a whole, has grown at a snail's pace. Successful lesbian stars don't declare their sexual preferences because they are scared of the possible impact on sales. And to make matters worse, as mainstream labels have offered more (and more lucrative) openings, it is becoming more difficult for the Olivia label to sign talented artists.

Dlugacz bristles when she recalls that Melissa Etheridge once sent a demo tape, only to be turned down with the reply that Olivia was not looking for new artists. Redwood Records, the label that Holly Near built, tried to sign Tracy Chapman when she was still in school in Boston, but could not compete with Elektra. As the producers of women's music see it, the new wave of sexual ambiguity signals the fact that the revolution has been stalled, gobbled up, and watered down by "the industry."

The terrain has shifted, they say, from lesbian-identified music created in the context of lesbian institutions and communities to music that blandly emulates women's music, playing with signifiers like clothes and hairstyle in order to gain commercial acceptance, but never really identifying itself as lesbian. "We've made the world safe for androgyny in the charts," said feminist singer-songwriter Deidre McCalla, referring, not so obliquely, to the likes of k.d. lang and Tracy Chapman. "But a few women musicians in the forefront is not what we wanted."

The dream of a body of music and art that expresses lesbian experience openly and honestly has not yet come to pass in the mainstream. Commercial broadcast and cable networks, film critic Martha Gever has written, see "the spectre of low ratings or outraged moralists."[4] Much the same can be said of the recording industry: "They may readily promote work that mobilizes sexual ambiguity as a titillating come-on—a common enough advertising ploy—but they see overt, unapologetic recognition of lesbian or gay cultures as poison."

The classic dilemma persists: a performer either becomes known as a "lesbian artist" and is thus doomed to marginality, or she waters down her lesbianism in order to appeal to a mass audience. The pioneers of women's music selected the former route. The new wave of androgynous women have chosen the latter. We have yet to see a lesbian artist who is able to integrate her sexuality into her art without allowing it to become either *the* salient fact, or else a barely acknowledged one.

Nonetheless, to call the new wave of artists assimilationists and sellouts is to do them a disservice. Such criticisms set women's music up as the only authentic voice of lesbianism, obscuring the efforts of women to make inroads into mainstream pop. For though they may not be overtly lesbian-identified, these women are not particularly heterosexually identified either. Many are no less "out" than their predecessors in women's music, and some are even more butch in appearance. Phranc and Two Nice Girls are the most obvious examples, along with k.d. lang, probably the butchest woman entertainer since Gladys Bentley.

If many of today's performers are ambiguous about their identities, it is not only because of industry constraints—frequently, their identities are ambiguous. Tracy Chapman, a black woman, is an obvious example of a complex personality with commitments to more than the lesbian community. So is Michelle Shocked, who is now rumored to be involved with a man. Ten years ago, Holly Near often hid her bisexuality in order to appeal to a women's audience, in the interest of providing a united front.

Today there may be greater tolerance for ambiguity, and even a certain attraction to *not* really knowing the "truth." Anyway, what *is* the truth? This is the 1990s, after all, an era in which "pleasure," says critic Larry Grossberg, "is replacing understanding."[5] David Letterman, the baby boomers' late-night talk-show host of choice, celebrates alienation with a mocking self-referentiality. MTV blurs the boundaries of pop music and advertising. Quick-change, recombinant pop jumps from style to style, integrating new sounds and textures, new identities and images, and blurring cultural categories of all sorts: a rap song samples the theme from *Gilligan's Island*; Peter Gabriel and Paul Simon borrow from African traditional music. Comedian Sandra Bernhard mixes and matches identities, alluding at times to her lesbianism without ever really embracing it. "I would never make a declaration of anything," she told Lawrence Chua of *The Village Voice*. "It's so stupid. Who even cares? It's so presumptuous."

Bernhard's smugness aside, her resistance to overt lesbian identifications, much like that of the androgynous pop stars, may be rooted in a critique of the notion of a shared lesbian identity—quite apart from career considerations. The notion of identity foisted on us by a century of scientific "experts" implies that all lesbians are alike, united by a common deviance, and locates us outside the dominant culture. Lesbian feminists attempted to universalize the possibility of lesbian experience by removing its grounding in biology, but in its place they often created rigid ideological prescriptions about who belongs in the lesbian community.

Today's lesbian performers in the mainstream must, like the rest of us, grapple with both of these legacies, and construct a position from which to speak that acknowledges both lesbian marginality *and* membership in the dominant culture, and the ways in which that position shifts over time. The charge that the "new breed" of women pop stars are sellouts is thus predicated on a rigid separation of "mainstream" and "margin," of dominant culture and lesbian culture, which may no longer apply—if it ever did. It understates the extent to which androgynous pop stars conspire in the making of their own images, working within the constraints of the industry to bring their message to an increasingly self-conscious and sophisticated lesbian audience.

This is not to say that we have been liberated, represented, and made visible. The new wave of androgynous artists reflects all the potential and all the ambiguity of our times. These artists signify a disaffection from the ranks of the Lesbian Nation, and a cynicism about the prospects for liberation. They embody the triumph of commerce over the small, alternative cultural networks, and signify a testing of the waters and a newfound freedom to maneuver. They reveal a new visibility of lesbian imagery in popular culture, and tell us, too, how much further we have to go.

QUEEN FOR 307 DAYS: LOOKING B(L)ACK AT VANESSA WILLIAMS AND THE SEX WARS

I

WATCHING THE SPECTACLE OF STAR-SPANGLED WHITE WOMEN compete for the ideological honor of being decreed Miss America was a ritual that frustrated me, my mother, and my two sisters every September. Nevertheless, we tuned the telly to NBC annually only to be disappointed annually—nary a Nubian princess strolled down the ramp of righteousness bikinied or gowned, much less crowned.

It is, then, a small, peculiar consolation to me that in 1983, before she died, my mother got to see a black woman win the Miss America pageant. Small, because the scarring prospects of radiation therapy all but confirmed my mother's worst projections of her dark-skinned self-image. (Who would want to behold and declare *beautiful* the sutured spot where her left breast once appeared, where the skin of her torso and right nipple were toughened from rads bombarding her chest?) Peculiar, because when my mother witnessed Vanessa Williams's victory, she got to see a black body, a black woman's body—her body—venerated as beautiful and *feminine*, qualities she feared she was losing and which I, her uncloseted dyke daughter, worried I didn't possess as I prepared to go to a black gay bar for the first time that same night.

Actually, my outing had been in the works for a couple of weeks. Hoping to find a scene not overrun by the sorority-pledging Karmann Ghia–driving dykes who were our peers on campus, a school friend suggested that we check out queer nightlife off the beaten (white) track. Fate shook the dice so that our date fell on pageant night. Neither of my sisters was at home to watch the show with my mother, thwarting my plan to slip out of the house unnoticed, unchecked by my mother's silent dissent. I shuddered to think of the long, quiet stare that would've told me everything my mother knew I knew she wanted to say at the sight of me with another woman. It was one thing to be out to my family as gay; it would be another challenge to be seen *being* gay. Scared to leave but unwilling to stay home that night, I showered and dressed for the evening, conflicted over the stand I was about to take. Time was of the essence. Eleven o'clock couldn't come soon enough. I also feared it wouldn't come at all.

I stalled my dread by fixating on the tube and the sizzling sistah from Syracuse University, Miss New York, who was *working* the pageant. Homegirl expertly fielded the banal interview questions, tossing back answers with a quick wit that scored with the audience. During the swimsuit competition girlfriend strutted her stuff like she had no concern for her straightened hair at the imaginary water's doo-defying edge. And then, Miss Thing sang some silly show tune like tomorrow was *not* another day. If snapping was as outrageous then as it is now, my fingers would've been blistered. My mother smiled incessantly. I anxiously eyed the clock, wondering if I had time to change my Benetton sweater and L. L. Bean button-down shirt for . . . what? At that moment, I longed to be a beauty queen—confident, radiant, beyond reproach; anything but a nervous, bookwormish college senior who wouldn't be given a second glance by the *serious* sisters I wanted to meet at the bar.

Those last minutes converged: Sue said she'd pick me up at eleven; only ten minutes remained between the last commercial break and the always-boring Saturday-night newscast. Those last minutes intensified: the crowd of fifty-two (including the beauties of the colonized commonwealths of Puerto Rico and the Virgin Islands) had been narrowed down to the final quintet, the four runners-up and the one queen. Those last minutes remain precious to me: three white girls smiled graciously as they were named second to fourth almost-wons. My mother edged forward on the couch. I found myself alongside her. Vanessa Williams and Suzette Charles, two black women, were vying for the title. *There was no way we could lose.* My mother held her breath and pulled me close. I checked the clock, hoping Sue would be late. When Suzette Charles's name was called first, my mother hugged me, beaming. "Finally," she half-whispered. "Finally." The doorbell rang.

II

On weekdays, the Maya Azteca was a Mexican restaurant that catered to white-collar types laboring under fluorescent lights in downtown Oakland. The menu changed on Saturday nights, Sue told me as she killed the ignition, when the space served as the hot spot for the city's black queers.

Waiting in the foyer to pay the cover fee, I could see beyond the crushed red velvet curtains to the TV perched above the bar. Glasses clinked and toasts were shouted over the flickering din of an anchor's voice announcing that Vanessa had made history. The dance mix soared around the room. In between the end of the pageant telecast and my arrival at the bar, in between my mother and Sue, Vanessa's victory aligned my worlds into Aquarian orbit. As Gary Collins serenaded Vanessa during her stroll down victory lane, my mother wept, gave me a kiss, and sent me out of the house with the quietly advised wish that I'd "have a good time with my friend." The black queers at the Maya Azteca were buoyed so high that when the club closed at two o'clock the party moved out and over to East Oakland, where the energy rode itself as far and long as it dared to go.

I even drummed up the nerve to ask an absolutely stunning woman to dance. And I wondered (as I tried not to stare too hard and long at her) whether, on that early-autumn night-turned-morning, all of black America, homo- and heterosexual, was reveling in the knowledge that the nationalists hard-lined during our second *fin de siècle*—after Malcolm and Martin were killed and before Watts/Chicago/Detroit burned: black *is* beautiful. Now America knew, I thought, as I spun around and faced my partner. *Yes, yes, yes. Wave your hands in the air like you just don't care.* Deal with it, Atlantic City: black is, as Nina Simone declared, the color of my true love's hair, and colored my love was that night. Vanessa Williams's triumph freed me to find every black woman in the house simply FINE.

III

July 20, 1984. Bob Guccione sits in his gilt gold *faux*-royal throne, wired for sound across the continent via the CBS, NBC, and ABC morning news. Leisurely situated, he aggressively defends *Penthouse*'s "journalistic duty" to publish photographs of Williams that would reveal our cultural icon to be less than virginally proper and morally irreproachable. With a sense of timing nothing short of suspicious, photographer Tom Chiapel has emerged with a set of incriminating pictures taken when Williams worked as his studio assistant in 1982. With two months to go before her reign ends, Chiapel sells the sexually explicit images to Guccione, who, on this date, announces his decision to feature them in the September 1984 issue of *Penthouse*. The American public deserves to know about Williams's past, Guccione insists. Pressing his obligation before the media, he waxes ethical:

> *She [Williams] committed a fraud on the pageant. . . .*
> *If she had not accepted the title then someone who*
> *was so much more deserving—who had nothing to*
> *hide—might have been Miss America in her place.*[1]

Feeling principled, Guccione rests his case and his back into the plush cushion of his chair.

Why did Vanessa do such a thing? Didn't she know that, whatever it was, it would come back at her?

July 23, 1984. The camera lights beam unbearably bright heat. Shutters snap furiously. Microphones cluster like a thorny bouquet in front of her. Williams fends off the volley of questions by insisting on reading her prepared statement:

> *It is apparent to me now that because of all that has*
> *happened during the past week, it would be difficult*
> *to make appearances as Miss America.*[2]

With these words, Vanessa Williams relinquished the crown and inscribed a large, peculiar place for herself in the history of the pageant. No sooner was she memorialized as the first black woman to earn the Miss America title than she was unceremoniously deposed, having been caught in various sexual acts with a white woman. How "bad" were the *Penthouse* photos? Bad enough to make Williams renounce the title and hand over the tiara to Suzette Charles. Bad enough to sell out the issue of the magazine in which the photos appeared. Bad enough to drive Williams out of public life and into near seclusion for years.

IV

Recalling this event now, what fascinates me is the seeming ease with which it has been forgotten. Black folks have turned on the force field of memory—which is to say, we've opted not to remember that it happened and instead elected to disregard that the episode bears something worth coming to terms with.

Leave the girl be. It wasn't her fault that white folks turned on her and put her down. Let her get on with her life and move past that ugly thing. Lesbians ignored the incident then and, by our continued silence about it now, perpetuate the "we-care-but-we-don't-know-how-to-explain-race" approach so annoyingly common to (white) feminist politics and scholarship. *We, as white women, cannot possibly talk about this issue because we, as white women, cannot fathom how black people, especially black women, must have felt about such a pernicious occurrence of racism.*

But Vanessa Williams's fall from social grace wasn't just about racism. In retrospect, lesbian feminism's absent response to the incident seems particularly disingenuous because, by July 1984, dyke activists and theorists were engaged in—indeed, we were embattled by—the very issues raised by Williams's ascent to, and abdication of, the Miss America crown. The buildup of Williams's public persona as Redeemer Queen and her subsequent demolition as Fallen Dyke encompassed some of the major themes contested in the "sex wars" debates of the 1980s: Just what constitutes sex work and what is its cultural value? Where does the line fall demarcating pornography from erotica? How does a viewer's gaze enable or circumscribe the subjectivity of the object (s)he beholds?

Lesbians kept mum about the incident, but our silence was heard at the time. In what remains the most perceptive analysis of the scandal, Barbara Ehrenreich and Jane O'Reilly astutely observed that Williams's downfall occurred during the same week as Geraldine Ferraro's nomination as Vice-President on the Democratic ticket in 1984. The electoral prospects of the Mondale-Ferraro pairing triggered a cultural panic over the threat of women's political power. This fear, Ehrenreich and O'Reilly explained, provoked a backlash of misogyny that expressed and justified itself in the persecution of a symbolic homosexual—Vanessa Williams, who had been "documented" in lesbian sex acts.

Writing in the right-of-center *New Republic*, they criticized sex progressivists for avoiding this important coincidence.

"Given the sexual anxieties aroused by the Democratic convention," Ehrenreich and O'Reilly wrote, "no one has come forth from the sexology profession, from the lesbian community, or from what is known to insiders as the 'pro-sex' wing of the women's movement to offer an exegesis of the photographs themselves."[3]

Perhaps Ehrenreich and O'Reilly were wrong. Perhaps lesbians *did* talk about the photographs among ourselves. Maybe we bought a copy of that September *Penthouse*, and maybe we looked at the pictures alone, with friends, or with lovers. Maybe we liked what we saw, and maybe we talked about why the pictures made us feel that way. Or, maybe the photographs angered us. Embittered us. Embarrassed us. Frightened us. Confused us. And maybe we talked about why the pictures made us feel that way. Who among us felt these (and certainly other) ways? Who among us thought these (and certainly other) things? To ask Who knows? is my point: no record exists detailing whatever monologues or discussions took place because lesbians were unwilling to defend or defame the episode publicly. To ask Why not? is the point of this essay.

Why was it that the black woman became the pariah? Starting with Vanessa Williams's shifting claims to the Miss America title, I want to read b(l)ack into the era of the sex wars, in order to interrogate the premises on which we assumed then and continue to assume now that "whiteness" figures the normative center of political and theoretical discussions about sexuality and identity. My questions don't depend on coercing racism out of this moment (that comes to the top, like flotsam) as much as they are concerned with locating *race* in a historical context in order to understand the effective silence which greeted and so defined Williams's fall, to consider why public discourse about colored sexuality remains conventional in its outlook on and response to boundary-shattering incidents such as this. Reviving the episode, then, I don't seek to demean Williams any more than she already has been demeaned. Nor do I intend to suggest that Williams is anything other than what she is: straight. It's not her person that interests me, but the institutional representation of her as a cultural persona, a sexualized type. In fact, the photographs of her matter more, and what they actually show means less than how meaning came to be ascribed to them.

The publication of Vanessa Williams's split images as the beauty-cum-porn queen marked a crucial moment wherein lesbian feminists could—and should—have theorized about the historic workings of *race* in relation to sexuality because it, and not racism, explains most critically why Williams met the infamous end she did. On that basis, by reading retrospectively, by looking b(l)ack into the event, I want to complicate some of the paradigms we currently claim define contemporary lesbian sexual culture. Or, put another way, I want to ask: Where and how do (mis)representations of black lesbian sexuality occur and so continue to inform racial antagonisms underlying lesbian feminism, even in the queer, lipstick, baby-boomin' nineties?

V

Williams's story begins with the issue of *legal* misrepresentation. From her point of view, she agreed to pose for the pictures under what turned out to be false assumptions. Williams believed Tom Chiapel's assurance that nude stills were common fare in models' portfolios and that the graphic scenes he wanted to compose of her would be discreetly shot—a screen was to have made Williams's face unrecognizable. Not only did the resulting proofs reveal Williams's face, it turned out that she had signed a loosely worded contract that authorized Chiapel to use the photographs for "promotional purposes." Once Williams won the pageant, Chiapel cashed in on the "slip" and the clause. After *Playboy* graciously bowed out of the bidding contest, *Penthouse* stepped forward in the queue, as publisher Bob Guccione secured the rights to copy Williams's image to the tune of $5 million in projected newsstand sales. The decision, for Guccione, was "a simple business choice; whether I get Vanessa into a rift with the pageant people versus the desirability

of these photographs in the eyes of my readers. Of course I
went with my readers."[4]

By doing so, Guccione also touched off arguments about
the nature of "desirability" itself. By purchasing and printing
the photographs of Williams's "modeling session," Guccione
not only engineered a monetary coup for his magazine, he also
leveled a body blow against the concept of the pageant itself:
the photos framed the Miss America contest as simply another
for(u)m for sex work. *Penthouse*'s publication of the images
implicated the pageant in its cultural practice of making a commodity out of sex. Pageant chairman Albert Marks, Jr., may have
decried the photographs as being unfit to show to his wife,[5] but
presenting Williams for his readers' consumption as a centerfold
treat, Guccione dealt back the pageant's card of respectability,
for the pageant, no less than *Penthouse*, exploited Williams as
an object of appeal. Indeed, Williams's status as the feminine-
elect established common ground for these seemingly opposed
venues of "womanhood," as the chaste queen and the salacious
poser became one and the same thing.

Seemingly siding with the feminist critique of beauty pageants, *Penthouse* also positioned itself in line with what would
ostensibly be the "sex radical" response to the crisis. Publishing
the photographs championed anticensorship politics and affirmed the legitimacy of the social display of sexuality. However,
linking these perspectives only served to isolate their weakest
points, which made them seem discontinuous, and so, illogical.
For *Penthouse* didn't merely print the photographs; the images'
resonance mattered as much as, if not more than, their literal
appearance on the magazine page. *How* they came to appear
when they did—*how* the images functioned to confuse their
own place in time, as history—constructed a meaning for the
images for which feminist theory couldn't account. Simultaneously conjoining with and upending the critiques of beauty
pageants and censorship politics (in other words, by fucking
with them), *Penthouse* dissed them both.

On one side, Williams's election knotted arguments decrying the exploitative nature of the pageant. The crowning of a

black woman deflected charges that the competition endorsed the sexist objectification of women; Williams's victory confirmed America's liberal promise of do-it-yourself political improvement. How could anyone complain that the contest's outcome was anything but "progress"? Didn't the nation have another racial "first" to add to the mythic melting pot of American achievement? Wasn't this a fulfillment of the Civil Rights dream state of affairs—a black woman representing the ideal of American femininity? *Didn't my mother cry at the thought of this affirmation? Didn't I see black women differently that night?*

Failing to condemn the racially specific iconography of "womanhood" promoted not only by the pageant but by the culture at large, antipageant feminists were hard-pressed to say anything about Williams's coronation one way or another. Once the scandal reared into view, these activists and theorists were left unable to address the complexities underlying her fall. Without the critical means to expose the racialized functions of patriarchal image-making, we settled for burning our memories of the year in the flames of conspiracy theories. *Why was it that a scandal cropped up when a black woman won? Was it just a coincidence or expedient that a black woman was also named first runner-up—that way, no one could say that the debacle was racistly motivated, right? How could the pageant officials not know about the pictures before the contest began?*

The existence of the photographs pinned the pageant's liability to the wall and exercised the discretion that contest officials presumably should have invoked. That is, the photographs functioned as a screening committee should have, dividing Williams's (then) present from her (then) past and judging her "fitness" to compete in troublesome accordance with the standards such distinctions imply. However, this break in process and time empowered the images to wreak havoc in Williams's world. The pictures were taken at a moment when, ostensibly, she had no idea that they would overdetermine her career. Once the photos hit the newsstands, though, their value and meaning transformed not around the fact of her ignorance, but around the *representation* of her knowledge.

The question of whether Williams knew what she was doing
is reflected by what it *looked* like she knew: how to eat snatch,
how to please herself. It becomes impossible to classify and so
withdraw the images as stock stereotypes from straight pornography precisely because Williams was the paragon of American
prenuptial chastity; the beauty queen became, irrevocably, the
derivative deviant that is the dyke. Though the pictures were
taken *before* the pageant, their publication and the consequences they exacted switched the order of the incidents. The
staging of the photographs consumed the moment of Williams's
televised coronation and replayed the instance of her crowning
as the specter haunting the scene. In terms of what caused
Williams more trouble, which came first—the crown or the
pictures?

The photographs didn't document history (as we might
expect), but rather sought to replace it, as they confused
temporality as a source of causality. The crown, not the representation of the earlier images, brought about Williams's
downfall. The images indicted the pageant as the culprit: if Williams wasn't Miss America, the photos wouldn't matter and
would mean nothing. From yet another angle, then, the publication of the photos revoked the pageant's license to moral
authority. At the same time, the images challenged feminist arguments promoting the value of sex as labor. The negatives
suggest this comparison. In its original state, raw film reverses
an image's codes—black objects whiten and white fields darken.

In this way, the sex acts Williams portrayed were inscribed
on the film stock in "white" terms—which is how most black
folks denied the incident altogether. *Her white boyfriend put
her up to it. A white photographer took the pictures. A white
woman posed in the photos with her and no one told her name.
A white media mogul published them. White folks are freaky
dekes, ain't they now?* As a product and form of technology,
film replaces the labor of representation. But how does race
condition the terms on which representation occurs? How does
race effect (and affect) one's agency within the marketplace of
sex?

Williams raised these questions herself when she repu-
diated the photographs as evidence of her abuse. "I feel as if I
were just a sacrificial lamb," she explained. "The past just came
up and kicked me. I felt betrayed and violated, like I had been
raped."[6] With her consent inconsequential to the proceedings
—indeed, the value of the pictures no doubt increased to the
extent that she couldn't claim ownership—Williams insisted that
the positions she took in the photos were "posed" and not
"spontaneous."[7] This distinction is remarkable not only because
it inverts what the two terms actually mean (posing becomes
an instance not of deliberation but of acting without will; spon-
taneity indicates the presence, not the abandonment, of intention), but because it opens for view the functions of race in
relation to the production of sex.

Williams was in no position to overturn the forces of consumerism that had been stimulated by Guccione's appropriation
of the pictures. Nor could she revise the racial symbolism of
film and the acts depicted in the images, precisely because the
historical construction of black sexuality is always already pornographic, if by pornography I mean the writing or technological representation and mass marketing of the body as explicitly
sexual.[8] Public auction ads, bills of sale, notices offering rewards
for the return of fugitive slaves, and probate records listing black
laborers as "assets" document the fact that, under chattel slavery,
black bodies were, literally, capital.[9] To perpetuate slavery efficiently, procreation became necessary, especially after the
trade was banned in 1808. Slaves' ability to reproduce compro-
mised the ideal(ism) of pleasure, since black desire was pressed
into service to generate wealth. Black babies meant more backs
to break over cotton, tobacco, rice, sugar, and indigo, which
meant more crop yields, which meant more cash flow. The mere
capacity to sire or bear offspring enhanced a black slave's price
on the auction block. Mammies and uncles, concubines and
studs, breeders all: slavery constituted a form of sex work.

That Tom Chiapel presided over an auction at which he
sold the photographs of Williams to the highest bidder; that
Williams's body was sold to (re)produce higher profits for her

"master," Bob Guccione, not only recalls the legacy of the sexual politics of American slavery, but also the sex radicals' labor theory of sexual value. To understand why Williams was pinioned between the ideological forces of the Miss America pageant and *Penthouse*, between liberalism and libertinism, we must return to the nineteenth century, to the moment when the terms and limits within which black sexuality was (and continues to be) publicly discussed were articulated and legitimated.

If black sexuality was, in the nineteenth century, the object of property, one meaning of "freedom" was the right to sex. For the fugitive slave-turned-author Harriet Jacobs, this proved to be a dilemma which, if it could be resolved, promised a hope of liberty that rivaled legal emancipation. Barred from pursuing a romance with a black carpenter and torn between yielding to the abusive advances of her master and consorting with another white man who took an interest in her, Jacobs observed:

> *It seems less degrading to give one's self, than to submit to compulsion. There is something akin to freedom in having a lover who has no control over you, except that which he gains by kindness and attachment. A master may treat you as rudely as he pleases, and you dare not speak; moreover, the wrong does not seem so great with an unmarried man, as with one who has a wife to be made unhappy. There may be sophistry in all this; but the condition of a slave confuses all principles of morality, and, in fact, renders the practice of them impossible.*[10]

In this, her autobiography published in 1861, Jacobs speaks profoundly, right on up to our own age. "The condition of a slave" did influence black "principles of morality," specifying "the practice of them" to be heterosexual. For slavery's logic suggested that mastery of one's self implied mastery not only of one's sexual desire, but one's capacity to reproduce. This ideology privileged and enforced heterosexuality as authentically "black" because the regulation of black reproductive rights demanded this definition.

No wonder, then, that black homophobes characteristically malign black homosexuality as a "white thing," as a relationship that, by definition, reenacts slavery itself.[11] No wonder, then, that black folks use "momma" and "daddy" or "brother" and "sister" as sexual references—"Come on, momma, and give me some sugar"; "Oh, daddy, don't stop now!"; "Brotherman got some boomin' boody"; "That sister is fresh": the alienation of black sexuality gets recuperated by the familiarity of the family, the historically constructed site of freedom.

That the photographs possessed the cultural value to compromise Williams's claims to her self and her authority is implicated in this history. Unlike her victory, it's neither a small nor a peculiar coincidence that she didn't own the copyright to her own image. Without legal standing, Williams couldn't freely choose to reproduce herself and so, again, was figured by the pictures as homosexual. These connections went unexamined, though, because "prosex" within black cultural discourse translates historically as "heterosex." On the other side, "prosex" arguments within lesbian feminist theories provide much-needed space to consider other social categories (in this instance, homosexuality) with which to describe historical experience. However, to the extent that feminist "prosex"-ists undertheorized black history in their various formulations, we were again left without an interpretative means to understand why the images of Williams took on the meaning and force they did.

Hence, Williams had nowhere to go but away. Unable to act on her own behalf, she could not compete against the needs either of the pageant (so she resigned from the throne) or of *Penthouse* (so she retreated from public scrutiny). So thoroughly exploited by the mass culture that offered to proclaim her one of its own, Williams accepted refuge—freedom—in the anonymity of private life.

VI

Since that time and between her twin triumphs of "Like a Virgin" and "Justify My Love"—between offering herself as a bridal queen and a demimonde dyke-type—Madonna has made a whole lot of money doing what Williams was castigated for: transgressing sexual boundaries and flouting gender/racial taboos. I would argue that winning the Miss America pageant defied, however problematically, the cultural maxim that black women are objects of desire meant only for backroom trysts and not living-room-mantel material, and that the *Penthouse* photos publicized the continually denied fact that black women do the nasty among ourselves and with female others. Why is it that Williams paid such a high price for striking her poses, and that Madonna, appropriating the practices of marginal cultures in her stage act, is rewarded so generously?

One reason, no doubt, would be the respective realms in which they work(ed): admittedly, the runway of the Miss America pageant is floodlit by an anachronistic conservatism that stadium rock has always opposed, what with its emphasis on rebellion and hyperbole (how else are you going to reach the cheap seats?). Williams wanted to make it by belonging; Madonna succeeds by refusing her prescribed place in the cultural order. The place where each situates herself, the genre each calls her own, levels the issue of gender with that of race, and it is there where a Madonna-like figure benefits from the sexual SOS sent up by lesbian feminism.

I happen to believe that the sex wars (not to mention the cultural logic of junk-bond capitalism) made Madonna plausible and profitable. As the boy-toy turned clit tease, she played out the notion of the gaze (who's looking at and getting off on whom and taking it to the bank?); proselytizing the joys of spanking on Arsenio Hall's show, the material girl got late-night America thinking about the pleasures of paddles and lite s/m, during that same interview thanking the "loose" black girls who encouraged her childhood defiance and, on vinyl and video,

ripping off voguing from black gay men. Part of Madonna's
glitter and glee is that she's a cultural robber baron, taking what
she wants from wherever she roams, incorporating it into her
rhetoric of self-presentation, without so much as an ethical
doubt as to the political implications of her gestures.[12]

Gazing on the prosex possibilities of a world beat without
the Third World, feminist discourses have, ultimately, given Madonna a body politic to deconstruct (and a racial aesthetic to
exploit) because they do, in fact, take race as their referential
starting point—only they position whiteness as the origin of all
theories postmodern, if not the very idea of theory itself. Though
other "post" theories (namely structuralism and, now, feminism) are on the politically correct tip since they propose a new
rationality based on pluralism, fragmentation, and nonlinear/
narrative world views, they nevertheless manage to leave race
less conceptualized than either gender or sexuality because
theorists misconstrue what "race" can mean.

This is why Madonna studies are now a cottage industry in
academia and a figure like Vanessa Williams is shunted to the
analytical wayside. Presuming that *racism* is the first and last
word bracketing the meanings and experiences of colored politics and culture foregoes understanding the complexities of
colored subjectivity. For example, what do I do with the fact
that, as I remember them, those photographs of Williams turned
me on? I know that part of my excitement came from the shock
of (for me, anyway) the new—I had never seen a black woman
being made love to by another woman. In that moment—as
much as on the night when she won the pageant—I felt affirmed
in my womanhood, my lesbianness, which, on both of those
occasions, reflected to me a self-image that I needed at the time.
And yet, I'm also aware that my pleasure wasn't entirely innocent; that, in fact, it depended on the expenditures of power
I've tried to describe in this essay. If we can deal with such
complications as they come to us in the figurative form of a
Madonna, why do we shy away from them in the symbol of a
Vanessa Williams? Accounting for racism is never wrong, but

it's necessarily limited and limiting, because it prevents us from seeing how the workings of race are fraught with ambivalences that empower us all, in sometimes discomfiting ways.[13]

There was—and still is—so much to say about the linkages between race and sexuality in American culture. However, our blindness to the political meaning of Vanessa's body, the abysmal silence enclosing her fall, describe this misunderstanding and underscore how the history of black sexuality informed Williams's calamity. It is neither a small nor a peculiar consolation to me that Williams's dark skin was seen and read in such a way that allowed her to pass from consideration, precisely because she lay right before our very eyes.

VII

As quiet as it's been kept, the (hi)story of Williams's fall from grace should have gotten air time during the sex wars debate. It didn't, partly because it happened so fast—without warning, without seeming cause, since her term was only weeks from its close. The main reason was that none of us knew how to talk about it, and that preemptive assumption resulted from the legacy of nineteenth-century sexual ideologies about race. If having the right to (hetero)sex constituted a form of freedom, so did the right to keep it private. As long as black sexuality was a market commodity, white voyeurism was an always-present threat, as black sex was subject to public inspection ("interventions" made in the name of rape and lynching). Silence, then, affords a measure of control; a strictly held confidentiality amplifies the pleasures of self-determination.[14] *If no one says anything, then no one will remember. What you don't remember you don't know and what you don't know can't hurt you.*

If history chronicles the facts and processes of transformation, the history of black sexuality must be written, in order to effect revisionary change. Otherwise, lives will continue to be lost: the silence burying the memory of Williams is the same silence that keeps the mortality rates of black infants, black crack addicts, and black AIDS victims abnormally and immorally high.

And this same silence renders black (homo)sexuality invisible both in lesbian feminist discourse and in black historiography.

At the very least, black dykes should have taken up Williams as an ascendant/fallen icon and viewed the episode as a textual moment to be, yes, intellectualized. It was an opportunity for us to create the language and discursive space we need to confront the ways in which sex is illin' our communities. That language and space require us to specify our sexuality as black and lesbian and to *define* what we mean by those terms; pictures, as the photographs proved, don't necessarily tell the one thousand truths those words can tell. Relying on fiction to do the work of historiography is a dangerous substitution to make, one that the Williams debacle and the novel-into-film projects of *The Color Purple* and *The Women of Brewster Place* demonstrate. While both brought black lesbianism to the Reagan-era masses, while we were right to take measured gratification in these well-meaning translations of our self-images and cultural expressions, the risk of rejection and betrayal was not resolved. Witness the dyke-bashing Alice Walker received on our behalf and the convenient erasure of "the two" from the TV series version of Gloria Naylor's book (black dykes are tolerable for the purposes of a one-shot miniseries but not on a weekly prime-time basis). Even if Spike Lee wouldn't let Opal Gilstrap have it, I took Nola Darling's nipple for my own, but I'd rather not rely on Spike, Walker, or Naylor to realize my desire onscreen or on the page. I don't want to cede that responsibility to others, and I want to pursue other expository forms that require me to claim it all—my race, my gender, my class, and my sex—at once.

VIII

Vanessa's coming back. Guest-starring on TV movies of the week. Hosting music-video shows. Starring in her own. Recording chart-busting, Grammy-nominated dance pop with the hottest producers in Hollywood. Marrying a righteously handsome black man with whom she's delivering beautiful children. Posing for the cover of Ebony *magazine. Doing all the right things. Consciously.*

Vanessa Williams's return is not—and should not be—contingent on her committing cultural amnesia and forgetting what happened to her. The point is not to remember her reign either as a triumph or as a failure, but to refuse the silence of critical complacency and to claim those parts of our history that are painful or otherwise difficult to account for.

As lesbian identity comes to be understood as a history with its own breaks and continuities, we must consider how race is and is not a seamless narrative as well. I'm trying to imagine how I would've told this story to my mother—she died before the scandal hit. And even if she had managed to live through it, she couldn't have seen it—the cancer had metastasized to her brain and shut down her sight. So I would have had to tell her, in words, that Williams had lost the crown. I would have had to discuss with her, in words, why the pictures banished Williams from further public view. I would have had to assert to her, in words, why what I do in bed with a woman is and is not, necessarily, what Williams did in the photographs. I would have had to risk, in other words, falling from grace in my mother's blind eyes. By writing this now, about us—Vanessa Williams, my mother, and myself—I see myself absolved.

PART THREE

LOOKING FOR HOME

COMING OUT HAS OFTEN MEANT PULLING UP ROOTS AND MOVING away, both literally and figuratively. Today many of us are trying to devise ways of being lesbian and maintaining connections with our families and cultures of origin—or we are at least trying to understand those connections better. The articles in this section explore the changing meaning of family—both families of origin and families we choose.

Dorothy Allison's "A Question of Class" is a personal recollection of growing up in a middle-class culture where being poor is a mark of shame. Allison managed to break the cycle of poverty and gain an education, which eventually brought her into the largely middle-class world of lesbian feminism. Participation in that world affirmed her sexuality but forced her to hide her Southern background, and its legacy of poverty, violence, and sexual abuse. "It is hard to explain how deliberately and thoroughly I ran away from my own life," Allison muses.

Creating fiction, she writes, has permitted her to reengage with that legacy, and to bring the voices of her past back into her life, into the lesbian community, and into her literary imagination. Her article reminds us that the injuries of class persist in our culture—even in communities that claim to transcend them. So do family ties.

For years, and in an amazing variety of contexts, writes Kath Weston, claiming a lesbian or gay identity has been portrayed as a rejection of "the family" and a departure from kinship. Indeed, we have often rejected our families because they have first rejected us. Today, however, lesbians (and gay men) are reconstructing kinship ties in new ways—through close friendships, same-sex partnerships, ties with ex-lovers, and the establishment of new biological families. In "Parenting in the Age of AIDS," Weston focuses on the last, on the lesbian baby boom of the 1980s and how it represents a creative response to the limitations of traditional family forms.

Catherine Saalfield expresses a dissenting view. While acknowledging that it is important that more and more lesbians are finding it possible to form families of their own, Saalfield is critical of rushing into a wholesale reconciliation with family life, decrying our tendency to emulate heterosexual institutions such as marriage.

Lourdes Arguelles broadens the agenda even further, mixing spiritual wanderings, personal testimony, and theoretical critique to argue for the importance of expanding our notion of lesbian kinship, culture, and community through the use of what she calls "crazy wisdom." Arguelles tells the story of her early youth in Cuba in the late 1950s, and of the lives of Teresa and Mercedes, two women who lived together and defied conventional notions of romantic love, sexuality, and personhood. Crazy wisdom, the embrace of an eccentric view of life, writes Arguelles, transcends personal and political solutions to our problems. Poised against the compulsion to fit in, to make communities that reproduce the ordinariness and conventionality of everyday life, crazy wisdom keeps alive the archetype of lesbian as "stranger, misfit, mysterious"—queer.

DOROTHY ALLISON

A QUESTION
OF CLASS

THE FIRST TIME I HEARD "THEY'RE DIFFERENT THAN US, THEY don't value human life the way we do," I was in high school in central Florida. The man speaking was an army recruiter talking to a bunch of boys, telling them what the army was really like, what they could expect "overseas." A cold angry feeling swept over me. I had heard the word *they* pronounced in that same callous tone before. *They*, those people over there, those people who are not us, *they* die so easily, kill each other so casually. *They* are different. "*We*," I thought, "*me*."

When I was six or eight years old back in Greenville, South Carolina, I heard that same matter-of-fact tone of dismissal applied to me. "Don't you play with *her*. I don't want you talking to *them*." Me and my family, we had always been *they*. Who am I? I wondered. Who are my people? We die so easily, disappear so completely—we/they, the poor and the queer. I hugged my bony white-trash fists to my stubborn lesbian mouth. The rage was a good feeling, stronger and purer than the shame that followed it, the fear and the sudden urge to run and hide, to deny, to pretend I did not know who I was and what the world would do to me.

My people were not remarkable. We were ordinary, but even so we were mythical. We were the *they* everyone talks about, the ungrateful poor. I grew up trying to run away from the fate that destroyed so many of the people I loved, and having learned the habit of hiding, I found that I also had learned to hide from myself. I did not know who I was, only that I did not want to be *they*, the ones who are destroyed or dismissed to make the real people, the important people, feel safer. By the time I understood that I was queer, that habit of hiding was deeply set in me, so deeply that it was not a choice but an instinct. Hide, hide to survive, I thought, knowing that if I told the truth about my life, my family, my sexual desire, my real history, then I would move over into that unknown territory, the land of *they*, would never have the chance to name my own life, to understand it or claim it.

Why are you so afraid? my lovers and friends have asked me the many times when I have suddenly seemed to become a stranger, someone who would not speak to them, would not do the things they believed I should do, simple things like applying for a job, or a grant, or some award they were sure I could acquire easily. Entitlement, I have told them, is a matter of feeling like *we*, not *they*. But it has been hard for me to explain, to make them understand. You think you have a right to things, a place in the world, I try to say. You have a sense of entitlement I don't have, a sense of your own importance. I have explained what I know over and over again, in every possible way I can, but I have never been able to make clear the degree of my fear, the extent to which I feel myself denied, not only that I am queer in a world that hates queers but that I was born poor into a world that despises the poor. The need to explain is part of why I write fiction. I know that some things must be felt to be understood, that despair can never be adequately analyzed; it must be lived.

As a feminist activist, I remember long conversations about the mind/body split, the way we compartmentalize our lives to survive. For years, I thought that concept referred to the way I had separated my life as a feminist activist from the passionate secret life in which I acted on my sexual desires, and I was convinced that the fracture was fairly simple and would be healed when there was time and clarity—at about the same point when I might begin to understand sex. I never imagined that it was not a split but a splintering, and that I would pass whole portions of my life—days, months, years—in pure directed progress, getting up every morning and setting to work, working so hard and so continually that I avoided examining in any way what I knew about my life. Busywork became a trance state. I ignored who I really was and how I became that person, continued in that daily progress, became an automaton who was what she did.

For years I tried to disappear, to become one with the lesbian feminist community so as to feel real and valuable. I did not know that I was hiding, blending in for safety the same way I had done in high school or college. I did not recognize the impulse to forget. I believed that all those things I did not talk about, or even let myself think too much about, were not important, that none of them defined me. I had constructed a life, an identity in which I took pride, an alternative lesbian family in which I felt safe, and I did not even realize that I had almost disappeared in order to become safe.

It is surprising how easy it was to live that life. Everyone and everything cooperated with the process. Everything in our society—books, television, movies, school, and fashion—is presented as if it is being seen by one pair of eyes, shaped by one set of hands, heard by one pair of ears. Even if you know you are not part of that imaginary creature, if you like country music, not symphonies, read books cynically, listen to the news unbelievingly, are lesbian, not heterosexual, and surround yourself with your own small deviant community—still you are shaped by that hegemony or your resistance to it. The only way I found to resist that homogenized view of the world was to make myself part of something larger than myself. As a feminist and a radical lesbian organizer, and later as a sex radical (which eventually became the term that referred to those of us who remained both feminists and lesbians but who insisted on the importance of arguing for a right to sexual diversity), the need to belong, to feel safe, was just as important in my life as in any heterosexual, nonpolitical citizen's, and sometimes even more important because the rest of my life was so embattled.

I have known I was a lesbian since I was a teenager, and I have spent a good twenty years making peace with the effects of incest and physical abuse. But what may be the central fact of my life is that I was born in 1949 in Greenville, South Carolina, the bastard daughter of a poor white woman from a desperately poor family, a girl who had left the seventh grade the year before, who worked as a waitress and was just a month past fifteen when she had me. That fact, the inescapable impact of being born in a condition of poverty that this society finds shameful, contemptible, and somehow deserved, has dominated me to such an extent that I have spent my life trying to overcome or deny it. I have learned with great difficulty that the vast majority of people pretend that poverty is a voluntary condition, that the poor are different, less than fully human, or at the least less sensitive to hopelessness, despair, and suffering.

The first time I read Melanie Kaye Kantrowitz's poems, I experienced a frisson of recognition. It was not that my people had been "burned off the map" or murdered as hers had. No, we had been erased, encouraged to destroy ourselves, made invisible because we did not fit the myths of the middle class. Even now, past forty and stubbornly proud of my family, I feel the draw of that mythology, that romanticized, edited version of the poor. I find myself looking back and wondering what was real, what true. Within my family, so much was lied about, joked about, denied or told with deliberate indirection, an undercurrent of humiliation, or a brief pursed grimace that belies everything that has been said—everything, the very nature of truth and lies, reality and myth. What was real? The poverty depicted in books and movies was romantic, a kind of backdrop for the story of how it was escaped. The reality of self-hatred and violence was either absent or caricatured. The poverty I knew was dreary, deadening, shameful. My family was ashamed of being poor, of feeling hopeless. What was there to work for, to save money for, to fight for or struggle against? We had generations before us to teach us that nothing ever changed, and that those who did try to escape failed.

My mama had eleven brothers and sisters, of whom I can name only six. No one is left alive to tell me the names of the others. It was my grandmother who told me about my real daddy, a shiftless pretty man who was supposed to have married, had six children, and sold cut-rate life insurance to colored people out in the country. My mama married when I was a year old, but her husband died just after my little sister was born a year later. When I was five, Mama married the man she lived with until she died. Within the first year of their marriage Mama miscarried, and while we waited out in the hospital parking lot, my stepfather molested me for the first time, something he continued to do until I was past thirteen. When I was eight or so, Mama took us away to a motel after my stepfather beat me so badly it caused a family scandal, but we returned after two weeks. Mama told me that she really had no choice; she could not support us alone. When I was eleven I told one of my cousins that my stepfather was molesting me. Mama packed up my sisters and me and took us away for a few days, but again, my stepfather swore he would stop, and again we went back after a few weeks. I stopped talking for a while, and I have only vague memories of the next two years.

My stepfather worked as a route salesman, my mama as a waitress, laundry worker, cook, or fruit packer. I could never understand how, since they both worked so hard and such long hours, we never had enough money, but it was a fact that was true also of my mama's brothers and sisters, who worked in the mills or the furnace industry. In fact, my parents did better than anyone else in the family, but eventually my stepfather was fired and we hit bottom—nightmarish months of marshals at the door, repossessed furniture, and rubber checks. My parents worked out a scheme so that it appeared my stepfather had abandoned us, but instead he went down to Florida, got a new job, and rented us a house. In the dead of night, he returned with a U-Haul trailer, packed us up, and moved us south.

The night we left South Carolina for Florida, my mama leaned over the back seat of her old Pontiac and promised us girls, "It'll be better there." I don't know if we believed her, but I remember crossing Georgia in the early morning, watching the red clay hills and swaying gray blankets of moss recede through the back window. I kept looking back at the trailer behind us, ridiculously small to contain everything we owned. Mama had, after all, packed nothing that wasn't fully paid off, which meant she had only two things of worth, her washing and sewing machines, both of them tied securely to the trailer walls. Through the whole trip, I fantasized an accident that would burst that trailer, scattering old clothes and cracked dishes on the tarmac.

I was only thirteen. I wanted us to start over completely, to begin again as new people with nothing of the past left over. I wanted to run away completely from who we had been seen to be, who we had been. That desire is one I have seen in other members of my family, to run away. It is the first thing I think of when trouble comes, the geographic solution. Change your name, leave town, disappear, and make yourself over. What hides behind that solution is the conviction that the life you have lived, the person you are, are valueless, better off abandoned, that running away is easier than trying to change anything, that change itself is not possible, that death is easier than this life. Sometimes I think it is that conviction—more seductive than alcoholism or violence and more subtle than sexual hatred or gender injustice—that has dominated my life, and made real change so painful and difficult.

Moving to central Florida did not fix our lives. It did not stop my stepfather's violence, heal my shame, or make my mother happy. Once there our lives became dominated by my mother's illness and medical bills. She had a hysterectomy when I was about eight and endured a series of hospitalizations for ulcers and a chronic back problem. Through most of my adolescence she superstitiously refused to allow anyone to mention the word cancer. (Years later when she called me to tell me that she was recovering from an emergency mastectomy, there was bitter fatalism in her voice. The second mastectomy followed five years after the first, and five years after that there was a brief bout with cancer of the lymph system which went into remission after prolonged chemotherapy. She died at the age of fifty-six with liver, lung, and brain cancer.) When she was not sick, Mama, and my stepfather, went on working, struggling to pay off what seemed an insurmountable load of debts.

By the time I was fourteen, my sisters and I had found ways to discourage most of our stepfather's sexual advances. We were not close but we united against our stepfather. Our efforts were helped along when he was referred to a psychotherapist after losing his temper at work, and was prescribed psychotropic drugs that made him sullen but less violent. We were growing up quickly, my sisters moving toward dropping out of school, while I got good grades and took every scholarship exam I could find. I was the first person in my family to graduate from high school, and the fact that I went on to college was nothing short of astonishing.

Everyone imagines her life is normal, and I did not know my life was not everyone's. It was not until I was an adolescent in central Florida that I began to realize just how different we were. The people we met there had not been shaped by the rigid class structure that dominated the South Carolina Piedmont. The first time I looked around my junior high classroom and realized that I did not know who those people were—not only as individuals but as categories, who their people were and how they saw themselves—I realized also that they did not know me. In Greenville, everyone knew my family, knew we were trash, and that meant we were supposed to be poor, supposed to have grim low-paid jobs, have babies in our teens, and

never finish school. But central Florida in the 1960s was full of
runaways and immigrants, and our mostly white working-class
suburban school sorted us out, not by income and family background, but by intelligence and aptitude tests. Suddenly I was
boosted into the college-bound track, and while there was plenty
of contempt for my inept social skills, pitiful wardrobe, and slow
drawling accent, there was also something I had never experienced before, a protective anonymity, and a kind of grudging
respect and curiosity about who I might become. Because they
did not see poverty and hopelessness as a foregone conclusion
for my life, I could begin to imagine other futures for myself.

Moving into that new world and meeting those new people
meant that I began to see my family from a new vantage point.
I also experienced a new level of fear, a fear of losing what
before had never been imaginable. My family's lives were not
on television, not in books, not even comic books. There was
a myth of the poor in this country, but it did not include us, no
matter how hard I tried to squeeze us in. There was an idea of
the good poor—hardworking, ragged but clean, and intrinsically noble. I understood that we were the bad poor, the ungrateful: men who drank and couldn't keep a job; women,
invariably pregnant before marriage, who quickly became worn,
fat, and old from working too many hours and bearing too many
children; and children with runny noses, watery eyes, and bad
attitudes. My cousins quit school, stole cars, used drugs, and
took dead-end jobs pumping gas or waiting tables. We were not
noble, not grateful, not even hopeful. We knew ourselves
despised.

But in that new country, we were unknown. The myth
settled over us and glamorized us. I saw it in the eyes of my
teachers, the Lions' Club representative who paid for my new
glasses, and the lady from the Junior League who told me about
the scholarship I had won. Better, far better, to be one of the
mythical poor than to be part of the *they* I had known before.
Don't let me lose this chance, I prayed, and lived in fear that I
might suddenly be seen again as what I knew I really was.

———

As an adolescent, I thought that the way my family escaped South Carolina was like a bad movie. We fled like runaway serfs and the sheriff who would have arrested my stepfather seemed like a border guard. Even now, I am certain that if we had remained in South Carolina, I would have been trapped by my family's heritage of poverty, jail, and illegitimate children—that even being smart, stubborn, and a lesbian would have made no difference. My grandmother died when I was twenty and after Mama went home for the funeral, I had a series of dreams in which we still lived up in Greenville, just down the road from where Granny had died. In the dreams I had two children and only one eye, lived in a trailer, and worked at the textile mill. Most of my time was taken up with deciding when I would finally kill my children and myself. The dreams were so vivid, I became convinced they were about the life I was meant to have had, and I began to work even harder to put as much distance as I could between my family and me. I copied the dress, mannerisms, attitudes, and ambitions of the girls I met in college, changing or hiding my own tastes, interests, and desires. I kept my lesbianism a secret, forming a relationship with an effeminate male friend that served to shelter and disguise us both. I explained to friends that I went home so rarely because my stepfather and I fought too much for me to be comfortable in his house. But that was only part of the reason I avoided home, the easiest reason. The truth was that I feared the person I might become in my mama's house.

It is hard to explain how deliberately and thoroughly I ran away from my own life. I did not forget where I came from, but I gritted my teeth and hid it. When I could not get enough scholarship money to pay for graduate school, I spent a year of blind rage working as a salad girl, substitute teacher, and maid. I finally managed to get a job by agreeing to take any city assignment where the Social Security Administration needed a clerk. Once I had a job and my own place far away from anyone in my family, I became sexually and politically active, joining the Women's Center support staff and falling in love with a series of middle-class women who thought my accent and stories thoroughly charming. The stories I told about my family, about South Carolina, about being poor itself, were all lies, carefully edited to seem droll or funny. I knew damn well that no one would want to hear the truth about poverty, the hopelessness and fear, the feeling that nothing you do will make any difference, and the raging resentment that burns beneath the jokes. Even when my lovers and I formed an alternative lesbian family, sharing all our resources, I kept the truth about my background and who I knew myself to be a carefully obscured mystery. I worked as hard as I could to make myself a new person, an emotionally healthy radical lesbian activist, and I believed completely that by remaking myself I was helping to remake the world.

For a decade, I did not go home for more than a few days at a time.

It is sometimes hard to make clear how much I have loved my family, that every impulse to hold them in contempt has sparked in me a counter-surge of stubborn pride. (What is equally hard to make clear is how much that impulse toward love and pride is complicated by an urge to fit us into the acceptable myths and theories of both mainstream society—Steven Spielberg movies or Taylor Caldwell novels, the one valorizing and the other caricaturing—and a lesbian feminist reinterpretation—the patriarchy as the villain and the trivialization of the choices the men and women of my family have made.) I have had to fight broad generalizations from every possible theoretical viewpoint. Traditional feminist theory has had a limited understanding of class differences or of how sexuality and self are shaped by both desire and denial. The ideology implies that we are all sisters who should turn our anger and suspicion only on the world outside the lesbian community. It is so simple to say the patriarchy did it, that poverty and social contempt are products of the world of the fathers. How often I felt a need to collapse my sexual history into what I was willing to share of my class background, to pretend that both my life as a lesbian and my life as a working-class escapee were constructed by the patriarchy. The difficulty is that I can't ascribe everything that has been problematic or difficult about my life simply and easily to the patriarchy, or even to the invisible and much-denied class structure of our society.

My Aunt Dot used to joke, "There are two or three things I know for sure, but never the same things and I'm never as sure as I'd like." What I know for sure is that class, gender, sexual preference, and racial prejudice form an intricate lattice that both restricts and shapes our lives, and that resistance to that hatred is not a simple act. Claiming your identity in the caldron of hatred and resistance to hatred is more than complicated; it is almost unexplainable. I know that I have been hated as a lesbian by both "society" and the intimate world of my extended family, but I have also been hated or held in contempt (which is in some ways more debilitating and slippery than hatred) by lesbians for behavior and sexual practices shaped in large part by my class background. My suspicious, untrusting, stubborn nature (characteristic of the Southern working class) has helped me survive but it has also made me a person who feels no safety within the lesbian community. The fact that my sexuality is constructed within, and by, a butch-femme and leather fetishism is viewed with distaste or outright hatred. I am presumed to be misguided, damaged by my childhood experiences, or deliberately indulging in a hateful and retrograde sexual practice out of a selfish concentration on my own sexual satisfaction. I am expected to abandon these desires, to become the normalized lesbian who flirts with fetishization, who plays with gender roles and treats the historical categories of deviant desire with humor or gentle contempt, but never takes any of it so seriously as to claim a sexual identity based on these categories.

One of the strengths that I derive from my class background is that I am accustomed to contempt. I know that I have no chance of becoming what my detractors expect of me, and I believe that even the attempt to please them will only further engage their contempt, and my own self-contempt as well. Nonetheless, the relationship between the life I have lived and the

way that life is seen by strangers has constantly invited a kind
of self-mythologizing fantasy. It is tempting to play off or engage
the stereotypes and misconceptions of mainstream culture
rather than describe a difficult and sometimes painful reality.

One of the things I am trying to understand is how we
internalize the myths of our society even as we hate and resist
them. Perhaps this will be more understandable if I discuss
specifically how some of these myths have shaped my life and
how I have been able to talk about and change my own understanding of my family. I have felt a powerful temptation to
write about my family as a kind of moral tale with us as the
heroes and the middle and upper classes as the villains. It would
be within the romantic myth, for example, to pretend that we
were the kind of noble Southern whites portrayed in the movies,
mill workers for generations until driven out of the mills by
alcoholism and a family propensity to rebellion and union talk.
But that would be a lie. The truth is that no one in my family
ever joined a union. Taken as far as it can go, the myth of the
poor would make my family over into union organizers or
people broken by the failure of the unions. The reality of my
family is far more complicated and lacks the cardboard nobility
of the myth.

As far as my family was concerned, union organizers, like
preachers, were of a different class, suspect and hated as much
as they might be admired for what they were supposed to be
trying to achieve. Serious belief in anything—any political ideology, any religious system, or any theory of life's meaning and
purpose—was seen as unrealistic. It was an attitude that bothered me a lot when I started reading the socially conscious
novels I found in the paperback racks when I was eleven or so.
I particularly loved Sinclair Lewis's novels and wanted to imagine my own family as part of the working man's struggle. But
it didn't seem to be that simple.

"We were not joiners," my Aunt Dot told me with a grin
when I asked her about the union. My cousin Butch laughed at
that, told me the union charged dues and said, "Hell, we can't
even be persuaded to toss money in the collection plate. An't

gonna give it to no fat union man." It shamed me that the only thing my family wholeheartedly believed in was luck, and the waywardness of fate. They held the dogged conviction that the admirable and wise thing to do was to try and keep a sense of humor, not to whine or cower, and to trust that luck might someday turn as good as it had been bad—and with just as much reason. Becoming a political activist with an almost religious fervor was the thing I did that most outraged my family and the Southern working-class community they were part of.

Similarly, it was not my sexuality, my lesbianism, that was seen by my family as most rebellious; for most of my life, no one but my mama took my sexual preference very seriously. It was the way I thought about work, ambition, and self-respect that seemed incomprehensible to my aunts and cousins. They were waitresses, laundry workers, and counter girls. I was the one who went to work as a maid, something I never told any of them. They would have been angry if they had known, though the fact that some work was contemptible was itself a difficult notion. They believed that work was just work, necessary, that you did what you had to do to survive. They did not believe so much in taking pride in doing your job as they did in stubbornly enduring hard work and hard times when you really didn't have much choice about what work you did. But at the same time they did believe that there were some forms of work, including maid's work, that were only for black people, not white, and while I did not share that belief, I knew how intrinsic it was to how my family saw the world. Sometimes I felt as if I straddled cultures and belonged on neither side. I would grind my teeth at what I knew was my family's unquestioning racism but still take pride in their pragmatic endurance, but more and more as I grew older what I truly felt was a deep estrangement from the way they saw the world, and gradually a sense of shame that would have been completely incomprehensible to them.

"Long as there's lunch counters, you can always find work," I was told by both my mother and my aunts, and they'd add, "I can always get me a little extra with a smile." It was obvious that there was supposed to be nothing shameful about it, that

needy smile across a lunch counter, that rueful grin when you
didn't have rent, or the half-provocative, half-begging way my
mama could cajole the man at the store to give her a little credit.
But I hated it, hated the need for it and the shame that would
follow every time I did it myself. It was begging as far as I was
concerned, a quasi-prostitution that I despised even while I
continued to use it (after all, I needed the money). But my
mother, aunts, and cousins had not been ashamed, and my
shame and resentment pushed me even further away from them.

"Just use that smile," my girl cousins used to joke, and I
hated what I knew they meant. After college, when I began to
support myself and study feminist theory, I did not become
more understanding of the women of my family but more contemptuous. I told myself that prostitution is a skilled profession
and my cousins were never more than amateurs. There was a
certain truth in this, though like all cruel judgments made from
the outside, it ignored the conditions that made it true. The
women in my family, my mother included, had sugar daddies,
not johns, men who slipped them money because they needed
it so badly. From their point of view they were nice to those
men because the men were nice to them, and it was never so
direct or crass an arrangement that they would set a price on
their favors. They would never have described what they did as
prostitution, and nothing made them angrier than the suggestion
that the men who helped them out did it just for their favors.
They worked for a living, they swore, but this was different.

I always wondered if my mother had hated her sugar daddy,
or if not *him* then her need for what he offered her, but it did
not seem to me in memory that she had. Her sugar daddy had
been an old man, half-crippled, hesitant and needy, and he
treated my mama with enormous consideration and, yes, respect. The relationship between them was painful because it
was based on the fact that she and my stepfather could not make
enough money to support the family. Mama could not refuse
her sugar daddy's money, but at the same time he made no
assumptions about that money buying anything she was not

already offering. The truth was, I think, that she genuinely liked him, and only partly because he treated her so well.

Even now, I am not sure whether or not there was a sexual exchange between them. Mama was a pretty woman and she was kind to him, a kindness he obviously did not get from anyone else in his life, and he took extreme care not to cause her any problems with my stepfather. As a teenager with an adolescent's contempt for moral failings and sexual complexity of any kind, I had been convinced that Mama's relationship with that old man was contemptible and also that I would never do such a thing. The first time a lover of mine gave me money, and I took it, everything in my head shifted. The amount she gave me was not much to her but it was a lot to me and I needed it. I could not refuse it, but I hated myself for taking it and I hated her for giving it to me. Worse, she had much less grace about my need than my mama's sugar daddy had displayed toward her. All that bitter contempt I had felt for my needy cousins and aunts raged through me and burned out the love I had felt. I ended the relationship quickly, unable to forgive myself for *selling* what I believed should only be offered freely—not sex but love itself.

When the women in my family talked about how hard they worked, the men would spit to the side and shake their heads. Men took real jobs—hard, dangerous, physically daunting work. They went to jail, not just the hard-eyed, careless boys who scared me with their brutal hands and cold eyes, but their gentler, softer brothers. It was another family thing, what people expected of my mama's family, my people. "His daddy's that one was sent off to jail in Georgia, and his uncle's another. Like as not, he's just the same," you'd hear people say of boys so young they still had their milk teeth. We were always driving down to the county farm to see somebody, some uncle, cousin, or nameless male relation. Shaven-headed, sullen and stunned, they wept on Mama's shoulder or begged my aunts to help. "I didn't do nothing, Mama," they'd say and it might have been true, but if even we didn't believe them, who would? No one told the truth, not even about how their lives were destroyed.

When I was eight years old, Butch, one of my favorite cousins, went to jail for breaking into pay phones with another boy. The other boy was returned to the custody of his parents. Butch was sent to the boys' facility at the county farm and after three months, my mama took us down there to visit, carrying a big basket of fried chicken, cold cornbread, and potato salad. Along with a hundred others we sat out on the lawn with Butch and watched him eat like he hadn't had a full meal in the whole three months. I stared at his head, which had been shaved near bald, and his ears, which were newly marked with fine blue scars from the carelessly handled razor. People were laughing, music was playing, and a tall lazy man in uniform walked past us chewing on toothpicks and watching us all closely. Butch kept his head down, his face hard with hatred, only looking back at the guard when he turned away.

"Sons-a-bitches," he whispered, and my mama shushed him. We all sat still when the guard turned back to us. There was a long moment of quiet and then that man let his face relax into a big wide grin.

"Uh-huh," he said. That was all he said. Then he turned and walked away. None of us spoke. None of us ate any more. Butch went back inside soon after and we left. When we got back to the car, my mama sat there for a while crying quietly. The next week Butch was reported for fighting and had his stay extended by six months.

Butch was fifteen. He never went back to school and after jail he couldn't join the army. When he finally did come home we never talked, never had to talk. I knew without asking that the guard had had his little revenge, knew too that my cousin would break into another phone booth as soon as he could, but do it sober and not get caught. I knew without asking the source of his rage, the way he felt about clean, well-dressed, contemptuous people who looked at him like his life wasn't as important as a dog's. I knew because I felt it too. That guard had looked at me and Mama with the same expression he used on my cousin. We were trash. We were the ones they built the county farm to house and break. The boy who had been sent home had been the son of a deacon in the church, the man who managed the hardware store.

As much as I hated that man, and his boy, there was a way in which I also hated my cousin. He should have known better, I told myself, should have known the risk he ran. He should have been more careful. As I became older and started living on my own, it was a litany that I used against myself even more angrily than I used it against my cousin. I knew who I was, knew that the most important thing I had to do was protect myself and hide my despised identity, blend into the myth of both the "good" poor and the reasonable lesbian. Even when I became a feminist activist, that litany went on reverberating in my head, but by then it had become a groundnote, something so deep and omnipresent, I no longer heard it even when everything I did was set to the cadence that it established.

By 1975, I was earning a meager living as a photographer's assistant in Tallahassee, Florida, but the real work of my life was my lesbian feminist activism, the work I did with the local Women's Center and the committee to found a Feminist Studies Department at Florida State University. Part of my role as I saw it was to be a kind of evangelical lesbian feminist, and to help develop a political analysis of this woman-hating society. I did not talk about class, more than by giving lip service to how we all needed to think about it, the same way I thought we all needed to think about racism. I was a serious and determined person, living in a lesbian collective, studying each new book that purported to address feminist issues and completely driven by what I saw as a need to revolutionize the world.

Fifteen years later, it's hard to convey just how reasonable my life seemed to me at that time. I was not flippant, not con-sciously condescending, not casual about how difficult remaking social relations would be, but like so many women of my gen-eration, I believed absolutely that I had a chance to make a difference with my life, and I was willing to give my life for the chance to make that difference. I expected hard times, long slow periods of self-sacrifice and difficult work, expected to be hated and attacked in public, to have to set aside personal desire, lovers, and family in order to be part of something greater and more important than my individual concerns. At the same time I was working ferociously hard at taking my desires, my sexuality, my needs as a woman and a lesbian more seriously. I believed I was making the personal political revolution with my life every moment, whether I was scrubbing the floor of the child-care center, making up a new budget for the women's lecture series at the university, editing the local feminist magazine, or starting a women's bookstore. That I was constantly exhausted, had no health insurance, did hours of dreary unpaid work and still sneaked out of my collective household to date butch women my housemates thought retrograde and sexist, never interfered with my sense of total commitment to the feminist revolution. I was not living in a closet, I had compartmentalized my own mind to such an extent that I never questioned why I did what I did. I trusted that it would all come clear in time, perhaps after the revolution—a mystical concept I took quite seriously—when I would also catch up on my sleep and, perhaps, radicalize my sex partners.

That oblivious concentration changed only when I began to write again for the first time since I had left college. The idea of writing fiction or essays seemed frivolous when there was so much work to be done, but everything changed when I found myself confronting emotions and ideas that could not be explained away or postponed for a feminist holiday. The way it happened was simple and completely unexpected. One week I was asked to speak to two completely divergent groups: an Episcopalian Sunday School class and a juvenile detention center. The Episcopalians were all white, well-dressed, highly articulate, nominally polite, and obsessed with getting me to tell them (without their having to ask directly) just what it was that two women did together in bed. The delinquents were all women, eighty percent black and Hispanic, dressed in green uniform dresses or blue jeans and workshirts, profane, rude, fearless, witty, and just as determined to get me to talk about what it was that two women did together in bed.

I tried to have fun with the Episcopalians, teasing them about their fears and insecurities, and being as bluntly honest as I could about my sexual practices. The Sunday School teacher, a man who had assured me of his liberal inclinations, kept blushing and stammering as the questions about my growing up and coming out became more detailed. When the meeting was over, I stepped out into the sunshine angry at the contemptuous attitude implied by all their questions, and though I did not know why, also so deeply depressed that I couldn't even cry. The delinquents were different. Shameless, they had me blushing within the first few minutes, yelling out questions that were partly curious and partly a way of boasting about what they already knew.

"You butch or femme?" "You ever fuck boys?" "You ever want to?" "You want to have children?" "What's your girlfriend like?" I finally broke up when one very tall confident girl leaned way over and called out, "Hey girlfriend! I'm getting out of here next weekend. What you doing that night?" I laughed so hard I almost choked. I laughed until we were all howling and giggling together. Even getting frisked as I left didn't ruin my mood. I was still grinning when I climbed into the waterbed with my lover that night, grinning right up to the moment when she wrapped her arms around me and I burst into tears.

It is hard to describe the way I felt that night, the shock of recognition and the painful way my thoughts turned. That night I understood suddenly everything that happened to my cousins and me, understood it from a wholly new and agonizing perspective, one that made clear how brutal I had been to both my family and myself. I understood all over again how we had been robbed and dismissed, and why I had worked so hard not to think about it. I had learned as a child that what could not be changed had to go unspoken, and worse, that those who cannot change their own lives have every reason to be ashamed of that fact and to hide it. I had accepted that shame and believed in it, but why? What had I or my cousins really done to deserve the contempt directed at us? Why had I always believed us contemptible by nature? I wanted to talk to someone about all the things I was thinking that night, but I could not. Among the women I knew there was no one who would have understood what I was thinking, no other working-class women in the women's collective where I was living. I began to suspect that we shared no common language to speak those bitter truths.

In the days after that I found myself remembering that afternoon long ago at the county farm, that feeling of being the animal in the zoo, the thing looked at and laughed at and used by the real people who watched us. For all his liberal convictions, that Sunday School teacher had looked at me with eyes that reminded me of Butch's long-ago guard. Suddenly I felt thrown back into my childhood, into all the fears and convictions I had tried to escape. Once again I felt myself at the mercy of the important people who knew how to dress and talk, and would always be given the benefit of the doubt while I and my family would not.

I felt as if I was at the mercy of an outrage so old I could not have traced all the ways it shaped my life. I understood again that some are given no quarter, no chance, that all their courage, humor, and love for each other is just a joke to the ones who make the rules, and I hated the rule makers. Finally I also realized that part of my grief came from the fact that I no longer knew who I was or where I belonged. I had run away from my family, refused to go home to visit, and tried in every way to make myself a new person. How could I be working-class with a college degree? As a lesbian activist? I thought about the guards at the detention center, and the way they had looked at me. They had not stared at me with the same picture-window emptiness they turned on the girls who came to hear me, girls who were closer to the life I had been meant to live than I could bear to examine. The contempt in their eyes was contempt for me as a lesbian, different and the same, but still contempt.

While I raged, my girlfriend held me and comforted me and tried to get me to explain to her what was hurting me so bad, but I could not. She had told me so often about her awkward relationship with her own family, the father who owned his own business and still sent her checks every other month. She knew almost nothing about my family, only the jokes and careful stories I had given her. Lying in her arms, I felt so alone and at risk, I could not have explained anything at all. I thought about those girls in the detention center and the stories they told in brutal shorthand about their sisters, brothers, cousins, and lovers. I thought about their one-note references to those they had lost, never mentioning the loss of their own hopes, their own futures, the bent and painful shape of their lives when they would finally get free. Cried-out and dry-eyed, I lay watching my sleeping girlfriend and thinking about what I had not been able to explain to her. After a few hours, I got up and made some notes for a poem I wanted to write, a bare painful litany of loss and grief shaped as a conversation between two women, one who cannot understand the other and one who cannot tell all she knows.

It took me a long time to take that poem from a raw lyric of outrage and grief to a piece of fiction that explained to me something I had never let myself look at too closely before—the whole process of running away, of closing up inside yourself, of hiding. It has taken me most of my life to understand that, to see how and why those of us who are born poor and different are so driven to give ourselves away or lose ourselves, but most of all, simply to disappear as the people we really are. By the time that poem became the story "River of Names," I had made the decision to reverse that process, to claim my family, my true history, and to tell the truth not only about who I was but about the temptation to lie.

The lesbian sex wars supposedly began in 1982, with the Women Against Pornography pickets who denounced Joan Nestle, Amber Hollibaugh, Pat Califia, and me at the Barnard Sex Conference. For me, however, the beginning was in the late 1970s, when the compartmentalized life I had created burst open. It began when I started to write and work out what I really thought about my family, and when I began to lose patience with my own fear of what the women I worked with—mostly lesbians —thought of who I slept with and what we did together. That was when I went back to my family. When schisms developed within my community; when I was no longer able to hide within the regular dyke network; when I was no longer able to justify my life by constant political activism or distract myself by sleeping around; when my sexual promiscuity, butch-femme roleplaying, and exploration of sadomasochistic sex became part of what was driving me out of my community of choice—I went home again. I went home to my mother and my sisters, to visit, talk, argue, and begin to understand.

Once home I saw that, as far as my family was concerned, lesbians were lesbians whether they wore suitcoats or leather jackets. Moreover, in all that time when I had not made peace with myself, my family had managed to make a kind of peace with me. My girlfriends were treated like slightly odd versions of my sisters' husbands, while I was simply the daughter who had always been difficult but was still a part of their lives. The result was that I started trying to confront what had made me unable to really talk to my sisters for so many years. I discovered that they no longer knew who I was either, and it took time and lots of listening to each other to rediscover my sense of family, and my love for them.

It is only as the child of my class and my unique family background that I have been able to put together what is for me a meaningful politics, gained a sense of why I believe in activism, why self-revelation is so important for lesbians, reexamining the way we are seen and the way we see ourselves. There is no all-purpose feminist analysis that explains away all the complicated ways our sexuality and core identity are shaped, the way we see ourselves as parts of both our birth families and the extended family of friends and lovers we invariably create within the lesbian community. For me the bottom line has simply become the need to resist that omnipresent fear, that urge to hide and disappear, to disguise my life, my desires, and the truth about how little any of us understand—even as we try to make the world a more just and human place for us all. Most of all I have tried to understand the politics of *they*, why human beings fear and stigmatize the different while secretly dreading that they might be one of the different themselves. Class, race, sexuality, gender, all the categories by which we categorize and dismiss each other need to be examined from the inside.

The horror of class stratification, racism, and prejudice is that some people begin to believe that the security of their families and community depends on the oppression of others, that for some to have good lives others must have lives that are mean and horrible. It is a belief that dominates this culture; it is what made the poor whites of the South so determinedly racist and the middle class so contemptuous of the poor. It is a myth that allows some to imagine that they build their lives on the ruin of others, a secret core of shame for the middle class, a goad and a spur to the marginal working class, and cause enough for the homeless and poor to feel no constraints on hatred or violence. The power of the myth is made even more apparent when we examine how within the lesbian and feminist communities, where so much attention has been paid to the politics of marginalization, there is still so much exclusion and fear, so many of us who do not feel safe even within our chosen communities.

I grew up poor, hated, the victim of physical, emotional, and sexual violence, and I know that suffering does not ennoble. It destroys. To resist destruction, self-hatred, or lifelong hopelessness, we have to throw off the conditioning of being despised, the fear of becoming that *they* that is talked about so dismissively, to refuse lying myths and easy moralities, to see ourselves as human, flawed and extraordinary. All of us— extraordinary.

KATH WESTON

PARENTING
IN THE AGE
OF AIDS

With a terrifying lucidity she had the vision of her corpse and she drew her hands over her body to go to the depths of this idea which, although so simple, had but just come to her—that she bore her skeleton in her, that it was not a result of death, a metamorphosis, a culmination, but a thing which one carries about always, an inseparable specter of the human form—and that the scaffolding of life is already the symbol of the tomb.

—PIERRE LOUŸS, *Aphrodite*

IN 1988 LOUISE RICE, A LESBIAN MOTHER OF TEENAGE SONS, spoke at a fund-raiser for *Choosing Children*, a film about lesbian parents and their families. "In the course of my talk," she wrote, "I asked how many there were considering motherhood. I remember my almost total disbelief as nearly every hand went up." Beginning in the mid-1970s on the West Coast, the fantasies and intentions of women like these gave way to the practice known as the lesbian baby boom. In the Bay Area, the impact of this novel concern reverberated throughout the lesbian population. The majority may not have been directly involved in raising a child, but everyone seemed to know another lesbian who was. Conferences and workshops abounded on the topics of whether to have children, how to have children, and what to do with them once you get them. Anthologies of writings about lesbian and gay parenting appeared in the bookstores.

Gay periodicals introduced columns that chronicled the adventures of new parents and offered advice on child-rearing. Even the progressive, politically oriented *Gay Community News* published a page of birth pictures from a "lesbians having babies" support group.

Women between the ages of thirty and forty-five seemed to predominate among those bearing, adopting, coparenting, or otherwise incorporating children into their lives. Most of these women were members of the relatively "out" cohort who came of age at the height of the women's and gay movements. Of course, lesbian and gay parenting is nothing new. A large number of gay men and lesbians have children from previous marriages, or were single parents before coming out. Support groups for gay fathers and lesbian mothers have existed since the 1970s. One thing that *has* changed, however, is the conviction, often reported by older gays and lesbians, that a person should get married or at least renounce gay involvements if he or she wants children. Writing in the 1930s, Mary Casal[1] anticipated the contemporary willingness to pursue parenting independent of marriage or an ongoing heterosexual relationship: "Had I been wise then as I am today and if the views of man had been different, I feel convinced that I might have had a child some time by a father chosen just for that occasion." Rather than maintaining a heterosexual facade or sacrificing gay relationships to raise children, more and more parents who identify as gay or lesbian have integrated their children into the gay families that are families we create. Those without children at the time they come out encounter a panoply of options, including foster care, surrogate parenthood, adoption, coparenting, alternative insemination, and "old-fashioned" (procreative, heterosexual) sex.

The popularization of alternative insemination among lesbians supplied the historical spark that set fire to this unprecedented interest in gay parenting. But gay and lesbian involvement in child-rearing must be viewed against the backdrop of growing numbers of single parents of all sexualities, coupled with the wave of pronatalism that swept the United

States during the 1970s and 1980s. The lesbian baby boom represents something more than a homosexual adjunct to this wider trend, insofar as it has developed and been meaningfully interpreted in the context of discourse on gay kinship. One result has been the subtle reincorporation of biology and procreation within gay families conceptualized as the products of unfettered creativity and choice.

THE LESBIAN MOTHER AS ICON

The characterization of lesbians as nonprocreative beings and the depiction of lesbian lovers as participants in "same-same" relationships render the image of the lesbian mother shocking and disconcerting, a veritable non sequitur. While I was attending a continuing-education class on a spring afternoon during fieldwork, one of the students—herself a single, heterosexual mother—could not contain her surprise when the instructor's lover brought their young children to visit the class. "She just doesn't seem like the type," remarked my classmate, having previously speculated about the teacher's sexual identity.

Many lesbian parents described motherhood as a status that made their sexual identity invisible. In their experience, heterosexuals who saw a lesbian accompanied by a child generally assumed she was straight and perhaps married. Before the lesbian baby boom, gay activists often challenged this presupposition by calling attention to the numbers of lesbians and gay men with children from previous heterosexual involvements. This information often surprised heterosexual audiences, but they were able to reconcile it with essentialist notions of homosexuality by treating these offspring as the product of earlier, "mistaken" interpretations of an intrinsically nonprocreative lesbian or gay identity.

If motherhood can render lesbian identity invisible, lesbian identity can also obscure parenthood. As the biological mother of three teenagers, Edith Motzko found it relatively easy to refute the popular notion that the term "lesbian mother" presents an oxymoron insofar as it joins a procreative identity (mother) to a sexual identity (lesbian) that is frequently represented as the antithesis of procreative sexuality. What Edith didn't count on was having to expose this sort of abstract thinking to her own father.

> When I told my father that I was gay ... his comeback was that society didn't demand it, that nature demanded that as a female that I would produce the species. I said, "I did it three times. I quit. That's it!" (laughter) So he gave me a big hug and said, "Be happy."

Numerically, adopted children taken together with children from heterosexual alliances still account for the majority of lesbian and gay parents. During the 1980s, however, the children of alternative insemination began to overshadow these other kinds of dependents, assuming a symbolic significance for lesbians and gay men disproportionate to their numbers. Insemination was the innovation many credited with motivating the lesbian baby boom, facilitating biological parenting without requiring marriage, subterfuge, or heterosexual intercourse. As the practice of alternative insemination spread among lesbians, relations conceived as blood ties surfaced where one might least expect them: in the midst of gay families that had been defined in *opposition* to the biological relations gays and lesbians ascribed to straight family.

In large part it is the prospect of physical procreation, the body of the child emerging from the body of the mother at a moment when she claims her lesbian identity, that renders "the lesbian mother" at once icon and conundrum. Babies conceived after a woman has come out demand a reconciliation of a nonprocreative lesbian identity with procreative practice. Any such reconciliation will be complicated by the notions of gender and personhood embedded in particular ideologies of kinship.

In the United States, new reproductive technologies have collided with ideologies that picture a child as the "natural" product of the union of a woman and a man in an act of sexual intercourse that gives expression to contrasting gender identities. Significantly, biological offspring conceived through alternative insemination need not necessarily be "conceived" as the product of two persons in this sense.

Most lesbians in the Bay Area used the gender-neutral term "donor" to describe a man who supplies semen for insemination. Because all parties to insemination theoretically construed the male contribution to procreation as a donation, freely given, a donor's continued involvement in a child's future was never assumed. Whether an individual donor would identify as a parent or participate in child-rearing had to be determined on a case-by-case basis. Some of the lesbians I met who were planning to have children specifically sought men who were prepared to coparent. For their part, not all donors were eager to assume the responsibilities of changing diapers or contributing money to a child's support. Ray Glaser, a gay man who intended to donate sperm to a lesbian friend, had no intention of becoming a father. Although he was willing for the child to know his identity, he had opted to become what he called an uncle or godfather, a more distant relationship defined by agreement with the child's lesbian parents.

With a view to possible legal complications or a desire to legitimate a nonbiological mother's claim to parental status, some lesbian mothers preferred not to know a donor's identity. A few went so far as to use sperm from several donors to make it difficult to trace a child's genitor. There was always the danger that a donor would have a change of heart, redefining his contribution from gift of sperm to possession of the shared biological substance that would give him grounds for a custody case. Though widely practiced, anonymous donor insemination remained highly controversial in the Bay Area. Lesbians who had been adopted as children and lesbian birth mothers who had once given up children for adoption took the lead in formulating a critique that portrayed anonymous insemination as detrimental to a child's well-being in a society that privileges biological inheritance.

Because insemination eliminates body-to-body contact, participants could minimize the male contribution to procreation with relative ease. Rather than focusing on donors, some lesbian parents-to-be referred only to "semen," making the procreative pair (if any) woman plus sperm, gendered person plus gender signifier. More is involved here than some strategic separation of genitor from (social) parent. To lesbian parents who had chosen an anonymous donor, their child might appear as the physical offspring of a single person, the child's biological mother. In this context, even so conventional a question as "Does he take after his father?" directed by a stranger toward the baby in the stroller forces the issue of coming out.

This separation of personhood and parenthood from the male's physiological contribution to procreation is in no way intrinsic to insemination as a technique. In her study of married heterosexual couples enrolled in an in vitro fertilization program, Judith Modell[2] found that women in the program considered adoption a preferable alternative to insemination in the event that the in vitro procedure failed. These women associated insemination with adultery and extramarital sex, believing that the method would introduce an unwanted third party into the relationship with a husband. For most Bay Area lesbians, in contrast, semen did not substitute for a contribution that would otherwise have come from their sexual partners. They defined the link to a donor as nonsexual, and insemination as an approach to procreation that circumvented any need for heterosexual intercourse or an ongoing heterosexual alliance.

Alternative insemination was initially associated with developments in biotechnology, although the syringe method favored by lesbians certainly represents a "low-tech," economical application. As insemination grew in popularity among lesbians, there was a corresponding move to change its linguistic modifier from "artificial" to "alternative," presumably in order to avoid invoking "natural" as a contrasting category. Labeling new reproductive technologies "artificial" resonated uncomfortably with the stigmatization of lesbian and gay sexualities as somehow unnatural. Were procreative sex reducible to methods of getting sperm to egg, this rhetorical shift might have proved adequate to avoid such associations. But the combination of two differently gendered persons destined to achieve substantive form in the new person about to be born, is as naturalized, as taken-for-granted, a part of procreation in the United States as the act of heterosexual intercourse symbolizing that union.

Viewed through the prism of a gendered difference predicated on the symbolic union of male and female in heterosexual relationships, the image of the lesbian mother can appear as much ironic as iconic. The butch stereotype of lesbians seems diametrically opposed to the nurturance and caretaking so closely associated with motherhood in the United States. If child-bearing stands as a sign of gender fulfilled, the mark of maturity and becoming a "real woman," how can it coexist with a category like "butch," popularly understood as a woman who desires to be a man? This perceived contradiction rests upon a contested ideology of womanhood, along with a very one-dimensional and inaccurate portrait of what it means to be butch. Although the majority of lesbians in the 1980s did not identify as either butch or femme, most had grappled with stereotypes about what it means to be gay, and developed a high degree of consciousness about issues of gender identity in the process of coming out.

Lesbian parents in the Bay Area were very well aware of heterosexual concerns about the effect of "same-gender" parents on a child's own gender and sexual identities. Joking about butch-femme contrasts accompanied lively debates over the importance of incorporating male "role models" into their children's lives. One woman might tease another about the inexpert styling of her young daughter's hair ("I never wore barrettes, and I *still* can't figure out where to put them!" protested the target of these friendly gibes). On another occasion, a woman who identified as a femme delighted in trading tips on makeup with the teenage daughter of a woman who had recently joined her household. A "mid-life butch crisis" was how Diane Kunin, in her late thirties, sarcastically referred to her recent, unprecedented thoughts of having a child. Humor aside, in cases where lesbian parents in a couple did identify as butch and femme, there seemed to be no preordained correspondence between biological motherhood and their respective gendered identifications. The femme-identified woman might or might not have physically given birth to their child(ren), contrary to what one would expect from a simplistic mapping of butch-femme categories onto the culturally constructed masculine-feminine contrast.

From radio and television talk shows to private conversations, one of the most frequently raised objections to lesbian and gay parenting invoked kinship terminology: What would the child call the (biological) mother's lover? The question assumes, of course, an idealized mother-and-father form of parenting in which the persons rearing a child coincide neatly with genetrix and genitor. In actuality large numbers of children in the United States have been raised by single or adopted parents, grandparents, aunts and uncles, older siblings, or multiple coparents. When heterosexual parents divorce and remarry, children often acquire more than two parents. Although they classify these relations as stepparents, "stepdad" and "stepmother" are not terms of address. Some children resolve the issue by calling their stepparents by first name alone; others apply the same kinship term to more than one individual; still others use different variants of a term for different parents (e.g., "Father" and "Dad").

Similarly, children in the United States have two sets of grandparents, yet they manage to avoid confusing one with the other. Terms of address vary regionally, but a common method of distinguishing between maternal and paternal grandparents employs some combination of kinship term plus first or last name. This strategy was the same employed by some lesbian mothers, whose children knew them as "Mama X" and "Mama Z." In other instances, lesbian parents marked a blood tie as primary by teaching the child to address the biological parent simply as "Mama" and the nonbiological parent(s) as "Mama (or Papa, or Mommy, or Daddy) So-and-So." Claire Riley[3] reported lesbian couples in New York City who used "Mommy" for one parent and a word for "mother" in a second language for her partner. Of course, the entire debate about kinship terminology ignores single lesbian parents, as well as lesbians who share child care with men who may or may not identify as fathers.

This widespread heterosexual preoccupation with nomenclature, coupled with an inability to imagine solutions to the terminological "problem," seems curious—curious, that is, unless one takes into account the belief that lesbian and gay relationships must resolve themselves into "roles" patterned on heterosexually gendered relations. Consider these all-too-typical remarks by Mark Grover, a columnist for the *Boston Ledger*: "It may be my ignorance, but I can't help but wonder what a child would do whose parents are two males; are they both referred to as 'Daddy?' Or does the child learn to refer to one of the men as 'Mom?' "[4] In his discomfort with gay parenting, Grover feared what seemed to him the inevitable outcome of a system of mutually exclusive gender categories—one man would have to be "the father," leaving "the mother" as the only identity available to the remaining partner.

Lest heterosexuals bear sole blame for perpetuating this line of cultural reasoning, listen for a moment to Paul Jaramillo, an interview participant whose opinions, while exceptional among gay men and lesbians, are not unknown:

> It seems like it's the latest thing now, to be a lesbian mother. And to me, that is so strange to me, two people of the same sex raising children. . . . It's gonna sound bad, but it seems to me there's no balance there. Maybe there is; I don't know. Again, focusing mostly in biology. I'm just so used to seeing a man and a woman. Sorts of masculine traits, sorts of female traits. Combining and raising this [child] together. And when it comes to lesbians, I'm totally ignorant. I admit that fact. I see them as being very good mothers, but I'm just curious as to how these kids are gonna be when they grow up. Is this gonna be a challenge, or a hard-

ship, or is it gonna be something that's wonderful for them?

Rather than wondering who would take which (presumably fixed and given) "role," Paul worries that a child could find it confusing to have two mothers. His account invokes cultural associations that link parenting and procreation to gendered difference, and not just any sort of gendered difference, but one constituted through a heterosexual relationship.

Paul's version of the terminological objection refracts relationships between lovers through the looking-glass imagery critiqued in an earlier discussion of lesbian and gay couples. There I argued that the abstract likeness which appears to characterize "same-same" (woman-woman or man-man) ties cannot be assumed for lesbian and gay relationships, but must be meaningfully specified and interpreted in context. To my knowledge most lesbian mothers who shared responsibility for raising a child made no special effort to minimize their differences, but with respect to parenting, they often formulated those differences in terms of a new and gender-neutral contrast. For lesbian parents who had practiced alternative insemination, the salient category shifted from "*the* mother" (a "role" that only a single individual can fill) to "*the one* having the baby." This reclassification still defined parental identities through difference, but it became a difference organized in terms of biological versus nonbiological parenthood rather than mother versus father. One effect of this shift was to underscore the congruence between procreative potential and lesbian identity, positioning lesbian mothers as mediators of these ostensibly contradictory categories. At the same time, it allowed for the possibility of coparents in excess of two, consistent with the fluid boundaries of gay families.

More relevant in this context than the construction of any sort of gendered contrast between parents is the notion, shared by some lesbians and gay men in the United States with their heterosexual counterparts, that children complete or legitimate a family. "What would make your relationship with Gloria a family?" I asked one woman. "If there were at least three people, like a child, involved," she replied. "I always felt that Nancy and I could be a family by ourselves," another woman with young children told me. "But she felt very strongly no, that being a family *meant* having kids. And [after having kids] I think I see what she means." In a play on the old song lyric "and baby makes three," and a poke at the proliferation of "alternative" families, a gay theater company in San Francisco recently produced a comedy titled "And Baby Makes Seven," which featured a pregnant lesbian, her lover, their gay male housemate and coparent-to-be, and several fantasy children. The lack of any prescribed number or gender for lesbian and gay parents, combined with the possibility (but *not* necessity) of a biological connection among those parents as contributors of egg or sperm, opened the way for some novel alliances between lesbian mothers and the gay men they had imaged as brothers previous to the lesbian baby boom.

MALE-FEMALE REVISITED: INSEMINATION AND AIDS

Generally speaking, gay men have been every bit as excited as lesbians about the baby boom and the prospect of becoming parents. If they had not personally donated sperm or assumed child-rearing responsibilities, many gay men in the Bay Area knew of others who had. Dick Maynes, for example, had a friend he described as "gaga" over the child he was coparenting: "All you have to do is mention the child, and he goes wild. Pulls out pictures and all the rest of it!" Craig Galloway had maintained a limited commitment to care for the son of a lesbian friend one weekend each month since the child was born five years earlier. Art Desautels got involved as a "bumblebee," the go-between who transfers semen from a donor to a lesbian trying to get pregnant when the two wish their identities to remain confidential. Meanwhile, Arturo Pelayo was searching for a lesbian of color who would want a gay man both to donate sperm and to play an active part in raising a child:

I've been really, really envious of lesbians for being able . . . for the options that they have. Just two weeks ago I went to see [the film] Choosing Children. *I was just in my mood again! But I did talk to someone who said that she had been thinking about that. She's a black woman, and she said she was thinking about at some point in her life, she'd like to consider having children with another Third World gay man. Of course I got excited! You know, whoa!*

Arturo's enthusiasm reflected the prospect of suddenly being able to envision something that had never before seemed possible, a parenthood categorically denied to lesbians and gay men in the past. His dream of one day having children encompassed the irony and the ecstasy of two persons culturally defined as nonprocreative beings uniting for the specific purpose of procreation. At one time, cooperation between lesbians and gay men as partners in alternative insemination and adoption seemed to offer the promise of healing some of the rifts in a "gay community" deeply divided by gender, race, and class.

As the vicissitudes of history would have it, it was AIDS, rather than AID (Alternative [Artificial] Insemination by Donor), that drew lesbians and gay men together after the 1970s. Lesbians adopted a variety of positions with respect to AIDS, as with any issue. There were those who stereotyped gay men by condemning them for "promiscuity," ignoring findings that linked the disease to unsafe sexual practices rather than number of sexual partners. Others, however, responded to the crisis by working together with gay men in hospice programs, political action groups, and AIDS organizations that offer support services to people with the disease. "It's changing," said Charlyne Harris, "to be on an empathetic level now with the men and know what they're going through. [There's] a closeness. . . . [Before] there was a barrier: gay men, they have their own lives—I'm a lesbian, I have my own. And it's not like that anymore. They experience the same things we do."

As they encountered the lack of government support for

AIDS research, programs, and drug trials, many newly politicized gay men learned firsthand the meaning of the feminist
slogan, "the personal is political." They began to build bridges,
however imperfectly constructed, to the feminist sector of the
lesbian population. Although some lesbians criticized the racism
and sexism within community-based AIDS organizations, renewed concern for the situation of gay men seemed to prevail.
Even lesbians not directly involved in AIDS organizing work
mentioned making gay male friends when previously they had
had few or none.

The onset of AIDS had a dramatic effect on the donor pool
available to lesbians for alternative insemination. Before AIDS
surfaced, the preferred means of facilitating lesbian motherhood
had been to ask gay men to contribute sperm. The general
feeling among lesbians was—and continues to be—that gay
men represent that category of males most likely to recognize
the lover of the biological mother as a full-fledged parent, and
to abide by any parenting and custody agreements reached in
advance of a child's birth. For many, economics was also a factor
in locating a donor, since informal arrangements are far less
expensive than paying the high fees charged by sperm banks.
But in light of the devastating losses AIDS has inflicted on gay
men in the Bay Area, and the risks for child and mother-to-be
of contracting the HIV virus through insemination, by the mid-
1980s most lesbians and gay men had become hesitant to pursue
this strategy.

In the absence of effective treatments for AIDS, many men
were reluctant to take the antibody test and skeptical about
claims that test results would remain confidential. "I don't feel
like I would want to be the biological father of anybody," Craig
Galloway told me, with the grim wit that has threaded its way
through this epidemic, "simply because I don't know whether
or not my sperm is radioactive." Louise Romero had originally
anticipated asking a close gay male friend to donate semen. "I
wanted to have his child, and I won't do it now because I'm
afraid of AIDS," she said. "Actually, that's kind of wrecking my
plans." Not everyone completely ruled out the combination of

gay male genitor and lesbian genetrix, but almost everyone regarded it as an option fraught with deadly hazard. Misha Ben Nun described the changes in her approach to becoming a biological parent:

> *I had definitely been looking at different gay men that were possibilities to me, or just feeling very secure that I would be able to find a gay man in the community who was into it. And then I gave that up completely. And then just recently, last week, my housemate was saying that you can feel safe enough, as long as he takes the [HIV antibody] test the day that you inseminate, each time you inseminate. And that's pretty intense to ask someone to do. But I'm also really interested in having whoever is the donor be also the father. So if someone's gonna make that kind of commitment, I expect them to be able to do something like take the test each time.*

Notice the usage of "father" in the exclusively social sense of a male who assumes active responsibility for parenting, a person quite discrete from a genitor or donor. Influenced perhaps by her strong desire to find a gay donor, Misha offered a somewhat inaccurate assessment of the risks involved in insemination. If HIV does indeed cause or contribute to AIDS, that virus has an incubation period during which exposure may not be detectable because the body has not yet manufactured the relevant antibodies. This picture is complicated by the unreliability of the HIV antibody test, along with ethical and emotional consequences of submitting to a diagnostic device with the potential to introduce severe stress and discrimination into a person's life if he or she tests positive or if test results become known.

The devastating impact of AIDS on gay men in San Francisco led many lesbians to look elsewhere for sperm donors. Toni Williams and her lover, Marta Rosales, had been seriously considering alternative insemination when they found themselves casting about for new possibilities.

*We wanted it to be a gay father. But with AIDS coming
around and stuff like that, I'm very afraid. . . . [Q: Why
did you originally want a gay father?] Because it
would be very difficult to have a straight person involved in a gay relationship, in a lesbian relationship.
It would take a very special person to be that understanding and accepting of how Marta and I are together. You're just this extra person here. You're part
of us, but—it's more tension than needs to be. And
plus, there's so many gay men that want to have children. And they can't because their lovers cannot have
babies. So we assumed that it would be nice for a gay
man, and that he would really want that child. . . .
And then, the whole fact that they are gay, and that
they accept that in themselves, would make it easier.
In the relationship that we have, all three of us or all
four of us. God, I don't know how it would work out!
(laughs) But now we just decided that we would try
to get one of Marta's brothers to donate sperm. God,
I don't know how that would work out legally.*

In legal terms relationships between gay and lesbian lovers
lack recognition in the United States, leaving lesbian and gay
parents dependent on the goodwill of authorities who oversee
nonbiological parenting arrangements like foster care or adoption and of sperm donors with a biological claim to parenthood.
There is little judicial precedent for granting custody or visitation
rights to nonbiological parents, whether lesbian, gay, or heterosexual, unless they have formalized their relationship to a
child through adoption. By 1990 most courts still would not
allow another person of the same sex as a biological parent to
adopt a child without causing the biological parent to forfeit all
legal relationship to that child. In only a very few cases had
courts allowed lesbian or gay couples to adopt children jointly.
Although lawyers urged lesbians and gay men to draw up contracts specifying the rights and obligations entailed in relationships with donors and coparents, such documents did not always

hold up in court. This precarious legal situation greatly accentuated the importance of finding sperm donors who would not challenge the status of gay people as parents.

During the 1980s the stigmatization of homosexuality and protective attitudes toward children continued to affect the courts' evaluation of what makes someone a "fit" or "unfit" parent. Judges handed down mixed rulings in custody cases, although more lesbian mothers seemed to be winning custody than in previous years, and in one instance custody of the adolescent son of a gay man with AIDS was awarded to his lover after his death. Such decisions came in the context of a broad range of legal challenges, from palimony suits to visitation rights for surrogate mothers, that sought recognition for relationships which seemed to fall between the cracks of laws framed with a genealogical grid and legally sanctioned marriage in mind.

When alternative insemination first became common, most lesbians chose gay male partners for their foray into procreation, regardless of whether they elected to minimize the donor's identity as a person or invited him to participate in child-rearing. By the 1980s lesbians were still likely to turn to gay men for prospective coparents. But the response of embattled gay and lesbian communities to AIDS has channeled gay fatherhood in the direction of a social rather than physical contribution. While the epidemic may have narrowed the options available for gay men wishing to become parents, it has not dampened their enthusiasm for raising children. Neither has AIDS changed the way alliances of lesbians and gay men as parents in one or another sense of the word embody a male-female symmetry between allegedly nonprocreative beings. Gay and lesbian parents invoke, only to disrupt, the unity of gendered opposites symbolically incarnated in the act of heterosexual coitus that represents a culturally standardized means to reproduction.

OF DEATH AND BIRTH

In conversations about the changes in their midst, gay men and lesbians in the Bay Area sometimes linked the lesbian baby boom to AIDS by juxtaposing the two as moments in a continuous cycle of life's passing and regeneration. New lives replaced lives lost, implicitly reasserting "community" as a unit which, like the disease itself, spanned divisions of gender, race, age, and class. Children (whether biological, foster, or adopted) brought generational depth to this community, along with the promise of a future in what some saw as genocidal times. To understand how deeply this sense of moving between the cultural poles of birth and death resonated in individual experience, one needs to understand something of the encompassing effects of AIDS in the Bay Area.

San Francisco differs from other urban locales around the United States in that the vast majority of its persons with AIDS are gay or bisexual. Because doctors diagnosed the first AIDS cases in the West in gay men, the disease was initially labeled GRID (Gay-Related Immune Deficiency). Although AIDS has disproportionately affected people at the bottom of class and race hierarchies in the United States, physiologically speaking the disease is no respecter of social classifications. Despite efforts to reshape public opinion, however, many people still associate AIDS with sexual identity rather than with unsafe sexual acts practiced across a range of sexualities. The very categorization of AIDS as a sexually transmitted disease (versus an affliction of the blood or immune system that may be transmitted in many ways) constructs particular images of the AIDS patient and divides the disease's so-called "victims" into innocent and guilty, morally responsible or irresponsible. While I was in San Francisco, "Here comes walking AIDS" was an insult of choice hurled by young heterosexuals at any man perceived to be gay. Gay organizations have shouldered the principal burden of AIDS education, with the unintentional effect of strengthening this association. Lesbians occupy the paradoxical position of facing discrimination at the hands of those who link AIDS with gay identity, while lesbians with AIDS and lesbians who test HIV-positive remain relatively invisible to service providers. Although lesbians as a whole fall into a low-risk category based on incidence of the disease, and no fully documented cases link sex between women to AIDS transmission, there are lesbians who have acquired the HIV virus through intravenous drug use (sharing needles), blood transfusions, or sex with men.

The rising incidence of antigay violence in the Bay Area, coupled with renewed discrimination in insurance, jobs, and housing, indicated a widespread tendency to view every gay man (and sometimes every lesbian) as a potential person with AIDS. Deeply resented, too, were the subtler indignities of being treated as a pariah in the course of everyday life. "People are less likely to offer a hug than they were a few years ago," said one man, the sadness in his voice almost palpable. Ronnie Walker, who cleaned houses for a living, had lost business in recent years. "Straight people are gonna be freaked out about some guy coming in and coughing on their toilet paper and then they're gonna die," he explained. "There's so much AIDS phobia going around." In his opinion, the phobia had proved far more contagious than the disease.

Like the baby boom among lesbians, AIDS has had an impact and significance reaching far beyond the numbers who have contracted the disease. Add the "worried well" to those who have tested HIV-positive and those diagnosed with AIDS or ARC (AIDS-Related Complex), and you have a group virtually synonymous with the population of self-defined gay men in San Francisco. Almost every gay man I met, as well as many lesbians, had friends or acquaintances who had died from AIDS. Some had the disease themselves. One of the few men who told me that he hardly ever thought about AIDS found himself face to face with it just six months later, when his closest friend developed ARC. A glance at the number of obituaries and articles on AIDS in gay periodicals, the constant round of funerals and memorial services, and the tremendous size of the AIDS contingent in the annual Gay Pride Parade offered other gauges of the epidemic's powerful presence in gay and lesbian lives.

At times of celebration like Halloween, the Castro Street Fair, and even Saturday nights, the mood in gay neighborhoods was subdued. No bubble machines sent their offerings up into the evening sky, and few men stood out on the balconies joking or flirting. While there were some men who practiced "safer sex" long before there was need for the term, others found it quite an adjustment. Confusion prevailed regarding whether monogamy effectively prevents individuals from contracting the HIV virus (it does not), while heated polemics examined the politics of "settling down" with a single partner. Initially some men were concerned that people would "go straight" for fear of AIDS or that gay communities would disappear, but no such trends developed. Central gay institutions such as the baths shut their doors, however, in response to loss of patronage and governmental decree.

While Simon Watney[5] has justly criticized media coverage of AIDS for its "slippage from 'gay' to 'Aids' to 'death,' " the epidemic has elicited an awareness among gay men of death as an ever-present possibility. Before AIDS, who would have mentioned dying as an experience comparable to claiming a gay identity, or portrayed encountering mortality as a second coming out? Some men tried to put AIDS out of their minds, feeling that beyond practicing safer sex they had little control over whether or not they would develop symptoms. Marty Rollins, who had had several close friends die from AIDS-related illnesses, adopted the philosophy of trying to "keep a good head on my shoulders and live each day one at a time." Others, like Brian Rogers, found themselves thinking about AIDS "every day. Almost every hour. Almost every minute. . . . Thoughts of mortality. Am I ready to die now? Have I done everything I want to do?" Drawing on his small income, Brian found a way to bring each of his brothers and sisters to spend time with him in San Francisco. He spoke about his plans for the future with the urgency and deliberateness of a man making a final settlement of his affairs. Experientially, AIDS had subjected gay men in the Bay Area to a kind of random terror. For them it was not homosexuality but death which appeared perverse, a formidable and elusive opponent that hunts down its targets and strikes without warning.

At the risk of succumbing to what Dennis Altman[6] has called a peculiarly "American" propensity to search for the silver lining in every cloud, I should emphasize that the epidemic has not left an unmitigatedly bleak landscape in its wake. Through self-help and educational activities, fund-raising, and provision of crucial services to PWAs, volunteers developed organizational skills and social ties. Persons with AIDS began to organize in an effort to formulate their own needs, rather than accept the role of clients passively shuttled through the byways of social service programs. They introduced the abbreviation PLWA—Persons Living With AIDS—to stress that they were not victims submitting to an automatic sentence of death, but people coping with the impact of serious illness on their daily lives. While Allan Bérubé[7] has rightly cautioned against the tendency to read positive meaning and intent into an epidemic devoid of reason or sense, credit must be given to those who have struggled to create something worthwhile from disaster.

Situated historically in a period of discourse on lesbian and gay kinship, AIDS has served as an impetus to establish and expand gay families. In certain cases blood relations joined with gay friends and relatives to assist the chronically ill or dying. Sometimes a family of friends was transformed into a group of caregivers with ties to one another as well as the person with AIDS. Community organizations began to offer counseling to persons with AIDS "and their loved ones," while progressive hospitals and hospices modified residence and visitation policies to embrace "family as the client defines family." Implicit in a phrase like "loved ones" is an open-ended notion of kinship that respects the principles of choice and self-determination in defining kin, with love spanning the ideologically contrasting domains of biological family and families we create.

When gay men and lesbians greeted the baby boom, then, it was in a lived context that presented contrasts between life and death as something much more than a cognitive opposition of transcendent categories. In practice, lesbian and gay parenting

countered longstanding associations of sex with death in Western cultures, including the nineteenth-century link between
homosexuality and morbidity that seems to have found a
twentieth-century counterpart in judgments that blame persons
with AIDS for their own affliction. According to the hygienic
ideologies that have blossomed periodically in the United States
since 1800, illness is not part of a "natural" order, but an evil
arising from individual violations of physiological laws, from
living contrary to one's "nature." Drawing on the characterization of homosexual sex as "unnatural acts," heterosexist com-
mentators have portrayed AIDS as the deserved product of some
mythically unitary "gay lifestyle." Lesbian and gay parenting
counters representations of homosexuality as sterile and nar-
cissistic by courting life, establishing new family ties where critics expect to find only tragedy, isolation, and death.

Parenting constructs a particular type of kinship tie, an age-
differentiated relationship that has added a generational di-
mension to gay "community." Before the baby boom, lesbians
and gay men were accustomed to speaking of generations in a
strictly nonprocreative sense that excluded biological referents.
In this context, age cohorts represented generations of a sort,
defined by symbolic events that incorporated new periodiza-
tions of history: the Stonewall generation, the lesbian feminist
generation, the AIDS generation. Generation and descent also
surfaced in transmission models that posited a unified "lesbian
culture" or "gay lore." Judy Grahn,[8] for instance, used the language of inheritance to describe peer relations through time
when she set out to record "oral history we heard in a line
passed on from our first lover's first lover's first lover." A notion
of gay generations also informed political struggles intended to
improve conditions for "kids coming out now." Their activist
elders depicted themselves working for a society in which
younger gays and lesbians "won't have to go through what we
went through." This is a rhetoric familiar from discussions of
class mobility, the hope voiced by parents seeking a better life
for their children. In many Western societies, at least before the
disillusionment of a postmodern era, the succession of gener-

ations had come to represent visions of unilinear progress fulfilled. This movement toward a world without heterosexism, which enlists the idealism of gays and lesbians to benefit generations yet to come out, looks with expectancy to the children raised within gay families for empathy and acceptance in the future.

Rather than grouping biological and adopted children together with blood family, lesbian and gay parents in the Bay Area considered both part of their gay families. For a child, belonging to a gay family did not depend on claiming a gay identity, any more than a straight adult would be expected to modify his or her sexual identity to be integrated into families we create. What qualified children for inclusion was being chosen by a self-identified lesbian or gay man. Contrary to the fears of some heterosexuals that gay men and lesbians will raise gay children, lesbian and gay parents tended to see themselves as substituting the freedom to choose a sexual identity for the generalized social pressure to be heterosexual. Craig Galloway, coparent to a young boy, emphasized that he took great care "to remind him that the door out is always open. Instead of saying, 'Yeah, you *better* be gay when you grow up.' You know, just like everyone told me when I was a kid: 'You *better* be straight when you grow up.' "

The spatial imagery of children growing up within lesbian and gay communities may offer a clue to the symbolic weight given to children who have been chosen after a parent has come out, children situated squarely within gay families in a manner uncomplicated by ties to former spouses or heterosexual partners. A fruitful parallel can be drawn between the straight children raised in gay families and the hearing children of deaf adults:

> *The only hearing people who are ever considered full members of the deaf community are the hearing children of deaf parents for whom Sign is a native language. This is the case with Dr. Henry Klopping, the much-loved superintendent of the California School*

> *for the Deaf. One of his former students, talking to me*
> *at Gallaudet, signed, "He is deaf, even though he is*
> *hearing."*[9]

In similar fashion, children raised by lesbian and gay parents
carry gay families forward into what for many will be a heterosexual future, moving through ideological space from families
we choose to blood family rather than vice versa, but accompanied by a firsthand knowledge of at least some sectors of the
diverse range of lesbian and gay experience.

BLOOD RELATIVES RESPOND

Like holidays and coming out, parenthood and AIDS have
opened opportunities to renegotiate relationships with blood
relatives. In these contexts, however, straight and gay families
tended to meet on the terrain of body and biology (adoption,
again, retaining a biological referent). When David Lowry's
mother, a staunch Catholic, wrote him one Christmas promising
to care for him if he ever developed AIDS, it was the first time
I had seen this friend of ten years cry. In many instances the
epidemic forced the issue of coming out to biological or adoptive relatives, which in turn meant facing the possibility of being
disowned at a time of acute need. "Living a lie is one thing,"
Joseph Beam[10] has written, "but it is quite another to die within
its confines." For Ronald Sandler, whose brother had already
died from an AIDS-related illness, what strengthened his relationship with his mother "almost overnight" was confiding to
her that he, too, had been diagnosed with AIDS. Not all stories
had such happy endings. The number of PWAs without homes,
family, or resources has grown year by year. When people told
relatives and friends they had AIDS, kin ties were reevaluated,
constituted, or alienated in the act, defined by who (if anyone)
stepped forward to offer love, care, and financial assistance for
the protracted and expensive battles with opportunistic infec-
tions that accompany this disease.

Kevin Jones took the threat of AIDS extremely seriously, having lived through the death of a good friend. Though he had already come out to his parents, when he contemplated the possibility of contracting the disease himself he felt pulled between two types of family:

> *I don't want my parents to go through me dying of AIDS. I'm almost more worried about them having to bury me dying of AIDS, than me catching AIDS. . . . I've thought about, would I tell my parents? Would I tell my mom and dad I have AIDS, or would I just wait and just die out here? It's scary to me.*

Contesting definitions of family can become all too evident in conflicts over a course of medical treatment or hospital visitation rights. Some people had drawn up powers of attorney authorizing persons they considered gay family to take charge of their affairs in the event of incapacitation or death, but these documents sometimes do not hold up under legal challenge by blood relations. When a gay man or lesbian dies, disputes over whether families we choose constitute "real" or legitimate kin can affect wills, distribution of possessions (including property held in common with lovers, friends, or housemates), listings of survivors in obituaries, and disposition of the body.

Tensions surrounding the legitimacy and kinship character of the social ties elaborated through families we choose also manifest themselves in struggles to define what relationship children raised in gay families will have to a lesbian or gay parent's blood relatives. Before the lesbian baby boom received widespread media coverage, the most common parental reaction when someone came out was to assume that having a gay son or daughter meant giving up any hope of grandchildren. Paulette Ducharme's father gave her sister with five children a piece of furniture he had originally promised to Paulette because he concluded that a lesbian would not be having children to whom she could "pass it down." Months after Amy Feldman came out, she felt it necessary to challenge her father's presumption that childbearing and child-rearing would be out of the question for her as a lesbian:

> *One thing my father did say to me about this thing, he said, one, he was sorry that I wasn't gonna be a mother, and I wasn't gonna have children. And I told him he was wrong. Even if I was straight, I wouldn't be having children right now. That's not the issue. . . . And he will get the chance to be a grandfather. And I told him that. He was jazzed about that!*

Others described parents urging them to "go straight" or arrange a marriage of convenience in order to have children. Those with a strong racial or ethnic identity sometimes associated pressure to have children with ethnicity, contending that not having children was considered anathema in categories ranging from "a traditional Italian family" to "Cuban culture."

In Rona Bren's case, both she and her brother had come out as gay from a sibling set of two. She felt sorry for her parents, who lived in what she portrayed as a very kinship-conscious Jewish community:

> *They can't go anywhere without people flashing baby pictures, grandchildren, wedding pictures. Everywhere they go it's children and children and children and children in their whole community. And everybody looks at them with sorrow. Everybody feels sorry for them—not that everybody knows their kids are gay, just the fact that we're not married and we haven't given them any grandchildren.*

Ironically, Rona was the proud nonbiological mother of a child her parents refused to acknowledge as kin:

> *They don't want anything to do with us. And I've been talking to them for years about having my own child. My mother says she's got enough trouble, she doesn't*

need a bastard to top it off . . . in the family. . . . When
I first told them that Sarah was pregnant, they just said,
"Well, she's not doing that kid any favors," and then
they stopped calling after she was born because they
didn't want to hear the baby crying, because it bothered
them. Because they want grandchildren so desperately
and to them it was just like another reminder that they
didn't have them.

Parents are surely no less complex in their reactions than their
lesbian daughters and gay sons. After their adult children presented motherhood or fatherhood as a possibility, some parents
had offered encouragement and support to see them through
the stresses of adoption applications or alternative insemination.
What these mixed responses by blood relatives indicate is that
the birthing and the raising, no less than the coming out and
the dying, have become arenas of contention in which discourse
on gay kinship is formulated even as transformations of kinship
ideologies are hammered out.

PARENTS AND PERSONS

Why should alternative insemination have dominated the discussions of lesbian and gay parenting that have arisen within a
wider discourse on gay families? The experience of coming out
to relatives convinced many that elements of choice shape even
the ostensibly fixed substance of biological ties. Selectivity man-
ifested itself in the discretionary power to judge the closeness
of relationships and to alienate kinship ties in response to revelations of a gay or lesbian identity. It should not be surprising,
then, to find families we choose capable of integrating biological
relations. Because insemination highlights physical procreation,
it subsumes notions of biology under the organizing metaphors
of choice and creation that have defined gay kinship in opposition to blood family. Such incorporations represent not con-

tradictions, but rather the interplay between any two terms that define an ideological contrast through difference.

When the gay men and lesbians I met spoke of blood ties, they did so in ways that generally did not challenge cultural notions of biology as a static, material "fact." However, they considered a nonbiological mother, father, or coparent no less a parent in the absence of legal or physiological connection to a child. Of those who responded with a simple "yes" when asked whether they wanted to have children someday, many envisioned a lover or close friend as the biological mother. Most did not consider a sperm donor to be intrinsically a parent, much less a partner, in relationship to a child conceived through alternative insemination; unless the donor shared parenting responsibilities, his semen tended to be spoken of simply as a catalyst that facilitates conception. Biological relatedness appeared to be a subsidiary option ranged alongside adoption, coparenting, and so on, *within* the dominant framework of choice that constituted families we create. At the same time, the distinction many gay people made between biological and nonbiological parents perpetuated the salience of biology as a (though not *the*) categorical referent for kinship relations.

There were those who felt that ethnicity was irrelevant, and those who dreamed of adopting "a child from every race" if money were no object. But had some method existed to fuse egg with egg, many lesbian couples planning to parent a child would have preferred that both partners contribute to the child's makeup biologically. The topic of parthenogenesis—procreation utilizing gametes of a single sex, which would completely obviate the need for sperm—came up in conversation from time to time. In the absence of such a method, many desired that children of alternative insemination bear a physical resemblance to the lover who would not physically be having the baby.

When searching for a donor, prospective parents frequently specified race or ethnicity: "[My lover] said, 'I really want an Hispanic to give me sperm so that the baby looks like you.'" Some, especially after AIDS complicated the task of finding a gay male donor, mixed metaphors in attempting to "create" a more direct "biological" link by asking brothers or cousins of a nonbiological parent to contribute sperm. At a workshop for lesbians considering parenthood, one participant recalled thinking about asking her adult son for sperm when her lover wanted to get pregnant. The arrangement would have created a legally recognized blood tie to the child that could have supported a custody claim if her lover were to die. After she realized that a genealogical mode of reckoning kinship would make her the child's grandmother, she rejected the plan as "too intense." Her fear was that perceived differences in generation would complicate her relationship to lover and child alike.

Appearance tended to carry as much symbolism as genetic connection. Resemblance between parent and child might signify an intention toward creating ethnic or cultural continuity (popularly understood as passing along "traditions"), as well as the union of the child's parents. Heterosexual couples, too, often sought their union and reflection in their children, with comments about which parent a child "takes after" in looks, likes, or behavior. Yet the situation of lesbian mothers choosing a donor for insemination differed in that they could very deliberately select for certain physical characteristics, sometimes in a conscious attempt to reinforce the legally vulnerable tie to a lover. By drawing on the social significance that infuses notions of biology, a lesbian couple can effectively make a statement about who constitutes the child's "real" parents. This subtle emphasis comes in the face of court decisions requiring the biological mother to alienate all legal right to a child in order for her partner to become its adoptive parent, and forbidding a newborn conceived through alternative insemination from assuming the biological mother's lover's surname. In the latter case, the New York State Supreme Court argued that assuming the mother's lesbian lover's name would not be in the child's best interests. For her part, "The child's mother called the use of her lover's last name important as a 'symbolism of family.' "[11]

An ideological stress on planning and choosing children pervades the titles for organizations, conferences, and films on lesbian and gay parents. Of course, heterosexuals can plan their children as well, but lesbians and gay men argued with conviction that they must choose in every case, effectively eliminating any contrast between "wanted" and "unwanted" children. In this context, biological ties no longer appeared as a given but as something consciously created, with choice representing a necessary and structural condition of parenting for anyone otherwise exclusively engaged in nonprocreative sex. By situating relationships between parent and child within the metaphor of choice that defines gay families, this argument underlined the implicit contrast between gay and straight parenting.

> *I think we think more than heterosexual people. I see some very thinking people [among lesbians and gays]. I see my sisters as, they didn't think about having kids. They just did it. And lesbians and gays, they think about* how *they want to raise that child. If they can afford it. They don't just go out [and do it].*

Prospective parents applied the notion of choice to the entire context of making a decision to have children, including the division of child-care responsibilities. Very often individuals engaged in extensive discussions and interviews before selecting coparents or sperm donors. Their own finances and job security typically came under scrutiny, especially when state agencies were involved. Many saw themselves enlisting "creativity" to work out the details of coparenting agreements.

The phrase "choosing children" also resonates with the variety of methods available for bringing children into one's life. Some gay men and lesbians would not consider parenting without a lover; others had elected to become single parents. Then there were those who assumed more restricted obligations, like Mara Hanson, who taught karate to children whom her lover cared for once each week. L. J. Ewing was not, as she put it, a "formal coparent," but she had helped care for a girl now age fourteen since the child was four years old. "She's my little buddy," boasted L. J., confident that this experience had given her a sense of what parenting her "own" child would be like.

Over dinner one evening, Brook Luzio surprised me by talking about a new desire to "help somebody who has kids already." When I saw her again several months later, the picture of a seven-year-old adorned her refrigerator door. After ending a long-term relationship with the biological mother of her daughter, Leslie Aronson continued to care for the child on a regular basis. On the other side of the city, Dave Vorlicek helped two lesbian friends through what he called a "family emergency" by letting their child live with him for the greater part of a year. Older gays and lesbians even had the option to become a grandfather or grandmother, as in this classified advertisement carried by *Gay Community News*: "Have Love Will Travel—Does your baby need a grandma? Middle-aged lesbian couple need grandchild to dote on." The very variety of these arrangements reinforced the belief that no models or code for conduct applied to gay families (aside from love), leaving lesbians and gay men freer than heterosexuals to experiment with alternative childrearing methods and novel parenting agreements.

The long history of state interventions into relationships among lesbians, gay men, and their children has supplied ample reasons for them to approach parenting with a healthy regard for tactical considerations. Custody battles remain a major concern. Former spouses, parents, and grandparents are the most frequent plaintiffs in custody cases that involve lesbians and gay men; such suits typically cite the parent's "life-style" as detrimental to the child or contest a lover's status as parent if the child's biological mother or father dies. Judges have mandated HIV antibody tests in some child custody cases, in one instance for heterosexual grandparents who had cared for a son with AIDS. Scattered custody disputes between lesbian coparents have arisen in conjunction with the baby boom, exacerbated by the uncertain legal status that positions gay relationships to one side of the "nature"/"law" divide. During the 1980s the Presidential Task Force on Adoption recommended against allowing lesbians and gay men to become adoptive parents, while foster care policy in several states became more restrictive, assigning lesbians and gay men to the status of parents of last resort. In the Bay Area the consensus seemed to be that planning and deliberation increase the chances that children will not be forcibly wrested from their parents at a later date.

Many lesbian and gay parents portrayed their children not only as the products of considered reflection, but as beings who *introduced* commitment and planning into everyday life. Rona Bren, the nonbiological mother of a two-year-old, spent much of her time and discretionary income on the child, caring for her three days each week in an apartment carpeted with toys:

> *She's totally a part of my life, totally, every single way. You know, I consider myself her parent. . . . I don't make decisions without thinking about her. I mean, I don't think, "She's with her mother," and I go through life and do what I want. She's very much a part of every decision, of every thought, everything that I do in my life. Every plan that I make.*

For all that Western societies have rooted kinship in a biological relatedness that invokes the act of heterosexual intercourse, becoming a genetrix or genitor has long carried cultural undertones of creation and responsibility for another human being. Among the lesbians and gay men in the Bay Area who had incorporated children into their lives, however, the persons who were parents rarely corresponded to genitor and genetrix. Although gay families have proved capable of subsuming childbirth along with adoption, erotic ties, and friendship, families we choose do not rest directly on a genealogical referent. By the time the lesbian baby boom entered the discourse on gay families, kinship in the United States could no longer be reduced to procreation, or procreation to the image of differently gendered persons locked in heterosexual embrace.

CATHERINE SAALFIELD

LESBIAN
MARRIAGE
. . . (K)NOT!

SUMMER 1988: AFTER COLLEGE I DROVE MY GIRLFRIEND ACROSS country so she could live in San Francisco while I returned east to New York. We wouldn't be joining the young dyke pioneers heading for suburbia in pairs with all their kids, carpools, and careers. We also wouldn't be telling each other about affairs and such, "unless one was going to have a direct impact on our relationship." She insisted, "Then I should know," and I agreed. In the end, there wasn't one particular person who drew us apart. Instead, the cumulative effect of new bodies, different turn-ons, and other people's morning patterns overburdened our already disjointed connection across three thousand miles.

But could a less stressed relationship survive nonmonogamy? Especially a relationship in which distance wasn't the easiest and most likely excuse for the open-ended state of things? One in which nonmonogamy was chosen on principle and not out of convenience?

Fall 1989: Denmark changed its laws to become the first country in the world to allow legal lesbian and gay marriages. I had spent a mid-September weekend in the woods with my lover. Sunday night was sweltering hot and clearly another difficult transition for all of us: me, the woman I just spent this intimate relaxing time with, and her other lover who was waiting for her to return to Brooklyn. We were trying to work out what it meant to us to do things differently, to try a difference that made sense in our separate lives. And open relationships, generally disdained and maligned by "married" couples, *are* a commitment. We are forced to do it without knee-jerk responses to social conditioning. It's never good enough to follow the example of Hollywood, rely on inappropriate sexual hierarchies, or relax into the patterns of "desirable but insensitive Casanova," "reliable but nagging wife," and "fun but unimportant affair." Our sheer exhaustion, headaches, impromptu tantrums, and churning anxiety reflect our lack of role models and an overwhelming dearth of support. Even comrades in other struggles casually and destructively play us off each other in this one with no regard for the time and love put into our work.

That particular Sunday afternoon, our car ran out of gas before we even left the farmhouse for the city. So, we're a couple of hours late back into town, again. She's preoccupied with her tardiness and explanations when we say goodbye in front of my building. Transitions are no one's forte and I'm wrenched into one of those all-too-familiar tailspins over quickly rearranged puzzle pieces. Nonetheless, in the scheme of things, this is where and when I step out. She's got a night ahead of her with someone she hasn't seen in a while, more sex, and undoubtedly more work to do. I've got loftmates, but no one is home when I walk in. The first phone machine message blares into a quiet room, breathy, frantic, a dyke: "This is for anyone, for all of you, even for just one, is it . . . like . . . is it OK for a P.C. person to . . . like . . . be married, to . . . want a house in the woods with 2.8 kids? I wanna ask you, is it fucked up? Is that it? You tell me what's goin' on. OK?"

Winter 1990: Two friends who had celebrated a three-year anniversary, who had been sharing the rent and a series of pets,
now faced the pain of breaking off a protracted term of nonsexual coupledom. The "security of monogamy" showed itself
for the smoke screen it was. As they pretended to be satisfied
with each other, they also pretended not to be "getting any"
outside the relationship. Both women had to admit that in a
dishonest or repressed relationship you're just as vulnerable on
Sunday nights as someone in a nontraditional situation.

Finally, the unfaithful member of the couple discovered
"the absolute worst thing is to be breaking up with two people
at the same time." Although her routine with the girls hasn't
changed, now she's up front from the jump about sleeping
around. In theory the honesty policy is more effective, but it
still doesn't necessarily breed responsibility. For example, being
late to dinner with one girl because she's making out in the
park with another ultimately makes her too late to the after-
dinner bar where she was supposed to meet the third she had
planned to spend the night with.

It definitely doesn't have to be that crazy. . . . There must
be an art in here somewhere.

Spring 1991: I still haven't been to a lesbian wedding. One of
my best pals from high school, who came out at the same time
as I did, has chosen a stable, long-term, monogamous relationship with a woman about ten years older. They exchanged rings
early on, before their first baby was born, and they had planned
a ceremony. My friend says, "A lot of what I needed to do was
let my family know that this relationship was important to me,
that [my lover] was marriage material." But it appears their bond
was secured by the birth of their little girl. "With the baby who
needs the other stuff. . . . It's like water under the bridge."

Her current sentiment seems eminently more sane given
the commercialism of weddings and the troubling traditions
they perpetuate. At most weddings I've attended (aside from my
mother's), rings were not exchanged, green cards were. (In

Australia, gay and lesbian relationships are recognized without the marriage drama for immigration purposes). But even without green card or visa transactions, weddings—like funerals— are a big business. People fly in from all over the place. Videos are made. Lots of money is spent. And afterwards the bank accounts are merged, the mortgages are shared, and so on. "Would you get married legally if you could?" I ask my high school buddy. Pause. I get nervous. Will we disagree? Whose choice would be more valid if we could marry and she did and I refused? Do we need this kind of hierarchy reinforced among queers? Rights for a few?

All sorts of alternative ceremonies aside, I don't believe government-sanctioned relationships are the answer to homophobia in this country. Not that it's going to happen anytime soon, but the intense lobbying for legalization of queer marriage really disturbs me.

Summer 1992: That plaintive call that echoed through my loft three summers ago asking if it's OK to be married, still runs crazy in my mind now and then, but I'm convinced that validation for "the best that I've got" can be achieved by other means than marriage. Why do lesbians in the early nineties want to get married to each other? Is this the only road to acceptance? community support? parental recognition? What are the great expectations of promised exclusivity? What meaning does "marriage" have when it's not legal? And how does all of this affect (or more accurately, disaffect) the rest of us? Besides, didn't feminists in the seventies and eighties already attack the institution of marriage, with its traditional sexual, political, and economic prerequisites, in their commitment to end sexual oppression? Has the conservative backlash of the Reagan/Bush era and the crisis of AIDS doomed alternative possibilities once and for all, leaving us to wallow in a whirlpool of cynicism and apology? I know there are more than three of us challenging the prescriptions and idealism of "The Brady Bunch," "Family Ties," and "The Cosby Show." I know many queers trying des-

perately to avoid the kind of family tragedy reflected in "Married
With Children," "The Simpsons," and "Divorce Court."

Marriage is embedded within heterosexuality, property relations, dependence, monogamy, and traditional parenthood, all
of which affect women in a particularly debilitating way. In Gayle
Rubin's seminal essay, *The Traffic in Women* (title borrowed
from Emma Goldman), the author exposes marriage as a sanitized knot of sexism. As Rubin examines the links between the
work of anthropologist Claude Levi-Strauss and Sigmund Freud,
she investigates the question "how does a female become op-
pressed as a woman?" She finds marriage and gender, boldly
organized around the exchange of women (in the marriage
system), to be at the root of sexual oppression. More than a
decade later, Rubin's basic analysis still rings painfully true (although I would add that insidious rumblings of compulsory
monogamy also serve much the same purpose as marriage).

Legal wedding ceremonies and the marriages that ensue
reverberate with unobstructed ties to the state. Nineteenth-
century bourgeois trends made marriage not only a convenience
but a necessity. Heterosexuality and the traditional nuclear family are all about property, all about economic and political arrangements: the shared income, the shared apartment—
"charters to rights of domicile and land use," as it were. Peace
and tranquility get yoked together in the dishonest fairy tale of
"family values," which disregards solutions for today's confu-
sions and challenges. But what should already be a relic of
heterosexuality is fast emerging as contested ground for queers.
It's about social validation, community support, and cultural
benefits, and we just want a piece of that pie, right?

Sure. And beneath the mask of state acknowledgment lies
emotional legitimization for both women and men. Despite
various sexual orientations, we're all on an ambiguous quest
for social validation since we've all been told that proper ad-
justments lead to cheerful lives. Why else do many young lesbians and gay men wait to come out to their parents (or

whomever) until they are in a stable, long-term, monogamous relationship? Why do they feel that open or short (even overnight) encounters are so unjustifiable? Why do we try to prove to the bigger-than-life mandates of society that we are no different, that we can be just like everyone else? Some previously straight and married, now lesbian women, especially, may recognize their struggle in this one. Why do we crunch ourselves up to fit into such traditionally oppressive structures?

Dykes in their forties and fifties who went through the experience of compulsory heterosexuality, the expected marriage, and the predictable divorce, have much wisdom about uphill battles against socialization. Their struggles to fit into accepted familial constellations are a dramatic reminder that women—who are so easily dismissed as useless by this culture—have a need (consequently, a desire) to be accepted, to escape disrespect and violence. But the role set out for women is a cultural imperative of "femininity": subordination, passivity, sacrifice. Who wants to be left alone, grow old alone, be called ugly, aggressive, difficult, selfish, unlovable? And even if they haven't been straight or legally married, anyone can identify with the fantasy: touching satin and imagining your wedding dress (billowing, with a very long train), the ceremony with loads of flowers (even in your hair), an adoring father to give you away (to your absolute soul mate), the spotlight on you, oh so much attention, the climactic kiss, the Happiest Day of Your Life.

These psychosocial pressures make us all start bad relationships, make us stay in bad relationships, make us settle for (almost) anything. Is this compulsory coupledom or compulsory heterosexuality? Perhaps I'm involved in two arguments here. One could be about heterosexuality as a detrimental prerequisite of and prescription for marriage, and the other might be about monogamy as not only the imperative for marriage but a repressive model for everyone. Nevertheless, I'm not sure they're that different. Any argument against marriage is an attack against the institution of monogamy. So my focus here is marriage because it's more concrete and it influences every corner of the cultural terrain very clearly. Marriage, which forces direct ties to the state in terms of inheritance, property co-ownership, and legal contracts, also creates gender relations (i.e., the sexual division of labor). The sexual-economic mandates are inextricable within such legally sanctioned unions.

The fantasy of marriage is one thing, the reality another. And romantic ideals fall short even for straight folks. They are up against the same morals and traditions as the rest of us: women are only valid when connected to a man, or when seeking a "mate." Take the example of mainstream AIDS research which has focused solely on women as vectors, as those who transmit HIV to babies and men. And how single women are also vilified when they have sex outside of marriage, before, after, *or* during. And marriage doesn't allow straight women any more independence, self-determination, or confidence than they are allowed otherwise; in certain ways, it limits them even further. The wedding ring isn't a viable promise or guarantee. Monogamy doesn't survive any better inside marriages than outside of them. The divorce rate is soaring. And there are plenty of still-married couples who would be better off apart. Trust, stability, and legitimization don't seem to emerge from these formalized unions. As Emma Goldman said, "Marriage is the antithesis of love, and will necessarily destroy it." It's hell to get it together in the first place, and then usually more painful doing the paperwork to get out of it.

So, lesbian rationalizations about how they will handle marriage differently don't satisfy me. Marriage isn't just a word but rather a whole system of values. For example, we all witness how aggressively the family unit is targeted for consumer items. Pick a TV advertisement, any advertisement. You'll most likely see parenthood, the nuclear family, the "happy homemaker" and her home improvement ideas, and kids with innocuous and irrelevant toys. And women are the ones socially positioned to administer the family's consumption. What kind of a world view are we trying to reinforce?

When I went to the "Children in Our Lives" conference in

Boston before I finished college, I saw lots of yuppie dykes with their perfect children, plenty of playthings, swimming lessons at two years old, tennis at three, the ideal kiddos. One closing statement, however, punctured the day's false tranquility. Angela Bowen, a grandmother, a Black woman, stood up and said that if she had it to do again she wouldn't have any kids. She said she couldn't stand seeing lesbians so eagerly participating in consumer culture, couldn't stand the nuclear family units with their awkward and exclusive notions of privacy, purity, and property. She suggested we explode this value system and make our homes reflect the diversity of the world around us by forming extended families, including people of different ages, races, sexual orientations.

Resistance takes many forms. If we play into the schemes of the dominant culture, we encourage the same ideological principles which govern our oppression, exclusion, invisibility, and the violence against us as lesbians. You tell mom that you're just like her, that you're married, that she doesn't have to accept lesbians or lesbianism, but if she can just see herself in your pseudo-heterosexual, familial scenario, everything will be all right. That leaves the rest of us dykes to be seen as difficult, unacceptable, disease-spreading, sex-crazed, pathological, unstable, adolescent, unfocused, unsuccessful, slutty perverts. Instead of the same old, predictable "validations" on their terms, we should use our gender socialization as the basis for critique and challenge.

One last point on the "inside-out approach" for people who want the benefits heteros enjoy when they tie the knot. It is a fact that thousands of queers got "married" at a mass wedding in October 1987 in Washington, D.C., and others are doing it in private settings with specialized rituals and personalized vows. So what about health insurance and other benefits of being legally married? The state certainly makes provisions for people who follow their rules. Even so, some marriages reap more benefit than others since only certain kinds of jobs provide spousal policies, let alone health insurance, in the first place. You say, "There's some form of domestic partnership (registration, health benefits, and sick and bereavement leave) now in sixteen cities nationwide." That won't even help at the airport ticketing counter where they shell out discounted fares to families and couples. But seriously, the health insurance predicament is a basic problem of the economic system in this country. You know something is wrong when you have to be monogamous to be treated in a hospital, when you have to live with a lover to afford primary care. If we had socialized medicine, everyone would be guaranteed health care regardless of status. We could stop rationalizing about benefits and start basing our decisions on the desire for companionship, respect, and love. Until then, we shouldn't play along with the exclusive, dollar-driven model, but fight for a change, a recognition of diversity.

Fall 1992: "And hey, the sex is a lot hotter in open relationships," says my favorite fuck buddy. She recently told me she'll never hang out with me again if I'm in a monogamous relationship because I turn cranky and neurotic and my skin takes on a greenish hue. She insists that when I'm in an open relationship I'm "more beautiful, fresher, certainly more fun, in a much better mood, and more alive." And then she becomes attracted to me. She may be exaggerating, but that's always worked for her before. I know I feel more out, more open, friendlier, sexier, happier when I can relate to people on a variety of levels, when I'm not bound to discourage myself, distance people, and generally shut down. My favorite long-term relationship models all include periods of nonmonogamy, lots of flirtations, three-ways once in a while, and separate bedrooms, which almost never get used. I would rather feel exhilarated about the loves that constitute the fabric of my life than nostalgic for some tame ideal of what it means to be family.

CRAZY WISDOM: MEMORIES OF A CUBAN QUEER

I'D LIKE TO FIRST TELL YOU A STORY AND THEN TRY TO EXPLAIN briefly its relevance for queers who, like me, are often personally misunderstood, theoretically excluded, and, more importantly, perceived as somewhat crazy. The story marks the first of my many encounters with people who have shown me the world through different lenses, until things became somewhat clearer—including gender, sexuality, and oppression. This story is undergirded by a vision different from those that govern mainstream lesbian certainties and uncertainties, a vision which draws from the teachings of many "crazy beings" and which still greatly upsets my conventional mind and the part of my being which continues to be absorbed in the lesbian fashions of the times.

The story begins in the city and period of my early youth, La Habana, Cuba, in the late fifties. It revolves around Teresa, who was for many girls of my generation a cultural heroine and for many other Cubans a trickster, a spiritual eccentric of sorts, a prostitute, and a fraud. Teresa, in turn, saw herself quite differently and might have described the story I am about to tell you as the tale of a *mulatta tortillera* who simply lived, laughed, and loved.

Teresa was thought to be the descendant of a family of unattached women deeply engaged in the exploration of Afro-Cuban and European traditions of spirituality and social protest such as Santería, Freemasonry, Espiritismo, and popular Catholicism. Teresa, however, always refused to validate the theories of her origin, and in a society and era consumed by a passion for genealogy, she never claimed any particular heritage.

I was barely thirteen when I found this enigmatic *entendida* (the preferred name by which Cuban and Cuban-American lesbians refer to each other), and she was well into her fifties, avidly practicing what was perceived to be a dangerous magical/spiritual craft while passionately engaged with a woman named Mercedes. Teresa was inseparable from Mercedes, her young, white, and wealthy apprentice, to whom she claimed to have been married in many other lives. Teresa lived in a mansion on the outskirts of La Habana, where her life seemed premised on the display of "crazy-wise" behaviors designed to break every racial, sexual, religious, and class taboo that one could hold onto in a society gripped by American neocolonial terror and consumerism and by Spanish colonial religion and prejudice.

No description of Teresa would be complete without mention of the fact that her house had served as a haven for urban *guerrilleros* as well as for the sick and the poor. Ironically, she routinely entertained members of the political establishment. When asked about this seemingly contradictory behavior, Teresa would shrug and, to everyone's consternation, say things like, "Oh, they are prick and balls underneath it all. And the women, all receptacles."

My first glimpses into Teresa's life came by way of a rumor, a joke, a melody that Tata, my milk mother, would hum throughout the day, saying that Teresa had composed it. Gradually, as my attraction to Teresa and her world grew, I began to spend hours watching from a nearby corner the comings and goings on her veranda. On each of the many days when I waited and watched, I could see Teresa with her legs spread wide apart sitting on an old rocker, her strong hands caressing Mercedes's long black hair, talking, singing, preaching, and laughing while smoking big thick cigars. I remember her powerful body covered by a simple white robe and her head by a red turban. She wore no jewelry or makeup, and I often wondered if one day she would do away with her robe and her turban.

At first, in the early stages of my voyeurism, I would stand staring at seemingly well-to-do white strangers to the island who paid homage to Teresa while dancing with each other and with "negros Ba-kongos" (blacks from an African ethnic group in Cuba) amid the rapturous sound of the sacred African double-headed bata drums, as Teresa and Mercedes handed plates of food to an endless parade of beggars, some of whom would be asked to join in the dancing. The gaudy images of Afro-Caribbean deities, trans-sexed and gender-blended gods and goddesses,[1] of a veiled picture which I was told represented Death, and of the bulging, sweat-ridden, black, brown, and white bodies of men, women, and in-betweens pressed against each other often followed me to my dreams.

Each day Teresa and Mercedes seemed different. At times Teresa looked like Mercedes and Mercedes looked like Teresa. Sometimes Teresa looked like someone I knew but could not quite place. Sometimes Mercedes's face looked quite masculine, as if she had begun to grow a mustache, but at other times her face was made up in stereotypical *criollo* feminine fashion. Occasionally when I watched them I had the impression that in some strange way they were fused.

Eventually I moved a bit closer to the house in the hope of immersing myself more deeply in the mysteries of the play on the veranda. I even dared to hope that one day I would peer behind Death's veil.

Earlier I had begun to feel my mind and my heart emptying out my bourgeois, adolescent racial and sexual assumptions, which were increasingly threatened by the continuing revolutionary war. But it was when I watched Teresa's veranda that I suddenly felt for the first time in my life fully awake and aware of the delusional nature of all the important structures and assumptions that made my world. I also felt poised to enter into those other realities in which Teresa seemed so comfortable. I intuited that life as she lived it, at the edge, afforded ways of existence unavailable to those who, like me, seemed stuck in the glue of social convention.

Months passed during which Teresa's crazy world continued to fuel my dreamlife. But the revolution of economy and society which began in 1959 changed all that: one day Teresa and Mercedes left abruptly for an unknown destination and their house stood empty. The following day it was taken over by several destitute families. I continued to stand near the abandoned veranda, guiltily wishing it all back. But Teresa's world had vanished.

Tata took pity on me and shared some of the teachings about life, death, and love she felt she had received on the days when she had been asked to join in the dancing on the veranda. She said that Death had taken everything away as He takes all that lives. Eventually I too left for one of many exiles, and Tata died soon thereafter.

The potential implications and the uses of crazy wisdom teachers and teachings for lesbian life and community are many and complex. I will attempt to explain a few of the implications which seem pertinent in this historical era and which have to do with transbiographical and spirit-based relationships, autonomy versus fusion in relationships, social hierarchy, difference, and change.

Some queers like me come from or have sought social and cultural circumstances in which independent teachers like Teresa, whom some call "crazy wisdom masters," are "on the loose."[2] Their lives constantly challenge conventional wisdoms and ordinary morality, eccentrically assisting in the process of understanding the play and transience of psychohistorical structures and conventions rooted in history and in the psyches of individuals. Such eccentric teachings seem to empty the body and mind of crippling biographical and cultural baggage as a necessary prerequisite to the development of understandings which may lie outside ordinary human judgment, free of cultural blinders.

The first assumption that left my mind as I watched Teresa's veranda was the notion of partnership in life as based only on romantic love, rational considerations, or initial sexual chemistry. Teresa and Mercedes opened for me the possibility of relationships based on the perception of a transbiographical experience or shared spirituality.[3] As a young girl, I witnessed Teresa and Mercedes in their relationship by becoming a part of their world, listening to their conversations, and observing their interactions. Such relationships appear to be inordinately joyful and creative and seem to endure in the face of numerous problems. They involve ways of relating that run contrary to Western notions of intimacy.

The most relevant implications for contemporary lesbians seem to revolve around issues of how these types of relationships can become vehicles to transmute problems and pain as well as instruments of joy and pleasure. When lesbian relationships can be predicated on the understanding that the psyches of the lovers are not limited to postnatal biography and that existence cannot be reduced to the material, the tangible, and the measurable, habits of perception tend to be activated and reinforced that can lead to viewing problems and hurts as challenging stages in the development of consciousness.[4] Such couples see this spiritual development as occurring across many lifetimes and at many levels. Pressure to resolve issues in the here and now therefore is not as intense. Though partners in these relationships may struggle to neutralize painful events and, in some cases, to dramatically change the course of their lives, their struggles may not be based on a sense of individual entitlement to feel specific emotions, to enjoy specific material conditions, or to control given situations. The demands of everyday life appear to weigh less heavily in relationships based on the perception that the ties that join the lovers will survive crises, changes in social circumstances, conflict, distance, or age. Boredom and the incessant quest for novelty, and hence an ever-widening search for new partners, seems less likely among these couples. There is a depth and resilience to these relationships, as well as a special evolving erotic pleasure that emerges from spirit-based purpose and transbiographical links between partners, that is difficult to explain but easy to recognize.

In later years my recollections of Teresa and Mercedes allowed me to question the current convention of assessing the health of a relationship by measuring the autonomy of each of the partners. Woven into the poetry of Teresa's songs and played out on her veranda were images of the blending of two strong women, the union of thoughts and feelings, the absence of boundaries. Fusion in relationships became a viable and acceptable possibility for me, as had spirit-oriented and transbiographical unions.

The lack of boundaries between self and other of women who have been involved in controlling or abusive relationships has made many lesbians fearful of voluntarily relinquishing boundaries in relationships, keeping them from viewing "fused" lovers as models and preventing them from understanding the pleasures involved in fusion between two strong women. This closing off to experiences of fusion may be contributing to making our lesbian communities into sites where autonomy and individualism are seen as the only acceptable options in relationships. Some lesbian writers take an even more extreme view that individualism within a relationship is not a realistic or acceptable option, proposing that total noncommitment is the only way to preserve a sense of freedom and adventure.[5] Crazy wisdom teachings remind us that autonomy and fusion are not mutually exclusive. Teresa and Mercedes were both autonomous individuals, yet they also achieved fusion in their relationship.

Another assumption that died for me as I watched Teresa's veranda was that social hierarchy or difference creates unsurmountable obstacles to compassionate action. On the veranda social and racial hierarchies and differences, rather than being flattened, ignored, or denounced, were systematically inverted, through continuous sharing, or used to illustrate an alternative reality, to create complementary polarities, and to afford protection from ordinary morality. This became possible due to a crazy wisdom not only capable of perceiving the interconnectedness and underlying sameness of all beings and the transitoriness of social positioning but capable of accepting the shadow, or dark side, of each being. Teresa was willing to act compassionately toward *guerrilleros*, beggars, and establishment politicians alike, precisely on the basis of their perceived shadow. The recognition and acceptance of the shadow parts of each being and of social groups seem to be necessary prerequisites for the building of compassionate communities and coalitions. Lesbian psychologies and sociologies seem to me to be essentially psychologies and sociologies of the "light" side of being, and tend to be unable to accept the tensions between the light and the shadow in each of us and in our communities. The emphasis on the good, the positive, and the elimination of the bad (an understandable response to society's pathologizing and vilification of same-sex eroticism and relationships) continues to lead dangerously to the systematic disowning of unacceptable thoughts and actions and their projections onto others "out there." One example is the denial or concealment of battering within lesbian relationships and the implicit projection of the image of the batterer onto the "other," which is male.[6] Shadow negotiation, recognizing and integrating the dark sides of our multiple individual and collective selves, remains a critical task.

In Teresa's house gender-blending and sexual role-play as people danced to the rhythm of primal sounds seemed to derive part of their charge from racial and class differences and perceived hierarchies. The presence of the wealthy and the powerful combined with the presence of feared African deities provided protection from conventional sanctions. The combined power of class status and spirituality guarded against police intervention. The public erotic union between the less affluent, aging, gender-blended *mulatta* teacher, Teresa, whose power derived from the creative appropriation of hybrid magical practices, and the white and wealthy student, Mercedes, whose condition as an apprentice was determined by her youth as well as by her whiteness and wealth, is as illustrative of erotic charge as of the suspension of social judgment. In that context, age conveyed power.

Other assumptions that might have dissolved in the power of Teresa's magic did not, and linger with me still, at least in remnants. The process of reflecting and writing has brought them into sharper focus. In recollecting Teresa's dismissal of the importance of origins and genealogy in herself, I am made aware of the salience of origins and backgrounds in my own and others' expressions of ourselves. Whatever our internal makeup, our outward expressions of ourselves are often designed for the purpose of "fitting in" to one or more categories. Teresa's lack of concern for fit into any sociocultural, spiritual, or even genealogical norms continues to challenge my searches for identity, community, and security. Further, the memory of her disdain for "fitting in" keeps alive for me the archetype of the lesbian as a stranger, a misfit, one who is homeless, mysterious, unpredictable, and barren. For me this balances the increasing "ladyfication" of our lesbian communities, with their penchant for ordinariness, procreation, and conventionality. The celebration of spaces free from political and social dogmas where we can love and dance in our difference seems of the essence for well-being and free flow within our stratified and conflicted communities.

I might also have reconsidered the illusion that anyone could, or should attempt to, change the world permanently. Teresa's fullest expression of self had nothing to do with attempting to alter the world or anyone in it. She lived and loved, danced and taught, and understood the delusional nature of "reality" sufficiently to know the folly of choosing to conform to it or trying to reshape it. When the dance that I was privileged to observe came to a close, Teresa and Mercedes moved on to find new music. To keep dancing, on or off the veranda, as various political or psychological generations seek the spotlight may be just the kind of crazy-wise behavior that could benefit lesbians of all colors, classes, ages, and abilities.

On some days the veiled picture on Teresa's veranda which I was told represented Death comes to mind. As I look back, and the sounds of bata drums pierce the soundless isolation of my suburban exile, I begin to suspect that there was not one image of Death, but many. I imagine Teresa and Mercedes each day selecting a different image to put behind the veil, a fitting recognition of the impermanence of gender, sexuality, class, ability, and race, and of life itself. I also suspect that these experiences of crazy wisdom may be a necessary component of the consciousness needed to make lesbian life and community unafraid of its own shadows and richer in fantasy and festivity, as much as in love and compassion, amid a forever-changing dark/light world.

PART FOUR

COMMUNITY AND ITS DISCONTENTS

THE IDEA OF COMMUNITY, A SAFE SPACE FAR FROM THE MAD-ding crowd, has long been a powerful one for many lesbians. The Lesbian Nation symbolized the possibility of inventing ourselves anew and dissolving the differences among us. This last section examines the shifting meaning of community, and the possibility of moving beyond the Lesbian Nation to build new forms of community, forms which acknowledge our differences as well as our commonalities, and which provide openings to the world beyond.

Our impulse to create safe space is noble. It emerges from a genuine desire to remake the world. But frequently, Alisa Solomon writes, the "call to compassion has been taken over by the will to regulate." Lesbian communities have been very good at laying down rules for proper behavior—rules which regulate sexual practices, romantic interests, and even, Solomon writes, "diet, dress, and aromatic emollients." As a result, we are often unsuccessful in engaging with pressing political issues beyond our communities.

Perhaps, writes Lisa Kahaleole Chang Hall, it's time to give up the idea of "the lesbian community" as a singular, monolithic entity. It's time to give up the idea of building community through exclusion—by decreeing who is a "real" lesbian and leaving everyone else out. For the vast majority of us do not fit neatly into those boxes. "Our lives," writes Hall, "are infinitely more complex than how we present them." These complexities can be the source of new political alliances—if we acknowledge them in positive ways. "Identifying as a lesbian," she writes, "potentially connects us to lesbians of all races, classes, and abilities and to a multiply gendered queer community."

Are we moving from the Lesbian Nation to the Queer Nation? Certainly new coalitions with gay men and other sexual minorities, centered on AIDS and other issues, are breaking with the gender-based politics of previous decades. Ruth Schwartz traces the history of lesbians in AIDS service and activist organizations, and examines how these alliances are making for strange bedfellows, and for new possibilities. In the 1980s, in many cities, many middle-class lesbians were drawn to AIDS-related work because of personal connections with gay men, because of their prior involvement in health care, or simply for the job opportunities. Lesbians, as a whole, were able to achieve more power in AIDS organizations than in relatively impoverished women's groups.

Through their work in the AIDS field, writes Schwartz, some gay men and lesbians have come to realize that they have fundamental things in common—namely their exclusion from the dominant heterosexual culture. But numerous divisions persist. As the epidemic has gone on, within many communities the experience of AIDS work—to quote sociologist Dennis Altman—has "increased the sense of community among gay men and lesbians, and at the same time sharpened the divisions." Today, more and more groups are fighting for fewer resources—not simply to battle AIDS, but also for other acute health-care needs such as cancer, and for other less acute needs as well.

Finally, Maria Maggenti reflects on her own role in the AIDS activist and queer movements, on our shifting alliances with gay men and straight feminists, and on the power of our passions. Historically, lesbians have been poised between the movements of heterosexual feminists and gay men—and as a result have become invisible. Today, writes Maggenti, "feminism has been absorbed by the same generation that so proudly claims to reject it," and instead of women's liberation, she hears "long live the Queer Nation." But the old problems persist: the map of the new Queer Nation has a white, male face; media representations of lesbianism fail to do justice to our long, complicated history. Maggenti describes a moment in which grappling for certainties seems futile, in which many of our preconceived notions about the meaning of lesbianism, and life in general, are being challenged.

ALISA SOLOMON

DYKOTOMIES:
SCENTS
AND SENSIBILITY

IN THE SUMMER OF 1989, A BOSTON-BASED NEWSLETTER called *Dykes, Disability & Stuff* published a three-year plan for improving access to "all lesbian, gay, feminist, and leftie events." In the "To Be Done Immediately" category the framers demand "good faith efforts to eliminate ableist language and images from our poems, prose, songs, dances, artwork, and hearts" (a process that would purge phrases like "blind to the truth" from the lesbian lexicon). In addition, "events should be advertised as scent-free, and 'sniffers' posted at the entrance to ensure that all who enter are in compliance. Anyone wearing scents should be turned away at the door." The reason: some women's sensitivity to perfumes. Some activists would extend the ban beyond patchouli to shampoo and commercial toothpaste.

Among the changes "To Be Achieved in One Year's Time": "Accessible seating should be provided for women of all sizes. Large sized women should not have to choose between not attending an event or being bruised by seating." "Food and drink should be available at all times. This should include sugar-free drinks for women who are diabetic or otherwise sugar-intolerant. Signs can be posted indicating that the presence of sugar-free drinks is not an endorsement of the diet industry. . . ." The aim is to meet the needs of all women without buying into the dominant ideology of feminine appearance.

I've been reading this manifesto to various lesbian activists over the last week, and though their responses have ranged from dismissal ("These women are so marginal, no one pays attention to them") to ridicule ("Give me a break. I get hay fever. Are music festivals supposed to move indoors?") to disappointment ("We've become a parody of ourselves") to anger ("If people need sugar-free drinks, let them bring their own fucking Perrier"), all have tempered their scoffing with sympathy. Indeed, most of the women whose knees jerked against the "authoritarian" tone of the demands were willing, as soon as they'd let off steam, to discuss the ethical complexities the manifesto raises. Sure, you might smirk at the image of sniffing-monitors posted at every door, but you've got to admit that the impulse of inclusion is a laudable thing. How admirable that women are trying to imagine and create a world where people traditionally regarded as impaired are treated with respect and care.

Still, the modus operandi often goes past consciousness-raising, and verges on behavioral control. This is what an increasing number of lesbians object to: an expansive system of regulations penalizing anyone who acts in a manner that can seem to others "patriarchal." This word is defined in ever more elaborate terms—especially in Boston, the Lesbos of political correctness, and Northampton, where guerrilla trashings of porn shops are a regular occurrence and separatist communities thrive. The Boston-based women's monthly *Sojourner* is one place where political lines are laid down, if not always debated, and new language constructions gain currency. In such publications, "nondominant" has replaced "minority," and "isms" proliferate: ableism, ageism, speciesism (meat-eating is a feminist issue for some), and the ultimate no-no, judging someone on the basis of their appearance: looksism.

We've all experienced too many occasions where the call to compassion has been taken over by the will to regulate. Rules for conduct get laid down, and soon after that, their enforcement becomes more important than the principles they were meant to ensure. The arena of semantic control encompasses not just sex and romantic impulses, but also diet, dress, and now, aromatic emollients. The body becomes a battleground: Women who dress too flannelly or too flouncy; who are too hairy or too sleek; who eat meat and drink wine or won't; whose erotic practices involve role-playing, porn, sex toys, or even men— all are subject to censure, and may even find themselves harangued at lesbian events.

Writers as politically diverse as Barbara Deming, Joan Nestle, and Audre Lorde have told dismayed tales of being ostracized because they thought the wrong things, wanted sex the wrong way, or had a child of the wrong gender. To this day, arguments rage over whether leather dykes and toddling male children should be allowed at lesbian music festivals; women's bookstores still get trashed for carrying *On Our Backs*, a journal of very incorrect lesbian erotica; audience members attending a recent performance by Holly Hughes in Washington, D.C., left the show to find their cars graffitied with red paint, labeling Hughes's work "pornographic"; a woman turned away from a recent reading by Andrea Dworkin at Judith's Room because of a dangerous overflow crowd wrote to the bookstore denouncing the "patriarchal" nature of its first-come, first-served policy.

At the Michigan Womyn's Festival in 1989, a white performer who sang about being cradled as a child in "ebony arms" was publicly condemned for condoning racism. A few summers ago, Brooklyn Women's Martial Arts *boycotted* the annual women's training camp, objecting to—among other things—an instructor who worked for her local police department. In both cases, a critique could well be made, but suppressing deviation and closing down discussion do not advance the cause. And more and more lesbian activists are convinced that the real motivation for these strictures is fear—of ideological contamination by the patriarchy, and even more disturbingly, of diversity. "These rules are about protection," says sex radical Amber Hollibaugh. "I didn't join a movement in order to be protected."

We dykes are rebels, after all. Our very identity has been shaped by our refusal to follow the rules set forth on billboards, in magazines, in movies, on TV; why, then, should we tie each other down with a new set of rules drawn up by our sisters? This is a question many young dykes are asking, with no small measure of venom. The result has been a new split in the lesbian community—between women whose analysis of sexuality was based on a model of oppression and victimization, and women whose model is Madonna—an emblem of autonomy and sexual taboo. My generation rebelled against patriarchy; the "new" lesbians are rebelling against *us*.

Perhaps author Sarah Schulman is right when she says that the sex radicals won the sex wars. After all, she points out, *On Our Backs* is the biggest-selling lesbian publication in the country. Over the last few years, an insouciant sort of dyke sexuality has penetrated mass culture as a radical woman's stance. Witness the Sandra Bernhard/Madonna faux confessions; the mainstream popularity of k.d. lang and Phranc; the way discoing till dawn has replaced the shadowy seductiveness of the old dyke bar scene; the "get over it" attitude of former *Outweek* columnists Liz and Sydney, whose idea of a hot lesbian night out was trendy barhopping with a couple of drag queens. So much for claiming women-only space.

Young dykes who lipstick up claim power by asserting traditional female coquettishness and withholding it from the traditional male beholder. In the giddy process of unleashing their libidos from the reigning, constraining hegemony of their lesbian predecessors, though, they fail to recognize a double bind: their appropriation of sluttish femininity is occurring at the moment when the dominant culture is rollicking with a heady antifeminism. Butch-femme dykes of the past dressed as an emblem of identity, but style-nomads—who wear lipstick tonight and Doc Martens tomorrow—are lost in the surfaces, and their ironic androgyny masks deracination. As twenty-seven-year-old writer/activist Maria Maggenti put it, "Most of the women I know who are my age or younger are cynical and alienated. They don't have any cogent analysis of where they stand in the world except that everyone should own a black bra. One side of me wants to say, 'Can't you stop calling us *girls* for one second?' At the same time, when I encounter older women who are rigid, I want to give them the finger and put on red lipstick."

Maybe young lesbians are making fun of our clothes and dissing our discourse precisely because political analysis has become equated with political correctness—as if hairy legs and flannel shirts had been reduced to an official lesbian-issue uniform and everyone lost sight of the underlying intentions to free ourselves from objectification and restricted movement. Working so hard to see to it that everyone shares in the liberating revelations of our analysis, we forget the political and obsess on the correct. Maybe the same could be said of the manifesto from *Dykes, Disability & Stuff.* Just the fact that they're setting rules makes it hard to take the reasons for the rules seriously.

Still, the reasons are important. Like any besieged community, lesbians have needed to tell our friends from our enemies. But unlike other nondominant folks—including gay men—lesbians must struggle to claim a sexual identity in a culture that doesn't allow women to do that. We're permitted to be ambiguous about who we are and what we desire, but when sexuality becomes the basis for an identity, we're public enemies, driven underground. And because we're often made invisible, the clues in the way we look—and even the way we might smell—have been crucial to our cohesion as a community. Beyond that, we make rules because we're trying to make our values concrete—that's how to make the political personal. If we want to build an alternative model of society, one not based on power, we need to live that model.

The result is not only a utopian impulse that veers toward the byzantine, but a genuine capacity to see the world beyond terms of strength and weakness. This clarity enables lesbians to respond to real dangers and possibilities—ecological as well as sexual—long before others. Dykes have been at the forefront of virtually every progressive movement, from civil rights to antinuclear activism. We battled for wheelchair accessibility long before the government caught on. And lesbians have led much of the way in AIDS activism. This is not just sensitivity, it's good sense.

More than three years have passed since *Dykes, Disability & Stuff* published its demands and as far as I can tell, the scents are wafting as heavily as ever at womyn's events. But to Catherine Odette, an author of the plan, time is on their side. "The lesbian community is miles ahead of the rest of the world on issues of access," she says. "This is the only place where environmental illness is even being discussed." To our utopian ears, Odette sounds perfectly reasonable when she explains, for instance, that the air is so toxic nowadays that women who react allergically to perfume are like the canaries sent into mine shafts: "If they're getting sick today, the rest of us are going to get sick ten years from now."

But this noble attempt to create a counterculture becomes an unintentional imitation of the oppression it's determined to replace. A lesbian can wag her fingers as righteously as any patriarchal puritan, defining what's acceptable according to what must not be ingested, worn, and especially desired. And these days, prohibitionism is more and more central to the American way. In a climate where a senator who doesn't like a couple of photographs tries to do away with the National Endowment for the Arts, censorious attacks within the lesbian community begin to sound a lot like fundamentalism. No matter that our bans—against s&m or butch-femme, dildos or lipstick, diet drinks or patchouli oil—are based, somewhere, on feminist analysis. They amount to a policing of the lesbian libido.

The Reagan years were preoccupied with policing pleasure. Consciousness was replaced by a touchy-feely sense of absolution, as twelve-step programs for practically any problem replaced CR groups. Defining temptations as addictions and addictions as sicknesses lets people off the moral hook and obscures the need for collective, political action. (We take our cue from the dominant culture here, too: Joel Steinberg got off easy because he was under the influence of cocaine when he murdered Lisa; Dan White became homicidal because he ate too many Twinkies.) If you take away people's moral responsibility, you can hardly count on them to make moral choices. No wonder the rules have been getting stricter.

There's an admirable sensitivity in the impulse to make accommodations not only for wheelchair users or deaf people, but for those who are "differently sized" or on restricted diets. But where do you draw the line on meeting individual needs, and what happens when they conflict? (Your accommodation to those who can't tolerate the chemical scent of deodorant might encroach on those who can't tolerate bad body odor in a hot, crowded room.) Legislating sensitivity equates disabilities that require systemic change—such as wheelchair ramps or signing—with ailments that people can deal with themselves, by bringing their own special foods or getting treatment for their allergies (which requires, of course, that we press for universal health care). By refusing to make distinctions, we end up valorizing helplessness and making a fetish of safety. The result, says Sue Hyde formerly of the National Gay and Lesbian Task Force, is that "we become suspicious of any lifestyle that is different from ours and see it as a threat or danger that must be shunned or controlled."

Loving other women *is* dangerous in this culture, and we can't afford to forget that. But we won't draw power by insisting on our weakness; we won't gain ground by claiming legitimacy from our status as victims. The greatest irony of decreeing politically correct action is that it ends up accomplishing the opposite. To "protect" a woman whose problem could be solved if she carries around a bottle of orange juice is to rob her of power. To tell women how to behave is to take away their agency. To define an identity by a group-think mentality is to rob the lesbian community of its most important asset: our diversity.

"Rather than saying we want to build a community that

reflects values we hope to have and opening discussion," says Amber Hollibaugh, "these rule-makers assume we're bad children who have to be told what to do. You end up with a movement made up of five people who can follow every single rule instead of fifty people in struggle. That's not a way to make change."

LISA KAHALEOLE CHANG HALL

BITCHES IN SOLITUDE: IDENTITY POLITICS AND LESBIAN COMMUNITY

I'VE BEEN A BIG FAN OF IDENTITY POLITICS SINCE THE FIRST TIME I realized the realities of my daily life were neither trivial nor irrelevant to what I wanted to do as an activist and to how I wanted to do it. For me, identity politics is about making connections between personal histories and a larger political and social context. Basic, but far from simple. Identity politics is important because it shatters the alienating split that we're taught exists between the realities of our personal lives and a public "political" reality. It's important because paradoxically, not recognizing and acknowledging where we're coming from makes it even harder to get beyond the limitations of our experiences. Both things are true: we are the world; we're just not all of it.

My first exposure to the concept of identity politics was as an undergraduate at Yale, not exactly a hotbed of social activism. As a student there, I often felt completely insane for reasons that are obvious now, but weren't then, that had everything to do with identity. As a mixed-breed, ambiguously middle-class potential lesbian who'd grown up in the socialist state of the U.S. military everywhere except the East Coast, my first encounter with this bastion of power and privilege was mind-bending. By my sophomore year, my friends and I came to understand that the institution was dedicated to the democratic proposition that everyone could be an upper-class WASP man. We began referring to the university as Male, in the city of No Haven.

There were many Yales; I went to the one for people who were accepted on sufferance, the tokens let in to prove that the elitism of Yale is based on quality, not status. My Yale was very small and suspicious, ironic and self-reflexive. It was taught by radical assistant professors who were on their way to being canned in three years, denied tenure for biting the hand that briefly fed them in their critiques of institutionalized power. It was attended by students who while being fed the myth of their superiority as "Eli"s were simultaneously called "faggot" and "nigger bitch" by fellow students and townspeople. It was about being both privileged and threatened, the locus of competing pulls between communities and the university.

I walked the tension-filled streets of impoverished New Haven, where the townspeople's hatred of the arrogant and non-taxpaying university spilled out in verbal and physical attacks. One day a car tried to run me down, as its driver screamed, "Fucking Yalie!" Other days, especially after dorm parties, I found myself identifying with the janitors forced to clean up afterwards—for valid reasons, it turns out. At a large faculty meeting a dean assumed that my mentor and another colored professor were maintenance workers. The dean was only a generation off; their mothers had both cleaned toilets to put their children through school. For them, and for me, there has never been anything simple about privilege—or oppression. Probably because of this, I have never assumed sisterhood with anyone.

The context for my first exposure to identity politics was my sophomore year, when my *nuyoriqueña* friend had the

ganas to find money within the university to bring Barbara
Smith, Cherrie Moraga, Chrystos, and many others to campus
for a conference on the newly published anthology, *This Bridge
Called My Back: Writings by Radical Women of Color*, edited
by Moraga and Gloria Anzaldua (Kitchen Table, 1984). Under
the portraits of the venerable white men, campus and community activists came together to explore just what the potential
of the newly accepted phrase "women of color" was and could
be. We had to convince a couple of the guest writers and artists
not to lift anything from the aptly named Master's Suites because
we were already stealing. We stole prestige for our lives and
our résumés and funneled it out with cash honoraria into our
larger communities. The layers of irony involved escaped no
one.

At the conference, my head exploded with new ideas, the
complexities of the lives revealed, and the connections among
them. The richness, the irony, and the ambiguities remain with
me as an integral part of my conception of identity politics.
Identity politics at its best is about making connections between
people and groups not normally perceived as related. Taking
seriously the idea that identity is a complicated mixture of sometimes contradictory layers of gender, racial, sexual, and ideological identifications means that there exists a number of
possible connections. Identity is as multiple as the communities
we form. Identifying as a lesbian potentially connects us to
lesbians of all races, classes, and abilities and to a multiply
gendered queer community. Working-class identification potentially links working people of all races and sexual orientations, and so on. That it doesn't work out this way too often is
obvious, but I don't think that's a result of taking identity too
seriously, but rather of not taking it seriously enough. The potential for positive identification and alliance is often wasted by
the racism, sexism, and homophobia that cross races, classes,
and genders so efficiently. A friend once told me of being in a
group of women of color working for university divestment
from South Africa who called themselves "Sisters in Solidarity."
Weeks of infighting accompanied their political accomplish-

ments. Near the end, they fought so bitterly because of one woman's homophobia that another was moved to declare, " 'Sisters in Solidarity,' shit. Y'all are gonna end up 'Bitches in Solitude.' "

There's no possibility of solidarity when people assume that identities are singular and fixed, self-evident and mutually exclusive. This is the foundation for the incredibly annoying questions asked of women of color that are all variations on "Which side are you on—race or gender?", as if one could pick and choose between the intersections of inseparable realities. In *In Search of Our Mothers' Gardens*, Alice Walker recounts the story of a white student questioning Walker's feminist commitment to the "black community" by asking why she didn't work with "women." When Walker reminded the student that of course there are black women, a puzzled silence followed. When feminists write about "women" in ways that it's very clear only certain women fit into, they are assuming a single meaning for the identity "women" that excludes most of its potential members. There is a power move that requires the security of being the "normal" center, whether racial/white or sexual/heterosexual. It doesn't work both ways; no one assumes that analyses by or about marginalized women cover the experiences of all "women." As the poet Gwendolyn Brooks reminds us, "The juice of the tomato is never just called juice/It's always called TOMATO juice."

There are at least two kinds of exclusionary identity-building. One is the exclusion based on power and privilege, the ability not to have to take other people's existences seriously. The other comes from the less privileged end of the spectrum. For some, identity becomes a fortress under siege that's protected by denying connections with others and oversimplifying connections with "their own." If people really took seriously their claims of solidarity within groupings like "all black people," "all lesbians," "all women," or "the working class," the entire planet would be linked in a web of overlapping networks around gender, race, sexuality, Marxism, or whatever, because each slice of the population contains members of all the others.

But there's little affirmation of this reality; instead the pressure comes from all sides to choose, choose. Pick a singular identity and then fit in: a lesbian identity that ignores cultural, racial, and class differences, a racial identity that represses sexual differences and multiracial histories, a gender identity that conflates it all. But our lives are infinitely more complex than the way we present them.

Identities focused around not being something else as opposed to being something are the result of feeling attacked on all sides; they're an attempt to consolidate ground that feels threatened. For lesbians this has taken the form of trying to regulate lesbian identity—who's a "real lesbian"; the rules have often changed but the desire to judge remains constant. I still believe that the most radical insight of the feminist movement is that "the personal is political," but I've never believed that that meant *only* the personal is political, or that the political begins and ends with the personal, or that personal change is equivalent to political change per se. The confusion of these three ideas has led to the creation of rigid prescriptions about everything from sex to food as a form of political activism, and to an assumption that feeling good is the necessary and desirable outcome of political organizing. This fits in nicely with traditional imperatives that women manage the personal arena, make nice, and be responsible for everyone's feelings.

There is an important distinction between trying to ensure equal access and trying to take care of people inappropriately. To see issues of language, assumptions, and physical access as being about making people feel better trivializes the significance of those issues. Framing them in terms of "political correctness" has not been illuminating. The attack on "pc" has become a total farce. In the first place, the term started as a self-critical in-joke of the left. No one ever seriously claimed it; it's always been a charge against someone else. Now "pc" has become a shorthand for knee-jerk thinking and rigidity, but only that of progressive activists. The backlash against it doesn't address the issues involved, only a style. Working against things that are both "normal" and oppressive is much harder than accepting an unequal status quo precisely because oppression is normalized. Consistently having to point out how some ideas and practices exclude your own and others' existences gets you the reputation of being a constant whiner and—my favorite—a "social fascist." For example, it's not a passion for making rules that motivates lesbian feminists to be concerned with wheelchair accessibility, sign language interpretation, and scent- and smoke-free environments, but a recognition that not having these conditions restricts the participation of all potential members in a community. Ensuring access to a broad variety of participants is not about doing for the poor unfortunates with special needs; it is about addressing barriers of language and physical ability that keep women apart. Inclusivity is important because exclusion impoverishes the experiences of both the excluded and those left in the inner circle without them. Ironically, this feels like unnecessary regulation only to those who don't have the personal experience of being excluded by those barriers. Being disabled or having disabled people in your life who matter to you means entering a world of inaccessible events, stairs where people swear there are none, migraine and asthma attacks from the woman drenched in Opium, tiny bathrooms that force you to pee in the streets, and more. Go through enough of this and you'll want to punch the next person who complains, "Is this another thing we're going to have to be 'pc' about?"

Working for the physical or ideological inclusion of as many lesbians as possible is coalition-building. This often means working with lesbians we can't stand, which is precisely why we often fragment into smaller and smaller circles that don't interact or communicate, but are collectively referred to as "the community." This is fine for a social life but not much good for developing ideas and actions that could change our world.

Actually, it's not even that great for a social life. Large-scale lesbian events like women's music festivals and conferences that have tried to encompass the diversity of lesbian existence have often been the sites of rage and alienation among participants who still feel excluded. The blowouts at the 1991 National Lesbian Conference in Atlanta about political correctness, exclusion, and lack of leadership were just a few of many well-publicized examples of lesbian dissension.

A fundamental issue is that lesbian events and "community" have been conceived of as "safe places," as homes. The primary problem in conceiving of the lesbian community as a singular monolithic haven was most eloquently put forth in Bernice Johnson Reagon's speech from the 1981 West Coast Women's Music Festival, "Coalition Politics," published in *Home Girls: A Black Feminist Anthology*, edited by Barbara Smith (Kitchen Table, 1984). Addressing the notion of a singular women's community, Reagon notes that we confuse "home" and "coalition." Home is where you want to feel safe with others like you; coalition is a deeply painful and difficult process during which you come to terms with others who are different in the pursuit of a finite common goal. We cannot have it both ways—either "the lesbian community" is a home that is only for "real lesbians," as defined by a particular ideology ("woman-identified," "feminist," "Queer National," or "real, not political") or by particular sexual practices (never with men, no penetration, no roles, only the right roles), or it's a coalition of women whose only assured commonality is a sexual love for women. If you look for home in a coalition you will always get hurt. The search for home is accompanied by the long-running lesbian metaphor of family, whether it's the "family," the "brethren and sistren," of gay slang or the particular "sisterhood" of lesbian feminism. But as I hear the strains of the rap remix of the 1970s gay disco hit "We Are Family" in the bars today, I consider the reality of actual families. Family is where we learn the deepest, most painful lessons about love, power, and abuse; sisterhood is a complicated mixture of love, jealousy, and profound betrayal, and all of this is played out when we make political and social communities into family.

The desire for a home is the desire for comfort. That desire is personally essential because no form of lesbian identity, no matter how privileged, is easy or safe in this society. No one values our lives, our beauty and worth except other lesbians and a very few nonlesbian allies. In the straight world we're either invisible or made monstrous, and this is the context from which we turn to each other for recognition and validation. But there's not necessarily any "us" there, because we haven't done the work it would take to cross the divisions between us. Assuming that "unity" inherently exists is a setup for major explosions when all our repressed differences surface with a vengeance.

Because no one has been able to agree on a single definition of what constitutes a "lesbian," it shouldn't be any surprise that the struggle to define or create a lesbian community has been so deeply problematic and painful, yet also, for many, lifesaving. When we speak of the lesbian community, we're almost always thinking of a very particular subset (not always the same one) of all the women who sexually relate solely or primarily to women. The lesbian community usually referred to is that of the visible lesbians who are connected with lesbian institutions—bars, newspapers, bookstores, sports teams, twelve-step groups, political groups, or whatever. But even among these subsets, the notion of a singular, unified lesbian community is absurd. If every lesbian in the United States was white, middle-class, able-bodied, Christian-raised, and living in an urban environment, there would still be bar dykes, sports dykes, women who aren't into roles, radical politicos, butches, separatists, s/m leather girls, those who aren't lesbians but are just in love with "X," believers in the Lesbian Nation, femme tops, Young Republicans, assimilationists, and piercing queens. And that's just for starters. What would a Lesbian Nation that could encompass all that look like?

One of the results of the 1991 National Lesbian Conference was the recognition that we don't really have a visible national leadership. Our diversity, relative poverty, and lack of national institutions are some of the reasons for this, but another is the ancient lesbian sport of "trashing" in which anyone who takes a leadership role, tries to create anything, or becomes moderately well known is fair game for brutal personal criticisms about her life-style, motivations, and actions. This is a major abuse of the concept "the personal is political." In this polarized version of reality, taking any power or responsibility within the lesbian feminist community often means being seen as all-powerful. Conversely, powerlessness and victimization are equated with innocence, and this has ugly implications for communication and organizing. If the only possibilities are good/bad or all-powerful/powerless, everyone is frozen on one or the other side of the dichotomy. This is what leads people to brandish any badge of oppression they can claim, in order to trump themselves into a position of nonresponsibility for anything. Everyone becomes the done-unto, never the doer. It's dangerous to rely on an identity founded on being innocent because none of us is ever completely innocent. Sweet Honey in the Rock, an African-American feminist choral group, sings a song about the manufacturing journey of a polyester/cotton shirt through several countries and groups of exploited women workers before its arrival at J.C. Penney's to be sold to working-class women in the United States. The last line of the song asks, "Are my hands clean?" It's critical that we remember—our hands are not equally dirty, but neither are they clean.

One thing that prevents many lesbians from taking action is the equation of power itself, rather than the abuse of power, with evil. This explains the old joke, "Why can't lesbians do ballroom dancing? They're always trying to lead from the following position." Seeing purity as the necessary condition for action means that not a lot gets done. Asking the question "What good is it?" is generally more productive when "what good" means how useful in the situation, rather than how correct. Trying to be the most powerless/innocent is a morality play whose only use is for personal redemption. It prevents making connections with others, first because it involves having to hide the often messy facts of our lives, and second because it usually involves making others guilty. Seeing power as inherently bad means having to deny and thus waste the power we have access to. The motivation for the deliberate downward mobility of some middle- and upper-class lesbians is that access to money and resources is seen as inherently bad.

This paralysis also stems from the idea that class, racial,

and sexual identities are basic and unchangeable; you either know who and what you "really are" or you're trying to discover it. This idea is a very interesting paradox for lesbians and other gay people if one considers the coming-out story. The entree into gay community is the coming-out story, the revisionist history of our lives in which we recount all the events leading to the magic moment when—ah—it finally all made sense. Identity and interpretation come together in one compact tale. Some people resolve the tensions around gay identification by looking for signs from their heterosexually identified pasts that they were always "really" gay (maybe they had heterosexual false consciousness); some were always gay-identified; some decide that their sexual identities fundamentally shifted; and some are completely uninterested in the question. The nature of identity is a loaded question for those who deviate from the mythical norm because to see identity as anything but fixed and inherent means having to defend the value of particular choices.

This is the basis of arguments about whether gayness is genetic or somehow biologically based; it comes down to "we just can't help it; we have no choice." But if there's anything that entering a gay community makes clear, it's that there are all kinds of choices to be made, and what a long strange trip it's been. Becoming part of a queer context is very different from following heterosexual norms. In queer communities the taking apart of traditional ideas about normal sexual and gendered behavior creates mind-bending moments of displacement and gender-fuck. There's certainly no agreement within a loosely defined community of lesbians, gay men, transsexuals, and bisexuals who either associate with each other or are associated with each other by outsiders, but there are an awful lot of interesting struggles. "Masculinity," "femininity," and the need for a two-party gender system are all up for grabs when self-defined drag queens, leather dykes, daddy's boys, lesbian separatists, the girls (and boys) next door, and the transgendered come into contact.

My roommate, your basic femme top who is convinced on alternate days that she's butch, all evidence to the contrary, frequents Latino drag bars in San Francisco's Mission District. At an AIDS benefit one night in her fishnets and miniskirt, she was approached by a somewhat inebriated male patron in eyeliner and tasteful foundation and asked to dance. The English translation of their interaction is as follows:

He: "What's your name?" She: "Lexi." He (knowing grin): "I'm Ana." She: "I'd be happy to dance with you but I hope you know I'm a woman. I'm a lesbian." He (much shock and mortification at his mistake): "Why are you a lesbian? You're pretty. Lesbians are ugly." More abuse, followed by his telling her the bar was for men only, while other male patrons dragged them apart and comforted her with, "Don't pay any attention to him; he's just a drunk asshole."

Many interesting questions are embedded in this story, and they all revolve around identity. Was the incident about straightforward misogyny? Did the man just hate women? Could it have been about his perceiving her as a slumming white girl in the Latino bar as opposed to a white boy with a sexual investment? Externalized homophobia? Jealousy at her being a better woman than he? Embarrassment at being unable to make an accurate assessment of sexual/gender identity in a social context in which it's fundamentally important? These are questions that don't make any sense outside the context of queer identity. They're unaskable of the majority of the straight world unfamiliar with a basic context of gayness. Unacculturated straight people are usually too caught up in the shock of relatively simple homosexuality itself—the fact of girls with girls and boys with boys —to be able to deal with the layers of complexity within a gay context.

Doris Fish, the late lamented drag impresario of the Castro, once said, "I don't dress like this to look like a woman. I dress like this to look like a drag queen." I've caught myself waving my hands like a drag queen and stopped dead on the street, struck by the multiple layers of irony involved in my making the gestures of a man making the gestures of a woman that no "real" woman would naturally make. As lesbians, we've often been told we're not "real women," but the truth is that we expose the fact that there's no such natural thing. "Real woman" is just another construct, another role. That's the subversive idea that connects us to drag; whatever other political critiques can be made of it, it dramatizes the constructed nature of traditional "femininity."

Gay men and lesbians are the people of drama. I have a theory that gay identity is really founded on storytelling and gossip, not sex, that in fact people often have sex so that they can talk about it. From the moment of that first entry into "the community" or "the life," we're embedded in a legendary network of gossip, tale-telling, and multiple interpretations of the same events. There are always layers upon layers and nothing should ever be taken for granted. Identity becomes an art form at times, a pastiche of meanings, affiliations, and self-parody that can be baroque.

The spiral of identity keeps coming around again. Former student, temporary professor, part-time organizer, and sometime diva, I'm sitting in an imaginary café with my friends—a faggot-identified dyke in her "I'm Not a Boy" T-shirt, a Radical Faerie friend in his camouflage khaki tutu, a Queer National in his "Dykes from Hell" shirt obtained from his sisters in LABIA, my queer yet heterosexual boys o'color auxiliary, my students who major in women's studies and go to sex clubs, where we try to avoid each other—and of course me in my newly acquired "It's *Mr.* Faggot to You" T-shirt. Artists, activists, academics, and the unaffiliated creating slices of community that have never existed before. I will always retain my fascination with "identity" and "community" because they're always in process and always provisional. Our identities never become final because new experiences continue to affect the way we see ourselves, and these new identifications in turn affect the kinds of experiences we can have and the kinds of communities we can create. Of course we're not completely free to be and do whatever we want, but the analogy I like best is gender theorist Judith Butler's improvisational theater: the set and props are in place but what happens after that is anyone's guess.

RUTH L. SCHWARTZ

NEW ALLIANCES, STRANGE BEDFELLOWS: LESBIANS, GAY MEN, AND AIDS

On opening night of the first Lesbian AIDS Caregivers conference, held in San Francisco in January 1989, Jackie Winnow—a lesbian involved in both AIDS and cancer work who was herself battling metastatic cancer—challenged her audience of nurses and doctors, social workers and educators:

> I'm in a roomful of lesbian AIDS caregivers, wondering why we're not also lesbian health caregivers. . . .
> In 1988, approximately forty thousand women are living with cancer in the San Francisco/Oakland area, at least four thousand of them lesbians. The forty thousand don't have the services that the one hundred women with AIDS have. . . . No one takes care of women or lesbians except women or lesbians, and we have a hard time taking care of ourselves, of finding ourselves worthy and important enough to pay atten-

tion to. . . . How is it that we are here today as lesbians
working on AIDS?

Winnow's talk left a palpable tension in the room. Some were
surprised and dismayed that conference organizers had chosen
a speaker who questioned as much as lauded us. Others were
simply uncomfortable because her questions were ones we had
often asked ourselves. What *had* led us, community-minded
lesbians, to such intimate involvement with an epidemic which
appeared to affect so few of our own?

Winnow attempted to answer her own question by citing
women's traditional role as healers: first as witches, later as
nurses—a role "subservient to doctors . . . subservient to men."
From nursing, women branched out into the fields of social
work, teaching, and counseling—all professions compatible
with an image of woman as nurturer. "As women," Winnow
reminded us, "we were raised to despise ourselves and belittle
our own needs, while holding those of men to be important."

Listening to her, I thought of my own journey to that conference room. In the early 1980s, my coming-out years, my life
focused on women's issues: I lived in an eleven-woman feminist
collective, worked on a women's newspaper, and majored in
—and later taught—women's studies. But since 1986, the year
I entered AIDS work, much of my time and energy had been
redirected toward an epidemic which, particularly on the West
Coast, overwhelmingly affected men.

I did not believe that my motivations and experiences, and
those of other lesbians doing AIDS work, could be reduced to
the simple habit of "taking care of men." Yet looking around
the room at the nearly two hundred lesbians gathered there, I
wondered: what *had* brought so many of us to work in this
epidemic? What had kept us there? How had we been changed
by our involvement with AIDS, individually and collectively—
and how, in turn, would our involvement change our community?

———

From the beginning, the early 1980s, lesbians were prominent in the community-based organizations that mobilized to respond to the "gay" epidemic. The forms our involvement with AIDS took—volunteering, activism, or paid service—were determined by our individual histories, skills, and priorities. But for many of us, an initial, powerful motivating force was knowing someone—most often a gay man or men—who had tested positive, gotten sick, or died. Gay activism in the late 1970s, particularly in San Francisco, had forged alliances between some gay men and lesbians, setting the stage for cooperation in this new crisis. Lesbians in their twenties and early thirties living in San Francisco in the mid-1980s were more likely to know a gay man with HIV than a lesbian with cancer (although this was less the case for many older women). Many of us were also spurred by a broader sense of concern for, and political identification with, the larger gay community.

While San Francisco's AIDS epidemic was picking up steam, I was in graduate school in Ann Arbor. I had already begun to move from identifying with a feminist community to considering myself part of a community which included gay men as well as lesbians, but I knew no one with AIDS. However, shortly after beginning work at the San Francisco AIDS Foundation, I learned that a male ex-lover had tested positive; within the year, one of my old college roommates received an AIDS diagnosis.

My master's degree was in creative writing, hardly a health-related subject, and I was first hired on at the AIDS Foundation as a clerical assistant. My first years at the foundation coincided with its period of most rapid growth; between 1986 and 1987, the organization nearly doubled in size. With expansion came opportunities; the epidemic was still young enough that there were no AIDS experts. Like many others without relevant degrees, or without degrees at all, I was quickly able to move into more challenging positions. By 1989 I was coordinating the AIDS Hotline, an information and referral line serving all of Northern California.

Like me, many lesbians who were working as paid staff in AIDS agencies found that we were offered a chance to do the kinds of service work women had long done—to use the skills many of us had honed working for women's causes while earning little or nothing—in a context which offered "goodies" on both sides of the fence. Thirty-two-year-old Veneita Porter went from volunteering in a Providence hospice to directing the state-wide Rhode Island AIDS Project in less than a year—and without any graduate degrees. "I'm on international and national advisory committees and boards," she says. "I know part of that is because I'm a woman of color. But it puts me in a powerful place that I would never, had it not been for this horrible fucking epidemic, have had a chance to be at."

Lesbians also flooded into positions as unpaid hotline operators, speakers' bureau members, and "buddies" to people with AIDS. There was tremendous camaraderie among volunteers, although some women were initially turned off by what they saw as a "gay boys' club" atmosphere. Those who stayed often had friends with AIDS in their personal lives as well—a motivator powerful enough to overcome the challenge of trying to enter what sometimes felt like an alien culture.

Ironically, there was even a measure of glamour in the work. When Rock Hudson was diagnosed in 1985, the straight world suddenly woke up to the disease—and panicked. At the San Francisco AIDS Hotline, calls from heterosexuals tripled, and HIV test sites were flooded. Heterosexual concern lent the epidemic a new prestige. For a brief time, TV crews came almost weekly to film the "gallant" hotline volunteers.

By 1987, the image of a fringe group working on a stigmatized disease was giving way to admiring media portrayals of heroes and heroines bravely battling on the front lines of an epidemic affecting "all of us." I noticed that I was beginning to get different reactions when I told straight people what I did for a living. Rather than an awkward silence followed, perhaps, by a timid, "Gee, that must be depressing," people now said things like, "Oh, how wonderful—what important work"—and then asked questions related to their own AIDS risk.

I, and other lesbians in AIDS work, watched our coworkers, our clients, and our volunteers receive positive test results. Begin to experience symptoms. Receive diagnoses. Lose their abilities—to work, to walk, sometimes to think. We saw people die. We witnessed, over and over, what can happen when people know they are close to death. And we saw people change their lives. Many who had been wealthy, complacent, and apolitical underwent changes in spirit as marked as the changes in their bodies. We witnessed, and became intimately involved with, a human drama of immense proportion.

I began to feel distant from many of my friends. The endless political debates which preoccupied many lesbian communities—the acceptability of sadomasochistic sex, whether or not to allow boy children at all-women events—began to seem rather petty. At times, it seemed as though I spent every day in a war zone which had forcibly reordered my priorities, yet so many other lesbians didn't even seem to know the battle was on. One night, in a women's café, I listened to a singer joke repeatedly about the diarrhea she had gotten at the Michigan Womyn's Music Festival. As the rest of the audience laughed, I sat silently, thinking about how, in the world which I now inhabited, diarrhea was nothing to joke about—and yet nobody in the room appeared to have any idea of that other world.

Michelle Carstens, a hospice social worker in San Francisco, felt similarly isolated. "After work, I'd be sitting on the couch with my girlfriend," she recalls, "and suddenly these images of her as emaciated would flash into my mind. It took almost a year before I could tell anyone about it." And when thirty-five-year-old Lisa Heft, an AIDS hotline and speakers bureau volunteer, mused aloud about what she'd want for her memorial service, or whether her lover would hold her hand if she were in a coma, her lover was horrified—and accused her of being morbid. " 'Why do you think about death all the time?' she asked. She didn't understand that death had become such a daily part of my life."

There was a price for living with such intensity. I heard lesbian coworkers begin to question our own motivations, linking our work with an "attraction to crisis," with being adult children of alcoholics, with unhealthy patterns from our pasts.

Others reported that their relationships suffered, that they stopped having sex, or that they became unable to have relationships more than a few years long—since life itself had come to feel so temporary. I found myself wanting to tunnel more deeply into my personal life, pushing my lover into buying a house together, to feel a sense of calm, refuge, and control.

Some of what I and others were experiencing was "survivor guilt." Our gay male coworkers were coping with losing their closest friends, caring for their sick lovers, and watching their own health deteriorate, all at the same time—while, as Jackie Winnow had pointed out, AIDS rarely touched us, our lovers, or our lesbian friends. No matter how close we were to the wounded, we still had a feeling of distance, safety. We always knew that if the work became too much for us, we could choose to walk away—although for many years, few of us did.

Our contact with gay men also affected us in other ways. Like me, many other lesbians had entered AIDS work with some identification with the larger gay community, but with few close gay male friends, or much contact with men at all. Often, to our surprise, we found that those men had something we wanted for ourselves—a feeling of entitlement, the ability not to hesitate, not to wonder whether you could get what you wanted or whether you deserved it, but just to go for it, whatever it was. There was something in that arrogant energy—which made gay male sexual culture so different from our own—that we craved.

I came to admire the way gay men talked about—and lived—their sexuality. Even as they battled a deadly sexually transmitted virus, many gay men remained unabashedly erotic. Although my objects of desire were different from those of my male coworkers, their enthusiastic embrace of the sexual made me experience my own gayness as a proud, *lustful* identity. I was fascinated when some late-night hotline shifts turned into sessions on women's sexuality for gay men. Many male volunteers were astonishingly ignorant about female anatomy (one volunteer asked me if stuff spurted out of women's breasts when we came). Yet they were open and curious as well. As I answered questions about clitorises and g-spots, vaginal lubrication, and why some lesbians liked dildos, I marveled at my audience's complete ease—in marked contrast to the way many lesbians seemed to talk about sex.

The epidemic which would dramatically restrict gay men's sexual lives had begun at exactly the same historical moment, 1981–82, when large groups of lesbians were beginning to chafe at the restrictive boundaries of "feminist" sexuality. Lesbian conferences and heated community debates about the "politics of desire" gave way, among some lesbians, to an attraction to gay male sexual directness. I knew I was not the only lesbian AIDS worker who felt secretly turned on by all the images of hard cocks which surrounded us. Yet in the midst of a lesbian community preoccupied with the threat of "lesbians who sleep with men," it was difficult to discuss my complex reactions to gay male sexuality.

Of course, while some of us were drawn to gay male sexuality, others remained ambivalent or critical. Christine Young, a thirty-one-year-old Bostonian who volunteered on the AIDS Hotline out of political identification with her "gay brothers," laughed at coworker Walt's tales of his weekly exploits, but noted, "It certainly didn't make me want to give blow jobs on the train!" San Francisco social worker Amanda Newstetter recalls her mixed emotions upon visiting one of her first clients in his apartment in the gay leather district. "There were penises everywhere—statues, posters, cards, ornaments. And here was this emaciated man, close to death. There was something grotesque about it, shocking." Another longtime social worker once confided to me, "Sometimes I wonder whether they *did* do something to deserve this. After all, it was their male sexuality which put them at risk for this disease."

THE AIDS INDUSTRY

To those of us who had worked in women's collectives, AIDS organizations seemed like a whole new world. Everything seemed to get done so much more quickly; we didn't have to worry so much about hurting the feelings of gay men, or making sure they had a chance to speak; they vigorously pursued their own agendas, leaving us free to pursue ours. Yet it was truly "every man for himself" in this organizational culture; we sometimes found our male coworkers interrupting us, and even making sexist or condescending comments after we spoke.

I had entered AIDS work with a bargain basement mentality. Having worked at a women's newspaper and a women's crisis center, I was used to thrift-store furniture and mimeographed flyers. Gay men brought with them greater access to money and other resources from the start. In the "AIDS industry," I encountered a professionalism which was both exciting and alienating.

It was great to be able to order all the supplies we needed, to feel a sense of relative plenty. Yet when we had professional focus groups evaluate our educational brochures, I was painfully aware that the money we spent on each focus group could have paid a month's salary for a street outreach worker.

I also found that some of my most basic assumptions about the world, understandings I shared with other feminist lesbians about the role of class, race, and gender in people's lives, were brand-new and highly disputed concepts for many gay men. The AIDS Foundation scheduled what was to have been a series of antiracism workshops for staff; during the first of the workshops, some white gay men were so offended by the suggestion that any of their actions could be racist that the remainder of the sessions were canceled.

In the spring of 1987, at the National Lesbian/Gay Health Conference held at a swanky hotel outside Los Angeles, many lesbians voiced our discomfort with the white, upwardly mobile, increasingly professionalized AIDS-work "culture." Many of us were infuriated when a plenary session on "lessons AIDS service providers can learn from the women's health movement" drew only a handful of male attendees. We asked ourselves and each other some hard questions. Once we were "world-renowned AIDS experts," were we still gay community activists? And if AIDS was not a "gay disease," why were the gay white men in charge of most AIDS organizations so loath to build coalitions with groups based in the communities of women and people of color?

For lesbians of color, who were relatively scarce in "mainstream" AIDS organizations and who tended to be ghettoized in organizations based in communities of color, these contradictions were glaring. Veneita Porter describes her sense of divided loyalties. "I got shit from the black and people of color community ('What are you doing around all these white men?'). I got shit from women ('What are you doing talking about sex with men?'), and I got shit from other men ('We don't need lesbians or women doing this work')." Before AIDS, Porter says she had watched people die from "drug abuse, from stupidity, from bad health care because they were poor." For lesbians of color, perhaps even more than for white lesbians, the issues raised by AIDS were familiar ones.

But even between white, middle-class gay men and lesbians, there were often stark differences in perspective. Amanda Newstetter recalls receiving phone calls from desperate-sounding clients and feeling "my heart go out to them." But on home visits, finding that these same clients "lived in these incredible castles with views and sunken bathtubs," she found herself struggling with anger, envy, and a sense of contradiction. "These men think AIDS is all there is," she thought. "Now that these white men are getting sick and having bad health care and having to deal with being ostracized—now they know how lesbians feel, or people of color, or women who have tried to get decent health care. . . . I felt like saying, hey, wait a minute here, this is not so new. You are not the only ones who are suffering."

While most new AIDS cases diagnosed in San Francisco through the 1980s continued to be among gay men, the situation in New York was markedly different. By 1988, more than half of New York City's people with AIDS were heterosexual men and women, mostly IV drug users or their partners. Gerry Pearlberg, who coordinated an AIDS project in New York in the late 1980s, experienced AIDS much more as a poor people's than a gay men's epidemic. "For me, the lessons were less about gay men's sexuality, and more about what poverty is really like," she recalls. Yet the "organizational culture" of the largest AIDS organizations throughout the country remained overwhelmingly male, white, and gay—and monied.

Late in 1987, amid growing political chasms between the gay men and lesbians involved in AIDS service work, a new breed of radicals—gay men, many of them HIV-infected and disillusioned with the AIDS bureaucracy, and a small but vocal minority of lesbians—appeared on the scene. ACT UP (AIDS Coalition to Unleash Power) shared the AIDS industry's white, male, middle-class bias but had none of its stodginess. It was loud, proud, outrageous, defiant. It made headlines; it made enemies; it got things done. And it attracted a new group of lesbians who had not previously been involved with AIDS, but were drawn to the vitality of the politic.

Fifty-year-old Maxine Wolfe, a longtime lesbian activist in the ranks of ACT UP New York, explains that she came to that organization because of "the inability of lesbians to organize around or even figure out what their issues were," and because of the "dead end of the identity-based politics of the early 1980s." ACT UP, she recalls, was composed of people organizing "not from some abstract concept but to save their lives and the lives of people they cared about. And, they were prosex at a time when sex was being connected to death." She stayed in ACT UP because it was a place where she could be "a lesbian, a woman, and an activist." For Wolfe and other women, ACT UP provided the chance to be daring, outrageous—and effective. It melded lesbians' skills in group process and community organizing with gay men's access to big bucks and media visibility—and held out the promise of political alliance between gay men and lesbians.

Many ACT UP women represented a new dyke generation, more queer than feminist. Next to their early-twenties bravado, punk haircuts, and sticker-plastered leather jackets, lesbian AIDS service providers often looked like the establishment. Yet despite the outward differences in style, lesbians found themselves in similar positions in both types of groups. Just as lesbian service providers had experienced financial culture shock in AIDS service organizations, many lesbian activists found themselves confronted by the new accessibility of a vast array of resources. In 1988, its first year of existence, ACT UP New York raised a quarter of a million dollars, $80,000 of it by marketing the group's T-shirts and posters: clearly, this was a new kind of "grass roots."

And, as in service organizations, tensions grew between proponents of different perspectives. The sides rarely divided strictly along lines of gender. Instead, in both service organizations and activist groups, an alliance of women (both lesbian and straight) and people of color often faced off against an "old guard" of white gay men. In service organizations, the conflict surfaced in a manner more in keeping with the organizational culture of gentility; meetings grew longer and more tense, and political differences were masked by seemingly benign questions of strategy (for example, should we do educational campaigns only in English, or in other languages as well?). Conflicts in ACT UP emerged more explosively. Thirty-two-year-old architect Randi Gerson, of ACT UP San Francisco, recalls, "Some gay men didn't understand what we [lesbians] were doing there." One man yelled at her, "You're not going to get [AIDS], I don't have to listen to you." As an individual, she felt respected and admired, but as a woman she remained suspect.

Meanwhile, within the larger lesbian community, most women seemed to maintain an ambivalent distance from AIDS. I saw articles and letters in community newspapers complimenting lesbian AIDS workers' dedication and in the same breath complaining that too many women chose AIDS work over more "authentically lesbian" issues. Lesbians not involved with AIDS often asked us: If the AIDS epidemic had primarily affected women, would gay men have mobilized in the same numbers to help us? We had often asked the same question of ourselves; always, the answer was a resounding no. Not one of us believed our efforts would have been reciprocated, yet this in itself was not a reason to withdraw. It was, after all, difficult to name a more "authentically" lesbian issue. The standard feminist causes—reproductive rights, domestic violence, women's health—all affected straight women far more than lesbians. I joked that the only *exclusively* lesbian issue I could think of was "Lesbian Bed Death."

The community also seemed confused about how to respond to the question of lesbian AIDS risk, and a scarcity of research kept actual information unavailable. Some women went overboard in their (at least rhetorical) commitment to safe sex. One of my housemates gave out dental dam party favors on her birthday, but I didn't know anyone who actually used them for sex. Other women shrilly proclaimed that any lesbian who had "too many" sex partners was a "danger to the community," and intolerance of bisexual women, on the grounds of AIDS risk, increased. There was also a brief flurry of fear about the risk of artificial insemination, since many lesbians in the early eighties had inseminated with the semen of gay men. However, once a lesbian-run research project failed to turn up any instances of infection via insemination, the issue died down.

On the other side, a different camp of women (including many lesbian AIDS workers) declared that lesbian sex *was* safe sex, that, in fact, any call for community discussion of safe sex arose from lesbians' "sex-negativity." New York novelist and AIDS activist Sarah Schulman, interviewed in *Gay Community News* in 1989, declared that she didn't see lesbian HIV transmission as an issue; after all, she hadn't met women sexually infected by other women on her cross-country book tours. Others argued that even if lesbian safe sex were an issue, the focus on dental dams was misplaced. Dams gave us a latex gadget, just like the boys had; but all evidence indicated that oral sex was extremely low-risk behavior. What *did* lesbians really do that might share body fluids, anyway? How many of us actually shared dildos, or had sex during our periods? Information about our own sexual practices was scarce.

An often-heard joke went, "If AIDS is God's revenge, then lesbians must be the chosen people." Among AIDS workers, this attitude was easy to understand. After all, we saw people with AIDS every day, and most of them looked nothing like us. The few lesbians we knew with AIDS had all used IV drugs, and many of us remained comfortably or willfully naive about the extent of drug use in our community. There was some realism in our scoffing, and also a measure of denial.

Yet as the epidemic neared its tenth year, increasing numbers of lesbians began to feel the effects of AIDS more directly, as brothers, friends, fathers, cousins, coworkers, and college roommates were diagnosed. My personal phone calls began to sound more and more like my professional calls. The epidemic was coming home.

In March 1991, just over two years after the first Lesbian AIDS Caregivers conference, remnants of the same group gather for a retreat at a hot springs resort seventy-five miles north of San Francisco. One AIDS social worker passes around pictures of her newborn and pumps her breasts between meals; other women discuss the fine points of artificial insemination. This time, in place of a controversial keynote speech, a photocopied article is distributed describing the dangers of "cross-transference in trauma work"—experiencing our clients' tragedies as our own. More and more of us are working with HIV-positive women, including lesbians.

Yet ironically, just as the line between AIDS and women's issues seems finally to be blurring, many longtime lesbian AIDS workers are leaving the field. For most of us, it's simply that, having been involved since the early or mid-1980s, we're burnt out, ready to move on to other things. New staff hired to replace us are much less likely to be lesbians. The grass-roots AIDS organizations are now professionalized; they are much less appealing to those with an activist bent; and those who do apply for jobs in the field often find themselves pushed out by applicants with a longer string of graduate degrees.

In the area of volunteer activism, too, things have changed. In San Francisco and on the East Coast, WHAM (Women's Health Action Mobilization), a grass-roots group with a broad health focus, counts many former AIDS activists among its members.

The San Francisco AIDS Hotline training attracts fewer lesbians and more straight men—another sign of the "mainstreaming" of the epidemic. Other lesbians have gone on to continue the work of Jackie Winnow (who died in 1991), providing emotional and practical support for women with cancer.

Those lesbians who leave AIDS work find themselves returning to a lesbian community whose landscape has been irrevocably changed. At least three local agencies are now offering services specifically for lesbians with HIV. At the same time, a new lesbian sex club is flourishing, testifying to the fact that, despite the AIDS epidemic, lesbian sexual possibilities have expanded. (Safe sex is the club's official rule, confusion about what that is notwithstanding.)

For those lesbians still in AIDS work, particularly those not on the West Coast, the changing demographics of the disease have transformed the experience of working to fight the epidemic. Thirty-year-old Sondra Johnson, a caseworker for the Chicago AIDS Project, is the only gay staffer in that organization. Most of her clients are heterosexual people of color, and the association of AIDS and homosexuality means that she frequently confronts homophobia on the job. "I find myself having to tell clients to stop using the word 'faggot.' " At the same time, Sondra says, she feels affirmed when she watches African-American families opening their hearts to their gay sons, brothers, and fathers with HIV.

Late in 1991, basketball star Magic Johnson's announcement of his HIV infection sparked a new wave of heterosexual concern. As in 1985, when news of Rock Hudson's AIDS diagnosis became public, the media again made AIDS its focus, at least briefly, and calls to AIDS hotlines throughout the country more than quadrupled. Although Magic's case appeared to be one of heterosexual transmission, his announcement also placed a brighter spotlight on gays with AIDS, particularly African-Americans.

In a sense, AIDS is now both more and less of a lesbian issue. Lesbians with HIV are far more visible in the community, and with their presence, discussions of lesbian safe sex, though still inconclusive, continue to resurface. But although some lesbians remain involved in all facets of the epidemic, the historical factors which brought so many of us to it seem to have receded. Now that AIDS is no longer a fringe political issue, our participation seems less crucial.

Our experiences in the field taught us—as individuals, and as a community—things we needed to learn: about coalition-building, about sexuality, disease, and mortality, and about accessing resources. These lessons helped Karen Thompson in her landmark court battle to gain custody over her ailing partner Sharon Kowalski, and they are helping the Women's Cancer Resource Center expand its services to an increasing number of women in need. With lesbians' propensity for being on the "front lines," we will take them with us to whatever new battles we find. The walking away is only partial. We don't leave behind our friends—neither those who are still alive, nor those who have died. We leave changed.

MARIA MAGGENTI

WANDERING
THROUGH
HERLAND

I

1990. THE HEADLINE OF THE *NEWSWEEK* MAGAZINE ARTICLE reads "The Future of Gay America" and the picture shows two white men holding hands. I scramble madly through the glossy pages to find the paragraphs that mention lesbians. Oh gee, there we are! In a sidebar—white, "married" lesbian couples with children in Columbus, Ohio, mumbling something about their semicloseted existence and their conventionally constructed relationships. The world *Newsweek* notices is not the world of *On Our Backs*, Pat Califia, girl bars, and out and proud dykes with long, complicated, and varied histories. The magazine trumpets "The Future of Gay America," but once again, we are somehow shadowy, unknowable, invisible, unthinkable. There is one quote from a young woman who says she represents that growing element of the lesbian community who wear makeup and feminine clothes and call themselves "lipstick lesbians or girlie girls." I think this is a crass distillation of the struggles that go on in our communities about who we are as lesbians. It's not so simple as who wears lipstick to be beautiful and who doesn't. I think *Newsweek* has missed the boat on lesbians, and then I wonder, well, what boat should it have been on, anyway?

II

A moment in the 1980s. As the 1980s begin to congeal and create a zeitgeist of cavalier conspicuous consumption on the surface and rumbling distress and despair underneath, it becomes more and more difficult to imagine a Lesbian Nation. The possibilities seem to have been reduced to 1980s polarities—extreme marginalization as an anachronistic up-yours to the white male power structure; or a sheepish but almost relieved dash for normality and assimilation through material and professional success, the consolidation of lesbian identity through monogamous coupling, joint property as an expression of mutual purpose in the world, and, increasingly in the latter half of the decade, a burgeoning movement toward lesbian parenting.

The Lesbian Nation can thus be pictured as a politically nonthreatening monogamous female couple, with a child, a dog, a house, and a Honda, or as an anachronistic Wanderground of wimmin all readying themselves for the Amazonian apocalypse. But though it seems that way on the surface, in fact it is far more creative and undefinable. Raw, contradictory energies and identities consume the lesbians I meet in New York at the exact halfway mark of the 1980s. From girl bars and "glamour dykes" to the still present politically correct lesbian behavior police, it seems all of us are going through changes, throwing off the legacies of the 1970s to discover things about ourselves that are far more ambiguous, frightening, and perhaps even unnameable than all our feminist theory and lesbian porn put together. Can this increasing individuality actually be called liberation, or is it simply the banal distillation of 1980s conformity? Does this supposed blossoming dissension among lesbians bode well for our future, auguring a new way for us to see ourselves and each other, or does this shifting pattern of relations and representation simply reflect an anxious and shrinking middle class, a disintegration of easily identifiable political goals, and a comfortable (again, almost relieved) return to individual comfort over group advancement? Or is it true that radicalism spreads its roots during periods of intense political repression?

III

1985. I do know that things are different now. Different than they were when I first kissed another woman's lips and whispered the word "lesbian" to myself. But it's like water or mercury; I can't catch it in my hands. I try to come up with things "lesbian" and I feel as though I am in the back of a cab staring out the window: the driver is going really fast down East River Drive at dusk and I know I am looking at Manhattan but all I get are the shapes, some colors; people are speaking in different languages. This is my home but I can't tell where my house is.

I am in a difficult place as a lesbian AIDS activist—almost as though I am standing on an island and other lesbians are standing on islands too and there are our brothers, gee, guess what, they are standing together on the mainland. I have one arm extended to ward off gay male sexism and another arm extended to keep away lesbian parochialism, the kind that says, "Be this way, womon, or else." The men are friendly and seem to take me for who I am; the women are suspicious, demanding, judgmental, critical. But the men don't seem to understand what I'm talking about half the time. *What do you think I am, anyway, some straight-girl fag hag?* And the women understand what I'm talking about but hate my ego, my clothes, my swaying butt when I walk. This island, where I often stand by myself, is a sometimes lonely and surreal place to be.

IV

1987. I chide men in ACT UP over and over when they say gay this or gay that and women have to interject, "Do you mean gay and lesbian or gay men?" and there is a moment of collective mental shuffling as though the axis of the earth had just been tilted to an extreme angle. Sheepishly the men reorganize the sentence and make an attempt at clarity and the men with seniority never make that faux pas again. In that hothouse called AIDS activism, where I spend two and a half steamy years screaming, getting my butt kicked, and loving gay men for the first time, I experience things that lesbian feminism has not prepared me for and I discover that without that feminism I never could have lasted so long in a community made up of so many men. Feminism has not taught me about that delicious outrageous queer decadence indulged in by gay men as a survival strategy. So I dance about in my leather jacket and help gay-boy friends zip up the back of their goofy dresses as we march off to close down the stock exchange. But feminism has given me a political discipline that is sometimes more useful than drag. Feminism keeps me from thinking that Robert's Rules of Order are a true form of human communication and that white racism can be eliminated by saying "people of color." Feminism, and lesbian feminism in particular, creates a world where only a desert existed before, and though I have long since given up romanticizing "the life," I feel proud of it anyway.

V

1990. When I am invited to the first meeting of a new group devoted to gay and lesbian activism I am so excited I can hardly stand it. Yippee! A new group, lots of old AIDS activist pals, and only gay and lesbian issues on the agenda. I sit in a circle with sixty other curious people, most of them men I already know with a handful of women I also already know. This may be it, I think when I sit down, this may be the birth of the Queer Nation.

I come to that meeting as a lesbian AIDS activist with a political education developed in the academy, refined through theory, and hashed out dramatically in the usually hushed hallways of a women's Ivy League college. Those politics have been refashioned, abandoned, polished, and reclaimed in the sweaty rough-and-tumble of the emerging AIDS activist movement of the late 1980s. Perhaps it is simply my decreasing level of energy and tolerance for the gritty work of direct action—the many arguments to refine a simple idea, the desperate attempts to apportion tasks equally, the delicate diplomacy required with more inexperienced or ignorant members of the group—but I come to believe that what I sensed on some visceral level during that first meeting was instead a kind of lesbian existential dread. That, in fact, the map of the new Queer Nation will have a male face and that my face and those of other women will simply be background. We will be the demographic cosmetics, as it were, posed in colorful formation like a Benetton advertisement to assuage and complement the deeply imbedded prejudices of so many urgent and angry young men.

I believe, like many women before me, that with hard work, enthusiasm, knowledge, and skill, not to mention the sheer force of personality, I will somehow be exempted from my status as girl, outsider, woman, bitch, cunt, other. I nurse this fantasy of my integral place in the burgeoning Queer Nation as a way to forestall my own consciousness that, in fact, it is nearly impossible to cross the million-year-old canyons that make men men and women women. I avoid my own late-night questions about what it means to be a lesbian in a gay male universe and prefer to believe in the united colors of the Queer Nation. But the fact that I cannot seem to remember when the meetings are or whom to call to find out reveals my increasing ambivalence. Soon it becomes apparent that I cannot join, I cannot participate, I cannot sit again in a room filled mostly with men and stand up confidently to argue for or against a specific proposal. Shameful as it feels to admit it, it is as though my heart has folded over, the way it does at the end of a relationship, and I wish only to retreat from the front lines. How convenient that at this same time I begin an affair with a woman whose participation in the political scene is relatively limited. She has been flexing her social and emotional muscles at the lesbian bars while I am at committee meetings until 2 A.M., arguing sentence by sentence for the right text for a fact sheet due at the printer the next morning. I envy her apparent freedom, for to me, she seems to be searching for the Queer Nation in the more knowable universe of dykes. I have been attempting to swim upstream in a river of gay men.

VI

1988. So feminism is dead, or it has changed, or it is still meaningful to some of us but its political currency in the world is weak, its radical heart excised, its plodding middle-class moderation now an acceptable way of life. Feminism has been absorbed by the same generation that so proudly claims to reject it, and instead of women's liberation I hear, "Long live the Queer Nation!" Then there are these "girl bars" with big-breasted women wearing strap-on dildos bending over so I can see their crotches as they dance to mean, loud music. Standing next to me are two women in a couple; they are wearing button-down shirts and "silence = death" buttons on their knapsacks. They share an apartment in Brooklyn's Park Slope, own a cat, they've been in couples counseling and try not to let people smoke in the house. One of them grins at me as the go-go girl does a slow grind down on her knees, teasing her nipples with her rose-red fingernails, sticking her round ass in the air. "Well, this sure is a long way from women's reading groups, isn't it?" she laughs. I imagine that she and I have the same books on our bookshelves, the ones that have a printing of 1,500 but somehow it seems everyone you know has read them. Then I am reminded of a former lesbian roommate, a few years younger than I, whose response to things feminist elicited a kind of glazed-over incomprehension. Boys, girls, girls, boys, her quizzical face said, as long as we're all queer and proud what's the big deal? But we need to be for us, I would say in my head, women as women, lesbians as lesbians, no one else cares about us except us. How can we be proud if we can't even see each other half the time? The boys are always in the foreground—oh, there we are, I spy a couple of dykes in the scenery over that guy's shoulder.

VII

1987. I read things about lesbians and by lesbians in a vain attempt to know something about us. I cruise women on the street and wear a pink triangle on my coat lapel when I ride the subway. No one ever seems to return my meaningful stares except gay men, who smile broadly, and straight male perverts, who interrupt my line of vision. I snort out loud about reproductive rights, dismissing any discussion that doesn't include lesbian sexual freedom, and fight with dykes who say that AIDS isn't "our" issue. If it says "women" I am skeptical—do they mean lesbians *too* or do they mean lesbians *only*? And why do we still say "women" when we mean "lesbians"? The new code is "girls." When I see the word "girls" it usually means "lesbians." I laugh about the screaming fights I would have with male strangers who called me a girl when I was twenty years old. Now I give them the finger, smile, and say, "Lezzie, you asshole."

VIII

1990. When I do attend Queer Nation meetings I experience one simple joy—that when you enter the room you don't need to ask, "Is she or isn't she?" the way a lesbian has to do in ACT UP. Few well-meaning straight women end up in lesbian and gay groups, so one is spared the alternately heartbreaking or irksome experience of trying to get together with a straight girl. I want to be able to look fiercely into another woman's eyes when the agenda gets boring or distract myself with sexual possibilities when arguments erupt about political strategy. I want to fall in love with the same fire I felt when screaming, "No justice, no peace," while getting arrested for civil disobedience. As with theater and other creative projects with lots of people involved, there is an erotic component to activism—it is all-encompassing, insular, hot, and demanding, creating a climate of supreme sexual and emotional intensity. Here you all are united against a common enemy, having to rely on each other in a way that ordinary circumstances rarely demand. Night after night you are locked in a common struggle to pull down the walls of oppression and soon the universe looks Manichaean, creating just the right energies for intense communion with strangers. This is what I read about in *Sisterhood Is Powerful* and the *SCUM Manifesto*, this heat, this anger, these fierce attachments. I could live in a Puccini opera.

Yet in Queer Nation I notice a number of lesbian couples. They sit next to each other, their knees lightly touching, their faces alert with the promise of liberation. They don't seem interested in waging an all-out revolution, just a little something to make it easier to get through the day. In other words, no one seems interested in rewriting *every rule* about what it means to be lesbians in a sexist, racist, homophobic culture. In other words, revolutions are better when they don't change domestic habits too much. In other words, coupling means taming. At least that's how it seems to me. I am strangely uncomfortable.

It is suggested that we all go to a straight bar and show that we're dykes and fags—you know, wear T-shirts or buy drinks for strangers of the same sex or make out on the dance floor, kinda take over the joint. I cross one leg over the other impatiently. Standing around as a bunch of open queers in a straight bar, wearing our dyke and fag finest, does not seem the most direct path to salvation. Then I feel the slow burn of self-righteousness peeling from my skin—maybe this is the way, or one way, that lesbians feel they are doing something on their own behalf. I talk to some of the women I see in Queer Nation. I want to know where they have been all this time, why this and why now? I am greeted nervously—"It's here, we're queer, and it's exciting," giggles one woman. It seems some women have been building their lives in Brooklyn, Manhattan, and the Bronx, they have just been waiting for the opportunity to get out and about, out of the house. Others are hot off their gender studies theses and are ready to put theory into praxis. Some have drifted in from ACT UP or have come because of the press they read about this new and different group. Some just happened to walk in from another meeting elsewhere in the cavernous gay and lesbian community center. I am astonished that I have never seen many of these women before. I leave the meeting feeling confounded and distant. It is as though everyone in the room is united in the effort to move somewhere but no one seems to know the destination.

IX

1988. A bunch of us, faggots and dykes, men and women, boys and girls, sisters and brothers (the language changes faster than our tongues untied can handle), are hanging out at my house drinking Rolling Rock and telling stories. Somehow my girlfriend and I begin laughing hysterically about the covers of lesbian novels from Naiad Press. How ugly and unappealing they are to a potential buyer, God, where is the art direction, how does the writer feel about those graphics, jeez! When one of the men joins in, we turn and say, "Listen, we can laugh at ourselves but you can't." My male friend has that look that I have seen on gay men's faces before—a kind of fearful, shameful, and indignant look that says, "Hey, I'm a sister too!" It's like this: I can say whatever I want about my mother but you can't, get it? It's like this: we bust our asses learning all about you and your lives, what you read, how you talk, who's who in the gay male universe, how you can fuck safely man-to-man, get it? What do you really know about us? What kind of effort have you made? In my head, I hear the usual rant: man-hater, separatist. We part easily, as true friends do when there is a disagreement, and later that week he calls to ask to borrow some of my books. Boys will be boys will be . . .

X

1991. Newsweek didn't miss the boat, it missed a whole flotilla. There we are paddling along, a whole million billion of us: lesbians, dykes, lezzies, bulldaggers, girlie girls, woman-identified women. So, everyone has different daytime drag and nighttime costumes, accents vary according to the region or the moment, lines are drawn and then redrawn, it still seems as though everyone you know has slept with everyone else you know and then it's as if there is simply not another dyke in the world like you and community is a big sham and sisterhood is dead and then some dyke miracle happens, right there out of the blue.

My body remembers what my mind forgets—all those soft lips, those rough fingers and swaying hips, a tongue on my thigh and easily holding hands in places where no one expects to see two lesbians being lovers. I think about how I want to be as out at Lincoln Center as I am at a dyke bar. I remember being called a classist, imperialistic, bourgeois pig when I mentioned my love of opera to a woman in a women's studies class. Now I am simply called an Opera Queen. I try to put words to those exquisite throbbing moments of women dancing close to me at Carmelita's on a Friday night. A broad-backed woman with rippling muscles raises her arms and the hair in her armpits is glistening with sweat. Her eyes are closed, she is feeling it, she almost looks like a boy with that strong chin and short shiny hair, but those hips, those legs. She is exquisitely beautiful. Maybe I have had too many beers or it is that girl's hands running up and down my ass pulling me toward her and pushing me away, but at that moment I think being a lesbian is the most glorious thing in the world. I forget about *Newsweek*, graduate school, sexist gay men and sexist straight men, the dumb world outside our existence, about how invisible we all are, about all the fights we have with each other about how we are and how we should be. I forget because there we all are moving swiftly forward. We all seem to be going in different directions. But no one paddles backward. Everything that rises, I say to myself, everything that rises, I sing to myself, everything that rises must converge.

EPILOGUE

1992. The girl with the rippling muscles became my lover and then my ex-lover and then my closest, most intimate friend. Queer Nation, ACT UP, and civil disobedience actions folded, one on top of the other, into deep memories as, one by one, many of us who had been there at the beginning found ourselves fanning out into other places where our queer selves could be seen and heard. I went to graduate school to learn to be a film director and let the straight women in my class argue with professors about the "male gaze" while I sat in the back of the room and wrote scenes where women took their clothes off and kissed passionately or female superheroes rescued whole towns from destruction. My lesbianism became louder, more distinct, strangely more glamorous in such a suburban rich-boy environment, and yet my films were taken as seriously as everyone else's. Girl bars are gone, and instead there are lesbian s/m nights where, the invitations say, "you may bring your favorite boys." Outing came and went, its arguments drifting into the air like a thin curl of smoke but its impact more lasting than anyone had imagined. The closet seems almost antique when I listen to women talking about themselves. Everyone I know wears Chanel lipstick and fantasizes about taking off in a car like *Thelma and Louise*, but instead of driving over a cliff at the end of the movie, we all want them to turn to each other, kiss like lovers, and be gorgeous outlaws forever. The lesbians I know and love seem to whisper less when in public, shout more when sitting around a table together, laugh better than we did when we first came out, struggle again and again over the same issues of race and class, move intrepidly sometimes alone and sometimes together, upstream into the rest of the decade, into the rest of the world. Everything that rises must converge.

ARLENE STEIN, "THE YEAR OF THE LUSTFUL LESBIAN"

1. JANICE IRVINE, *Disorders of Desire: Sex and Gender in Modern American Sexology* (Temple, 1990).

2. CINDY PATTON, "Brave New Lesbians," *Village Voice* (July 2, 1985).

3. JOAN NESTLE, "Butch-Fem Relationships: Sexual Courage in the 1950s," *Heresies* (1981).

4. SAMOIS, *Coming to Power: Writings and Graphics on Lesbian S/M* (Alyson, 1982).

VERA WHISMAN, "IDENTITY CRISES: WHO IS A LESBIAN, ANYWAY?"

1. YVONNE ZYLAN, "Letter to the Editor," *Out/Look*, no. 8 (Spring 1990) p. 4.

2. DEL MARTIN AND PHYLLIS LYON, *Lesbian/Woman* (Bantam, 1972) p. 66.

3. RADICALESBIANS, "The Woman-Identified Woman," in Karla Jay and Alan Young, eds., *Out of the Closets: Voices of Gay Liberation* (Douglas Links, 1970) p. 172.

4. ADRIENNE RICH, "Compulsory Heterosexuality and Lesbian Existence," *SIGNS*, vol. 5, no. 4 (1980) p. 648.

5. CHERYL CLARKE, "Lesbianism: An Act of Resistance," in Cherríe Moraga and Gloria Anzaldúa, eds., *The Bridge Called My Back* (Kitchen Table, 1981) p. 128.

6. JACQUELYN ZITA, "Historical Amnesia and the Lesbian Continuum," *SIGNS*, vol. 7, no. 1 (1981) p. 173.

7. JOANNE LOULAN, quoted in Jorjet Harper, "Lesbians Who Sleep with Men," *Outweek* (February 11, 1990) p. 48.

8. JAN CLAUSEN, "My Interesting Condition," *Out/Look*, no. 7 (1990); responses by Robyn Sadowski in no. 8 (1990) p. 4; Lucia Conforti in no. 9 (1990) p. 7.

9. LILY BRAINDROP, quoted in *On Our Backs*, vol. 7, no. 1 (September–October 1990) p. 35.

10. INGRID NELSON, quoted in Steve Cossan, "Queen," *Out/Look*, no. 11 (1991) p. 20.

11. CHARLES FERNANDEZ, "Undocumented Aliens in the Queer Nation," *Out/Look*, no. 12 (1991) p. 21.

12. SUSIE BRIGHT, "Boss City," *On Our Backs*, vol. 2, no. 2 (Fall 1985) p. 6.

13. JACKIE GOLDSBY, "What It Means to Be Colored Me," *Out/Look*, no. 9 (Summer 1990) p. 15.

14. SHANE PHELAN, *Identity Politics* (Temple, 1989) p. 156.

15. ANN SNITOW, "A Gender Diary," in Marianne Hirsch and Evelyn Fox Keller, eds., *Conflicts in Feminism* (Routledge, 1990).

LIZ KOTZ, "ANYTHING BUT IDYLLIC: LESBIAN FILMMAKING IN THE 1980S AND 1990S"

1. For recent writing on lesbian media, see Teresa de Lauretis, *Technologies of Gender* (Indiana, 1987); Judith Mayne, *The Woman at the Keyhole* (Indiana, 1990); Martha Gever, "The

Names We Give Ourselves," in Russell Ferguson et al., eds., *Out There: Marginalization and Contemporary Cultures* (New Museum/MIT, 1990); and Bad Objects Choices, eds., *How Do I Look? Queer Film and Theory* (Bay Press, 1992).

2. JOHN D'EMILIO, "Capitalism and Gay Identity," in Ann Snitow et al., eds., *Powers of Desire* (Monthly Review Press, 1983) p. 111.

3. SCOTT MACDONALD, "Su Friedrich: Reappropriations," *Film Quarterly* (Winter 1987–88) pp. 41–42.

ARLENE STEIN, "ANDROGYNY GOES POP: BUT IS IT LESBIAN MUSIC?"

1. JON SAVAGE, "Tainted Love: The Influence of Male Homosexuality and Sexual Divergence on Pop Music and Culture Since the War," in Alan Tomlinson, ed., *Consumption, Identity, Style* (Routledge, 1990) pp. 153–71.

2. SIMON FRITH, *Music for Pleasure* (Routledge, 1988).

3. GINNY Z. BERSON, "Who Owes What to Whom? Building and Maintaining Lesbian Culture," in *Windy City Times* (June 22, 1989).

4. MARTHA GEVER, "The Names We Give Ourselves," in Russell Ferguson et al., eds., *Out There: Marginalization and Contemporary Cultures* (New Museum/MIT, 1990) pp. 191–202.

5. LAWRENCE GROSSBERG, "MTV: Swinging on the (Postmodern) Star," in Ian Angus and Sut Jhally, eds., *Cultural Politics in Contemporary America* (Routledge, 1989) pp. 254–68.

JACKIE GOLDSBY, "QUEEN FOR 307 DAYS: LOOKING B(L)ACK AT VANESSA WILLIAMS AND THE SEX WARS"

1. Bob Guccione, quoted in BARBARA EHRENREICH AND JANE O'REILLY, "Sexual Forboding," *The New Republic* (August 27, 1984) p. 11.

2. Vanessa Williams, quoted in *The New York Times* (July 24, 1984).

3. EHRENREICH AND O'REILLY, p. 12.

4. W. PLUMMER, "Haunted by Her Past," *People* (August 6, 1984).

5. Marks's exact words were as follows: "As a man, as a father, and as a grandfather, as a human being, I have never seen anything like these photographs. Ugh. I can't even show them to my wife." See ibid., p. 80.

6. "Vanessa's Story," ibid., p. 87.

7. "Ex-Miss America Endures Pain," *Jet* (August 6, 1984) pp. 60–62.

8. Erotica seems to me to be defined by a presumed rarity and ascribed aesthetic of scarcity and restraint. Pornography, by contrast, displays itself as common, abundant, and excessive. Erotica "testifies" and pornography "confesses."

9. Credit for this original insight is due to Ida B. Wells, who advanced this argument in her brilliant report, *Southern Horrors: Lynch Law in All Its Phases* (Arno, 1969 [1892]).

10. HARRIET JACOBS, *Incidents in the Life of a Slave Girl*, Jean Fagin Yellin, ed. (Harvard, 1987) p. 55.

11. For example, the television series "In Living Color" reinforces this assumption through the snapping predilections of the show's gay culture critics, Blaine and Antoine. Whether the men are on film or books, they invariably proclaim their lust for white men. They never ogle, for example, Denzel Washington or Wesley Snipes or Kid (of Kid 'n Play).

12. It stuns me that Madonna can brazenly assume, due to the marketability of her name, that the roles of Evita Perón and Frida Kahlo should be hers for the film option taking.

13. For a politically brave and theoretically rich discussion of this point, see Kobena Mercer's essay, "Skin Head Sex Thing: Racial Difference and the Homoerotic Imaginary," in *How Do I Look? Queer Film and Theory*, Bad Object Choices Staff, eds. (Bay Press, 1991).

14. I want to be clear here: I'm not proposing a "definitive" interpretation of the conditions affecting expressions of black sexuality, nor do I mean to be deterministic. To believe that slavery decided everything closes off the possibilities for—and the truth of—resistance and change. I'm sure that black men

and women had pleasurable encounters with each other beyond the master's desirous eye. Indeed, in my own unsystematic wanderings through academic scholarship and popular culture, I've been amazed at the abundance of joyfully bold depictions of black sexuality in literature, film, music, magazines, and newspapers. My point is that history matters insofar as it constitutes a profound, formative influence which produces the language we use to describe what happens to us, and certain words are given more credence than others.

KATH WESTON, "PARENTING IN THE AGE OF AIDS"

1. MARY CASAL, *The Stone Wall* (Arno, 1975).

2. JUDITH MODELL, "Last Chance Babies: Interpretations of Parenthood in an In Vitro Fertilization Program," *Medical Anthropology Quarterly*, vol. 3, no. 2, pp. 124–38.

3. CLAIRE RILEY, "American Kinship: A Lesbian Account," *Feminist Studies*, vol. 8, no. 2, pp. 75–94.

4. Quoted in KIM WESTHEIMER, " 'Right Thinking' at the *Ledger*," *Gay Community News* (January 4–10, 1987).

5. SIMON WATNEY, *Policing Desire: Pornography, AIDS, and the Media* (Minnesota, 1987).

6. DENNIS ALTMAN, *AIDS in the Mind of America* (Doubleday, 1986).

7. ALLAN BÉRUBÉ, "Caught in the Storm: AIDS and the Meaning of Natural Disaster," *Out/Look*, vol. 1, no. 3, pp. 8–19.

8. JUDY GRAHN, *Another Mother Tongue: Gay Words, Gay Worlds* (Beacon, 1984).

9. OLIVER SACKS, "The Revolution of the Deaf," *New York Review of Books* (June 2, 1988).

10. JOSEPH BEAM, "Brother to Brother: Words from the Heart," in Joseph Beam, ed., *In the Life: A Black Gay Anthology* (Alyson, 1986) pp. 230–42.

11. REGINA GILLIS, "You Call My Name (But I'm Not There)," *Gay Community News* (October 26, 1985).

LOURDES ARGUELLES, "CRAZY WISDOM"

1. For the most complete studies of these gods and goddesses, see Lydia Cabrera's original writings, published by Chicheruku Editorial in La Habana in the 1950s and available in major Caribbean collections in the United States.

2. Two valuable books on crazy wisdom are Georg Feurstein, *Holy Madness* (Paragon, 1991) and Wes Nisker, *Crazy Wisdom* (Ten Speed Press, 1990). Feurstein's book in particular includes a cautionary discussion of inauthenticity and gurumania associated with crazy wisdom masters. Unfortunately, neither book includes crazy wisdom stories of Caribbean or U.S. people of color or delves in detail into same-sex erotic practices among crazy wisdom masters.

3. For additional examples of these types of relationships, see Lourdes Arguelles, "Same Sex Eroticism and Spirituality: Conversations with Some Women in India." Paper presented at the first Lesbian, Gay and Bisexual Studies Conference, Harvard University, Cambridge, Massachusetts, October 1990.

4. For a critical and nonheterosexist analysis of methods of accessing transbiographical experiences without blindly accepting dogma or pop psychology, see Roger J. Woolger, *Other Lives, Other Selves* (Bantam, 1988).

5. SONIA JOHNSON, *The Ship That Sailed into the Living Room: Sex and Intimacy Reconsidered* (Wildfire Books, 1991).

6. At least one study has found that the rate of abuse within lesbian relationships was not significantly different from that of heterosexual relationships. See P. A. Brand and H. Kidd, "Frequency of Physical Aggression in Heterosexual and Female Homosexual Dyads," *Psychological Reports*, 59 (1986) pp. 1307–13.

ABOUT THE CONTRIBUTORS

DOROTHY ALLISON is a fiction writer, poet, and essayist whose work has appeared in numerous publications, including the anthologies *Disorderly Conduct*, *Reading Black*, *Reading Feminist*, and *High Risk*. Her collection of short stories, *Trash*, won two Lambda Literary Awards. *Bastard out of Carolina*, her first novel, was published by Dutton in 1992 and was nominated for a National Book Award for fiction.

LOURDES ARGUELLES was born in Cuba and teaches in the gender and feminist studies and Chicano/Latino studies departments at Pitzer College in Southern California. She is also a psychotherapist in private practice and a consultant in AIDS prevention, education, and ecology in U.S. communities of color and in Latin America. Her work has appeared in numerous academic and popular publications. An earlier version of "Crazy

Wisdom" was presented at the First Queer Theory Conference at the University of California at Santa Cruz, February 1990.

S. BRYN AUSTIN is an award-winning journalist, the managing editor at *The Advocate*, and an editor of *Scream Box*, a lesbian 'zine.

JACKIE GOLDSBY is a doctoral student in American studies at Yale University and a former editor of *Out/Look*.

PAM GREGG is an independent curator and grants assistant at the Museum of Contemporary Art in Los Angeles. She is, with Bryn Austin, an editor of the lesbian 'zine *Scream Box*.

LISA KAHALEOLE CHANG HALL is a graduate student in ethnic studies at the University of California at Berkeley, and a former editor of *Out/Look*. She works at Aunt Lute Books and was the conference coordinator for Out/Write, the national lesbian/gay writers' conference, in 1990 and 1991.

LIZ KOTZ is a critic and curator who writes on film, video, and visual arts for *Artforum*, *Art in America*, *The Advocate*, and *Aftermath*. She is a graduate student in comparative literature at Columbia University and is co-editing an anthology of lesbian writing with poet Eileen Myles for *Semiotext(e)*.

MARIA MAGGENTI is a student at the New York University Graduate Film Institute. Her work has appeared in *Outweek*, *Outlook Quarterly*, *OUT*, and *Interview* among other publications. She was involved in ACT UP from its inception in 1987 until 1990 before devoting herself full time to making movies.

TRACY MORGAN is currently working toward a Ph.D. in American (homosexual) history at the City University of New York Graduate Center. For many years she worked part-time jobs, devoting most of her time to AIDS, lesbian and gay and reprodutive rights activism. One of several founders of WHAM!, and a contributing author to ACT UP/NY's *Women, AIDS and Activism*, her writings have also been published in *NYQ/QW* and the fanzine *Word!* "Butch-Femme and the Politics of Identity" was originally published in *NYQ*, December 1, 1991.

CAMILLE ROY writes plays, prose, and poems. Her work has appeared in several anthologies, including *Women on Women 1* and *Deep Down*. Her first play, *Bye Bye Brunhilde*, was produced at the WOW Cafe, at Theatre Rhinocerous, and also at New Langton Arts. A book of selected plays is forthcoming from O Books. She was an editor of the queer art & lit 'zine *Dear World*, and has another book of selected poems and prose, *The Rosy Medallions*, forthcoming from Kelsey Street Press.

CATHERINE SAALFIELD, a co-author of *Women, AIDS & Activism*, writes on independent film and video, AIDS, and other lesbian and gay issues for various publications, including *The Independent*, *The Advocate*, and *Outweek*. A film/videomaker, curator, and consultant, she co-facilitates the Seeing Through AIDS media workshops in New York City. An earlier version of "Lesbian Marriage. . . . (K)Not!" appeared in *Outweek*, #13 (September 18, 1989).

RUTH L. SCHWARTZ worked for six years at the San Francisco AIDS Foundation and is currently volunteer coordinator for the San Mateo County AIDS Program. Her poetry, including much AIDS-related work, has been widely published, and she is the recipient of a 1992 Astraea Foundation Award for Emerging Lesbian Writers.

ALISA SOLOMON writes essays, criticism, and reportage on a variety of topics for *The Village Voice*, where she is a staff writer and where "Dykotomies: Scents and Sensibility" first appeared. She is also an assistant professor of English/Journalism at Baruch College CUNY.

ARLENE STEIN holds a Ph.D. in sociology from the University of California at Berkeley. She writes about politics and sexuality for such publications as *The Nation*, *On Our Backs*, and *Out/Look*, and has taught at Berkeley and the University of Essex. An earlier version of her article "Androgyny Goes Pop: But Is It Lesbian Music?" appeared in *Out/Look*, Spring 1991.

KATH WESTON is an assistant professor of anthropology at Arizona State University West in Phoenix. She is the author of *Families We Choose: Lesbians, Gays, Kinship*, which was awarded a 1990 Ruth Benedict Prize in anthropology, and a coeditor of *The Lesbian Issue: Essays from SIGNS*. She is currently working on a book on butch-femme and gender theory.

VERA WHISMAN studied sociology at New York University, where she taught courses in sexuality and women's studies, and recently completed a doctoral dissertation on lesbian and gay identities. She lives in Tulsa, Oklahoma, where she is studying lesbian culture in the Bible Belt.

A

Abortion, 36
Access issues, 223
Aché, 82
ACT UP (AIDS Coalition to Unleash Power), 37–38, 46, 86, 239–40, 248, 251, 255
Adoption, 159, 160, 161, 170–71
Advocate, The, 83, 94
African Americans, 82, 243
AIDS, 29, 31, 41, 46, 55, 86, 90, 172–78

activism, 208, 209, 247–48
care workers, 230–44
and insemination, 166–71
and parenting, 156, 175–78
research, 193
All Girl Action (road show), 18
Allison, Dorothy, 131, 133–55
Altman, Dennis, 175, 208
Androgyny, 42, 96–109
Anstey, Jo, 77
Antifeminism, 213–14
Antiporn feminism, 86–87

Antisex attitudes, 55
Arguelles, Lourdes, 132,
    196–204
Aronson, Leslie, 185
Arts, xii, 64, 68, 86. *See also*
    Film; 'Zines
Asian women, 78, 82
Assimilationism, 99, 107
Association of Women's Mu-
    sic and Culture, 105
Austin, Bryn, 64, 65, 81–95
Autobiographical genres,
    71

B

Babies, 30, 189. *See also*
    Lesbian baby boom;
    Parenting
Baby boomers, 106
Bad Attitude, 20, 88
Barbie doll, 92–93
Bar culture, 39, 40
Barnard Sex Conference
    (1982), 153
Battered women's shelters,
    52
Battering, 202, 262*n*6
Beam, Joseph, 178
Bechdel, Alison, 18
Behind the Green Door II
    (film), 18
Bentley, Gladys, 107
Bernhard, Sandra, 108, 213
Berson, Ginny, 98, 101

Bérubé, Allan, 175
Bimbox, 83
Bisexuality, 4, 28–30, 49, 54,
    87, 107, 241
Black historiography, 127
Black Lace, 82
Black Narcissus (film), 75
Black sexuality, 121, 122–23,
    126–27, 260*n*14
Black women, 22, 44, 66,
    100, 110–28. *See also*
    African Americans;
    Women of color
Bleiweiss, Rick, 104
Blk, 82
Bookstores, 16, 82, 212
Boston Globe, 102
Boston Ledger, 164
"Bound and Determined,"
    31
Bowen, Angela, 194
Bowie, David, 102
Braindrop, Lily, 94
Brat Attack, 90
Bren, Rona, 180, 186
Bright, Susie, 4, 13–22, 23,
    27, 28, 29–30, 34, 58
Brooklyn Women's Martial
    Arts, 212
Brooks, Gwendolyn, 221
Brooks-Brody, Nancy, 39, 43
Brown, Judith, 75
Brugmann, Danielle, 96
"Butch-Femme Relation-
    ships and Sexual Cour-
    age in the 1950s"
    (Nestle), 39

Butch-Femme Society, 39–
    40, 41, 45
Butch-femme tradition, 4, 8,
    10–11, 27, 31, 32, 213
  contempt for, 143, 215
  and culture, 64
  and motherhood, 162–63
  and politics of identity,
    35–46, 49, 51, 154
Butch identity, 11, 38–40,
    43, 44–45
Butler, Judith, 229

C

Cabrera, Lydia, 262*n*1
Califia, Pat, 24, 32, 88, 153,
    245
Carstens, Michelle, 234
Casal, Mary, 157
Censorship, 118
"Challenge of a Highly For-
    malized Martial Art,
    The," 89
Chang, Cathy, 42
Chao, Milyoung, 39
Chapman, Tracy, 97, 98, 102,
    105, 106, 107
Charles, Suzette, 112, 114
Chiapel, Tom, 113, 117, 121
Chicago AIDS Project, 243
Children
  abuse, 90, 137
  and choice, 183–85
  male, 212

  sexuality, 90
  See also Lesbian baby
    boom; Parenting
"Children in Our Lives"
    conference, 193–94
Choosing Children (film),
    156, 167
Chrystos, 220
Chua, Lawrence, 108
Clarke, Cheryl, 51
Class, 49, 59, 133–55, 167,
    202–03, 237
  and butch-femme identity,
    44
  and identity politics, 220,
    222, 226–27
Clausen, Jan, 28, 54
Clips (film), 15
Coalition building, 223–25
"Coalition Politics"
    (Reagon), 224
Code language, 8, 65, 97
Cohen, Ronda, 44
Colette, 13
Color Purple, The (Walker),
    127
Coming out, 131
Coming-out story, 71, 227
Coming to Power (Samois),
    88
Cool Hearts, Warm Heart
    (film), 74
Coparenting, 160, 166, 170,
    177, 182, 184
Corinne, Tee, 24
Crazy wisdom, 132, 196–
    204, 262*n*2, 263*n*2

Crazy Wisdom (Nisker),
    262*n*2
Cross-dressing, 38–39, 40,
    50
Crossover artists, 104
Cultures of origin, 131, 222
Cunt, 88
Custody cases, 171, 185

D

Damned If You Don't
    (film), 74, 75–76
Daughters of Bilitis (DOB),
    51
David, Madeleine, 39
Declet, Marie, 44
Del Valle, Desi, 42
D'Emilio, John, 71
Deming, Barbara, 212
Denenberg, Risa, 40
Desautels, Art, 166
Disability, 223
Dlugacz, Judy, 105, 106
Dobkin, Alix, 54, 98
Dolo Romy, 85
Dominance and submission,
    77
Dominant culture, 64
    lesbianizing, 91–95, 108
Donahue, Phil, 40
Double Strength (film), 70
Drag queens, 228–29
Dress styles, 39, 43, 51, 56
Ducharme, Paulette, 179

Dworkin, Andrea, 212
DYKES, Disability & Stuff,
    210, 214, 215
Dyketactics (film), 69, 70

E

Ehrenreich, Barbara, 115–16
Erotica, 260*n*8
Etheridge, Melissa, 97, 98,
    106
Ethnic identity, 58, 80, 180,
    182–83
Ewing, L. J., 184

F

Fact Sheet Five, 94
Family, xii, 131, 132, 144,
    154
    and AIDS, 178–79
    and biology, 181–84, 186
    and children, 165–66
    and coalition building,
        224
    and lesbian baby boom,
        179–81
    and lesbian marriage, 195
    See also Parenting
"Family values," xiii
"Fanzines," 82, 94
Feldman, Amy, 179–80

"Female homosexual" idea, 51

Femininity, 4, 39–40, 43, 44–45, 229

Feminism, xii, 4, 135, 240, 248, 250
  and beauty pageants, 118–19
  and femininity, 44
  lesbianism and, xiv, 31, 39, 48, 51–52, 59
  and lesbian pornography, 14–15, 16–17, 19–21, 22
  and race, 221
  and sexuality, 9, 21. *See also* Lesbian feminism

Feminist documentaries, 71

Feminist health-care movement, 21

Feminist press, 82, 84, 85–86

Femme identity, 36–38, 40, 44, 45
  lack of visibility, 45–46
  and motherhood, 162, 163

Fernandez, Charles, 56

Ferraro, Geraldine, 115

Feurstein, Georg, 262*n*2

Film, 64, 67–80, 258–59*n*1

Fish, Doris, 228

Flipside, 82

Foster, Jodie, 91

Four Girls (film), 91

Freaks, 81–95

Freud, Sigmund, 191

Friedrich, Su, 74–76

Frith, Simon, 100

Frye, Marilyn, 33

G

Gabriel, Peter, 107

Galoway, Craig, 166, 168, 177

Gardner, Kay, 99

Gay Community News, 103, 156–57, 185, 241

Gay generations, 176

Gay/lesbian press, 83

Gay male culture, 32, 71
  sexual directness, 235–36
  sexual institutions, 86

Gay male press, 83

Gay men, 4, 31, 45, 56, 247
  and children, 166–71
  coalitions with, 208, 209, 230–44
  impact on culture, 63
  and lesbian identity, 46, 48, 51, 55, 56, 57, 228–29

G.B.F. (Gay Black Female), 88

Gender, 237
  conventions, 4, 51, 167
  as game, 55–56
  and identity politics, 222
  and marriage, 193
  and motherhood, 162–63

Gently Down the Stream (film), 74
Gerson, Randi, 240
Gever, Martha, 106
Gino, Janet, 44
Girl bars, 246, 250
Girlie Mag, 92
Girljock, 94
"Girls Just Want to Have Fun" (song), 103
"Glamour dykes," 246
Glaser, Ray, 160
Goldman, Emma, 191, 193
Goldsby, Jackie, 58, 66, 110–28
Gonzalez, Alida, 41, 45
Grahn, Judy, 17, 176
Great Goddess, The (film), 70
Gregg, Pam, 64, 65, 81–95
Grossberg, Larry, 107
Grover, Mark, 164
Guccione, Bob, 113–14, 117–18, 121–22

of butch lesbians, 44–46
Harris, Charlyne, 167
Harris, Jill, 42
Health care issue, 238
Health insurance, 194–95
Heft, Lisa, 234
Helms, Jesse, 86
Heresies, The, Sex Issue, 8, 9
Heterosexual
  conversion, xii
  culture, 4
  porn, 21
  relationships, 53, 55
Hollibaugh, Amber, 9, 153, 213, 217
Hollywood, 99
Holy Madness (Feurstein), 262n2
Home, desire for, 224–25
Home Girls (Smith), 224
Homocore, 94
Homophobia, 26, 38, 104, 122–23, 220, 221, 243
Hudson, Rock, 233, 243
Hughes, Holly, 212
Hyde, Sue, 216
Hysteria, 84

H

Hall, Lisa Kahaleole Change, 208, 218–29
Hall, Marny, 33–34
Hall, Radclyffe, 50
Hammer, Barbara, 69–70, 78
Hanson, Mara, 184
Harassment, 45–46

I

Identity politics, xii
  butch-femme and, 35–46
  and community, 218–29
  and who is a lesbian, 47–60

Immodest Acts: The Life of a Lesbian Nun in Renaissance Italy (Brown), 75
Incest, 90, 136
"Incest Spread, The," 90
Inclusiveness, 223
Indigo Girls, 97, 98, 105
"In Living Color" (TV series), 260*n*11
In Search of Our Mothers' Gardens (Walker), 221
Insemination, 159–62, 165, 181, 182–83
  and AIDS, 166–71, 241–42
"Invert," 50
Invisibility, 10, 45–46
In vitro fertilization, 161
Irigaray, Luce, 13
Irvine, Janice, 23

J

Jacobs, Harriet, 122, 260*n*10
Jaramillo, Paul, 164
J.D.s, 82, 91
Jennings, Tom, 94
Jetsons (TV series), 92
Jobs, 44
Johnson, Jill, 52
Johnson, Magic, 243
Johnson, Sondra, 243
Jones, G. B., 82, 91
Jones, Kevin, 179

"Justify My Love" (song), 103, 124

K

Kahlo, Frida, 91, 260*n*12
Kantrowitz, Melanie Kaye, 136
Kennedy, Liz, 39
Khush (video), 79
Kinney, Nan, 18
Kinship
  networks, 132
  terminology, 163–64
Kinski, Nastassia, 91
Klein, Howie, 104
Kotz, Liz, 64, 67–80
Kovick, Kris, 23
Kowalski, Sharon, 244
Kunin, Diane, 162

L

La Bruce, Bruce, 82
Ladder, The, 18
lang, k.d., 65, 96–97, 98, 104, 106, 107, 213
Larson, Elizabeth Rae, 33
Lauper, Cyndi, 103
Leather fetishism, 143, 212
Lee, Spike, 127
Legal issues, 193
  and death, 179

Legal issues (*cont.*)
  of parenting, 170–71, 183
Lesbian AIDS Caregivers'
    Conference (1989),
    230–31, 242
Lesbian and Gay Studies
    Conferences, 40
Lesbian baby boom, 132,
    156–57, 171–72, 175–
    76, 179–84, 186
Lesbian community, xiii–
    xvii, 207–09
  and film and video, 67–68
  future of, 245–55
  and identity politics, 218–
    29
  loss of, xii, xiv–xv, 29
  political rigidity of, 84–85
Lesbian culture, 63–66, 91,
    108
  prefeminist, 31, 32
Lesbian dialect, 11
Lesbian Erotic Dance (Lou-
    lan), 23, 27
Lesbian-feminism, xii, xiii,
    37, 135, 248
  and class, 155
  and culture, 64, 84–90
  and film, 68–70
  and lesbian identity, 51–
    52, 53–55, 59
  and music, 99–102
  and pc, 215, 223
  and race, 117, 126
  and sexuality, 57, 66, 123,
    124–25
  vs. younger styles, 48–50

Lesbian/feminist press, 52,
    83–84
Lesbian identity
  and art, 80
  and bisexuality, 29
  and butch-femme visibil-
    ity, 46
  carving out, xi–xii, xiv
  and class, 131–55
  and community, 208,
    218–29
  desexualization of, 17–18
  minimizing vs. maximiz-
    ing, 59
  and motherhood, 158–66
  and music, 106–07, 108
  and new lesbians, 59–60
  politics of, 9, 35–46, 222
  question of who is les-
    bian, 47–60, 222
  and race, 44
  redefined in 'zines, 84
  and sexual revolution, 4,
    34
  See also Identity politics
Lesbian Nation, 207, 208,
    225, 246–55
Lesbian Passion (Loulan),
    23, 25–26, 28
Lesbian separatism, 71, 99
Lesbian Sex (Loulan), 23, 25
Let's Play Prisoners (video),
    67, 77–78
Letterman, David, 107
Levi-Strauss, Claude, 191
Lewis, Lisa, 103
Lewis, Sinclair, 144

Liberace, Ina, 91
"Like a Virgin" (song), 124
Liz and Sydney, 213
Lorde, Audre, 18, 212
Loulan, JoAnn, 4, 15, 22–28,
    30, 33, 53
Lowry, David, 178
Luzio, Brook, 184–85
Lyon, Phyllis, 51

M

McCalla, Diedre, 106
MacDonald, Scott, 76
Macho Sluts (Califia), 88
McNichol, Kristy, 91
Madonna, 65, 66, 103, 123–
    25, 213, 260*n*12
*Madres: The Mothers of the
    Plaza De Mayo, Las*
    (film), 72
Madwoman, 83
Maggenti, Maria, 209, 214,
    245–55
Mainstream culture, 64, 65,
    96–109
Male-identification, 55
Male sexuality, 57
Mannerisms, 39
Marginality, 10–11
Marriage, 187–95, 245
Martin, Del, 51
Masochism, 10, 20, 77
Mass media, 91
Masters & Johnson, 23

Maude (TV series), 92
Maximum Rock N Roll,
    82
Maynes, Dick, 166
Media, lesbian, 258–59*n*1
Men
    and butch posturing, 44–
        45
    lesbians who sleep with,
        53–54
Menses (film), 170
Mercer, Kobena, 260*n*13
Michigan Womyn's Festival,
    212, 234
Middle-class
    culture, 32, 131, 136,
        155
    lesbians, 40, 44, 48, 131,
        208, 226
Miss America, 110–28
Mitchell Brothers, 18
Modell, Judith, 161
Monogamy, 189, 191, 193,
    246
Moraga, Cherrie, 71,
    220
Moral responsibility, 216
Morgan, Robin, 100
Morgan, Tracy, 35–46
Morrison, Toni, 260*n*10
Motzko, Edith, 158–59
Ms. magazine, 100
Munoz, Susana Blaustein,
    71–74
Music, 64, 96–109
Myth, internalization,
    144

N

National Lesbian Conference (1991), 223–24, 225–26
National Lesbian/Gay Health Conference (1987), 237–38
Naylor, Gloria, 127
Near, Holly, 106, 107
Negativa, 89, 92
Nestle, Joan, 8, 31, 39, 63, 153, 212
New Republic, 115
Newstetter, Amanda, 236, 238
Newsweek, 245–46
Nisker, Wes, 262n2
Nonbiological parent, 183
Nonmonogamy, 187–95
Nun, Misha Ben, 168–69
NY femmes, 39

O

Odette, Catherine, 215
off our backs, 18, 29, 83, 85, 86, 96
Ofrenda: The Days of the Dead, La (film), 72
Olivia Records, 98, 101–02, 106
On Our Backs (OOB), 14, 15, 18, 19–21, 30, 33, 34, 56, 57, 86, 88, 96, 212, 213, 245
On Our Rag, 86
O'Reilly, Jane, 115–16
"Outcasts," 32
Outlines, 105
Out/Look magazine, 23, 28, 48, 83, 94
Outrageous Woman, 20, 88
Outweek, 94, 98, 213
Out/Write Conference (1990, 1991), 94

P

Parenting, 156–86, 246
Parkin, Joan, 40, 44
Parmar, Protibha, 78–99
Parthenogenesis, 182
"Patriarchal" behavior, 211–12
Patton, Cindy, 31
P.C. Casualities, 87, 92
Pearl, Monica, 42
Pearlberg, Gerry, 238
Pelayo, Arturo, 166–67
Penthouse, 113, 114, 116, 117–18, 122, 123, 124
Penthouse Forum, 14
People of color, 93
and AIDS, 237–38, 240
Perón, Eva, 260n12
personal as political, 222, 225–26

Phelan, Shane, 59
Phillips, Gretchen, 103
Phoenix Rising, 82
Phranc, 102, 103, 104, 105,
    107, 213
Platt, Karen, 85
Playboy, 117
Pokorny, Syndey, 103
Political corectness, 211–17,
    222–24, 246
Politics
    of identity, 35–46
    and pornography, 21
Popular culture, xii, 63, 65
    music, and androgyny,
        96–110
    and 'zines, 91–95
Pornography
    lesbian, 3, 4, 14–21, 34
    mainstream, 19–20, 99,
        260*n*
    and Vanessa Williams,
        119–22
Porter, Veneita, 233
Portillo, Lourdes, 72
Postmodenist theory, 125
Poverty, 131, 133–55
    and AIDS, 238–39
Power, 9
    and identity, 221
    and love, 78
    and self-control, 9
    and sexuality, 16, 39
    and trashing, 226
"Power and Trust," 32
Power Exchange, 20, 88
Powerlessness, 226–27

Privilege, 221
Property, 191, 192–93, 194,
    246
Pro-sex theory, 116, 123
Prosser, Amanda, 44
Prostitution, 146
Puerto Rican women, 44
Punk, 64
    and music, 100, 103
    'zines, 81–82, 84–86, 93,
        94–95

Q

"Queen for 307 Days"
    (Goldsby), 66
Queer culture, 4–5, 17, 48
    and lesbian identity, 56–
        59
Queer Nation, 56, 57, 83,
    208, 209, 248–55

R

Race, 49, 58, 78–79, 143,
    155, 237
    and butch-femme identity,
        44–45
    and identity politics, 220,
        221–22, 226–27
    and insemination, 182
    and lesbian culture, 65–
        66

Race (*cont.*)
  and postmodern theory,
    125
  and sexuality, 116–17,
    120–21, 125–27, 128
Racism, 78–79, 115, 117,
    125, 145, 155, 168, 212,
    220, 237, 248
Radicalesbians, 51
Radical feminists, 31
Rape hotlines, 51–52
Raymond, Janice, xiii
Reagan/Bush era, xiii, 190,
    215
Reagon, Bernice Johnson,
    224
"Real Life Barbie," 92–93
"Real" vs. "false" lesbians,
    53–54, 224
Redwood Records, 106
Reuben, Dr. David, 49
Rhode Island AIDS Project,
    233
Rice, Louise, 156
Rich, Adrienne, 51
Right wing, 86–87
Riley, Claire, 163
"River of Names" (Allison),
    153
Rock Against Sexism, 101
Rogers, Brian, 174
Rollins, Marty, 174
Romero, Louise, 168
Rosa, Josephine, 41, 42, 45
Rosales, Marta, 169
Roy, Camille, 3, 6–12
Rubin, Gayle, 31, 191

S

Saalfield, Catherine, 132,
    187–95
Sadomasochism (s/m), 3, 4,
    11, 26, 31–32, 39, 49,
    77–78, 87, 88, 154, 215
  publishing, 88–90
Safe(r) sex, 90, 174, 241,
    243
Samois, 88
Sandler, Ronald, 178
San Francisco AIDS Founda-
    tion, 232, 237
San Francisco AIDS Hotline,
    233, 243
San Francisco Lesbian and
    Gay Film Festival of
    1990, 13–14
Sari Red (video), 78
Savage, Jon, 99
Scent-free events, 210–11,
    215
Schneider, Yvette, 40, 43,
    45
Schulman, Sarah, 213, 241
Schwartz, Ruth, 208, 230–44
Scream Box, 87–88, 90
Second Wave label, 101
Sendgraft, Terry, 70
Sex debates, 4
Sex experts, 51
Sexism, 22, 26, 168, 220
Sexology, 23, 38, 50, 116
Sex progressivists, 115–16
Sex radicals, 136, 213
Sex therapy, 4, 23–28, 33

Sexual abuse, 131

Sexual boundaries, 29–30

Sexual codes, 39

Sexual dialect, 3, 7–12

Sexual literacy, 24

Sexual revolution, 30–34

Sexuality, xii, 3–47
 and black women, 116–17, 120–23
 and butch-femme, 35–46
 female, 49–50
 and feminism, 16–18
 in film, 69–71, 79–80
 and gay men vs. lesbians, 235–36
 and lesbian identity, 47–60
 new climate in 'zines, 86–90
 new, vs. political correct-ness, 213, 236
 and politics, 21
 and politics of identity, 35–46
 and pop music, 103–04
 and pornography, 12–23
 and race, 66
 and sex therapy, 23–28, 33
 See also Pornography; Sex wars

Sexual preference, 57

Sexual role playing, 32

Sexual violence, 22

Sex wars, 126, 153–54, 213

Sex work, 115, 118, 121–22

Shamakami, 82

Shocked, Michelle, 65, 97, 101, 102, 104–05, 107

Simon, Paul, 108

Single parents, 157, 184

Single women, 193

Sinister Wisdom, 33

Sink or Swim (film), 74

Sister Nobody, 84, 91

"Sisters in Solidarity," 220–21

Slavery, 121–22

"Sleep Keeps Me Awake" (song), 105

Slut Mag, 88

Smith, Barbara, 220, 224

Smith, Patti, 91

Snitow, Ann, 59

Socialization, 192

Social validation, 193

Sojourner, 211

Solomon, Alisa, 207, 210–17

Sontag, Susan, 19

"Southern Kink," 31

Southern working class, 143, 144–46, 155

"Spew: The Homographic Convergence" conven-tion, 95

Stein, Arlene, 13–34, 96–109

Stein, Gertrude, xvi

Steinberg, Joel, 216

Stonewall rebellion (1969), 36, 81

Straight men, 50
Straight women, 58
  feminists, 48, 209
  vs. femmes, 44
  and real lesbian issue,
    54
Style nomads, 213–14
Subcultures, 81, 93, 103
Sundahl, Debi, 18
Superdyke (film), 70
Susana (film), 71–74
Sweet Honey in the Rock,
  226

T

Taste of Latex, 88, 94
Television, 92
Thing, 94
This Bridge Called My Back
    (Moraga and Anzaldua),
    220
Thistlewaite, Polly, 41
Thompson, Karen, 244
Ties that Bind, The (film),
    74
Tillery, Linda, 100
Traffic in women, The
    (Rubin), 191
Trashing, 225–26
Treut, Monika, 19
Trull, Teresa, 101
Two Nice Girls, 103,
    107

U

Up Our Butts, 90
Upper classes, 50, 226
"Urania," 32

V

"Variant," 51, 56
Videos, 64, 67–82
Violence, 131, 137
Virgin Machine, The (film),
    19
Vorlicek, Dave, 185

W

Walker, Alice, 127
Walker, Ronnie, 173
Walker, Valerie, 42, 44
Watkins, Mary, 100
Watney, Wimon, 174
Wedding, 189–91, 194
Well of Loneliness (Hall),
    50, 83
Wells, Ida B., 262*n*
West Coast Women's Music
    Festival (1981), 224
Weston, Kath, 132, 156–86
WHAM (Women's Health Ac-
    tion Mobilization), 242
"When I Grow Up" (song),
    105

Whisman, Vera, 4–5, 47–60
White, Dan, 216
Whites, 44, 49, 50, 66, 115, 120
  and AIDS organizations, 238, 240
Whorezine, 94
Williams, Toni, 169
Williams, Vanessa, 66, 110–28
Williamson, Cris, 101
Wilson, Ara, 41, 43
Wilson, Susan, 102
Winnow, Jackie, 230–31, 235, 243
Winters, Lisa, 46
Wolfe, Maxine, 239
Women Against Pornography, 14–15, 153
Women-identified women, 58, 99–100
Women I Love (film), 70
Women of Brewster Place, The (Naylor), 127
Women of color, xv, 44, 50, 58, 66, 68, 79, 100, 166, 230–31
  and AIDS organizations, 238–39
  See also African Americans; Black sexuality; Black women; People of color

Women's Cancer Resource Center, 244
Women's centers, 52
Women's communities, 68
Women's culture, 64–65, 70
Women's music, 51, 65, 96, 97
  and androgynous pop, 99–102, 105–09
  festivals, 212, 223
Women's studies programs, 37
Working class, 4, 50, 152, 220
  and butch-femme identity, 44
  and sexuality, 32

Y

Young, Christine, 236
Younger women, 68, 81, 213–14

Z

Zando, Julie, 67, 77–78
" 'Zines," 64, 81–95
Zita, Jacquelyn, 52